SOCIOLITERARY PRACTICE
IN LATE
MEDIEVAL ENGLAND

Socioliterary Practice
in Late
Medieval England

HELEN BARR

OXFORD
UNIVERSITY PRESS

OXFORD
UNIVERSITY PRESS

Great Clarendon Street, Oxford, OX2 6DP

Oxford University Press is a department of the University of Oxford.
It furthers the University's objective of excellence in research, scholarship,
and education by publishing worldwide in

Oxford New York

Athens Auckland Bangkok Bogotá Buenos Aires Cape Town
Chennai Dar es Salaam Delhi Florence Hong Kong Istanbul Karachi
Kolkata Kuala Lumpur Madrid Melbourne Mexico City Mumbai Nairobi
Paris São Paulo Shanghai Singapore Taipei Tokyo Toronto Warsaw

and associated companies in Berlin Ibadan

Oxford is a registered trade mark of Oxford University Press
in the UK and certain other countries

Published in the United States
by Oxford University Press Inc., New York

British Library Cataloguing in Publication Data

Data available

Library of Congress Cataloging in Publication Data

Barr, Helen, 1961–
Socioliterary practice in late Medieval England / Helen Barr.
p. cm.
Includes bibliographical references (p.) and index
1. English literature–Middle English, 1100–1500–History and criticism. 2. Latin
literature, Medieval and modern–England–History and criticism. 3. Literature and
society–England–History–To 1500. 4. England–Social conditions–1066–1485.
5. Social history in literature. I. Title.

PR275.S63 B3 2001 820.9'001–dc21 2001036728

ISBN 0-19-811242-4

1 3 5 7 9 10 8 6 4 2

Typeset in Bembo
by Regent Typesetting, London
Printed in Great Britain
on acid-free paper by
Biddles Ltd, Guildford and Kings' Lynn

Acknowledgements

THIS BOOK HAS been so long in the making that I am tempted to dedicate it 'to the memory of my lost youth'. I am grateful to OUP for keeping faith in a project which has undergone considerable metamorphosis since the initial commission more years ago than I dare record. The original readers for the book read a revised proposal and sample typescript. Their warm encouragement and constructive criticisms have been invaluable in enabling me to bring a project to fruition which, at many points, looked in point of foundering. Where I have departed from their sage advice, I apologize for my pig-headedness.

If I had not been dispensed of teaching, lecturing, and administrative duties for two terms by the Oxford Faculty of English, and Lady Margaret Hall, I doubt when I would have found the space to gather together the materials of this book into publishable form. I am also grateful to the editors of *Medium Aevum* for permission to reproduce a revised version of my article '*Pearl*—or the Jeweller's Tale', 69 (2000) as Chapter 2 of this book, and to Helen Cooper for very helpful advice and comments on the original essay which went well beyond the call of editorial duty.

Personal and professional debts are numerous and often inextricable. Many students, both undergraduate and graduate, have contributed greatly to the formation of ideas (indeed, Chapter 2 was stimulated in response to a question from an undergraduate, 'Why can't we read *Pearl* like Chaucer?'). Much of the impetus for writing this book came out of preparing lectures in Oxford which I conducted jointly with Kate Ward-Perkins. I am indebted to Kate's critical sharpness, for introducing me to challenging discursive terrains, and for Kate's continued intellectual companionship and support, and for that of her family while I have been writing this book. I also want to thank the following: Ralph Hanna, Ananya Kabir, Sally Mapstone, Francis O'Gorman, Vincent Quinn, James Simpson, and John Watts. They may not be aware of how much they have contributed, but the book is the richer for their input and insights. I am deeply grateful to Matthew Fisher and Joanna Martin for their help with checking at a late stage.

I do not wish to erect a hierarchy of gratitude, given how thankful I am for all the different kinds of assistance I have received, but it would be equally unethical not to record how I am especially indebted to Paul Strohm and Anne Hudson. In this, I have been remarkably lucky. The writing up of this book coincided with the arrival of Paul as Tolkien Professor in Oxford, and I thank him warmly for attending lecture versions of some of these chapters, and also for reading a sample version of Chapter 4, and for the enabling discussion that ensued. Anne inspired me to specialize in early literature as a result of her tutoring me while I was an undergraduate, and it is fair to say that, without her continued, but unobtrusive influence, this book would not exist. I thank her for her insightful reading of Chapter 6, for locating a crucial source at the eleventh hour, and for generally providing me with every encourage-ment and practical advice. I am sorry, given all the help I have received, that this book contains so many 'errores and hereses', for which I claim sole responsibility. The heresies that I am conscious of I secretly rather welcome; the deplorable errors, for all my best attempts to extirpate them, will remain as a source of irritation to others, and as a source of lasting embarrassment to me.

It remains to thank my very dear friends, apart from those already mentioned. Without their luring me to more and less disreputable activities, this book might have been finished sooner. But, truthfully, without them, I wonder if I would have finished it at all. A huge thank you to all my friends and companions, both human and feline.

Contents

Abbreviations

A Note On Conventions

In the footnotes, where two numbers are given, separated by an oblique, the second is a line reference.

Introduction: Socioliterary Practice

IN THIS BOOK I examine a selected variety of writings produced in late medieval England as examples of socioliterary practice.[1] My starting point is that language, whether written or spoken, is a material form of social practice.[2] That is, far from language existing either as some kind of autonomous organism *independent* of 'reality', or as a *passive reflection* of anterior 'reality', language *exists* as material reality because it is a form of social behaviour.[3] Social structures and behaviour determine language practices but language practices also have effects on social structures and behaviour. This is because the materiality of language inheres in orders of discourses which produce, and are produced by, social institutions and conventions. These institutions and conventions encompass the most intimate and informal social situations alongside those which are the most public and powerful.[4]

Literary texts are part of these orders of discourses.[5] They are forms of social language practice every bit as much as a legal document or a

[1] My use of the term 'socioliterary practice' is an attempt to '"locate" the production of literary effects historically as part of the ensemble of social practices'; see Etienne Balibar and Pierre Macherey, 'On literature as an ideological form', in Robert Young, ed., *Untying the text* (London, 1981), 79–99, p. 83. My title, and mode of enquiry, is heavily influenced by Gunther Kress, *Linguistic processes in sociocultural practice* (Oxford, 1989), 2nd edn. Kress observes at the outset that while there is nothing particularly original about the view that language is a social phenomenon, it is extremely difficult to write about the topic in a way that does not separate language from society as though they were discrete objects. He notes that 'the somewhat awkward title . . . reflects . . . the problems', p. 1.

[2] See Norman Fairclough, *Language and power* (London, 1989), 22; Roger Fowler, *Literature as social discourse* (London, 1981), 21; and Robert Hodge and Gunther Kress, *Language as ideology* (London, 1979), 1–14.

[3] Cf. Deborah Cameron, 'Demythologising sociolinguistics: why language does not reflect society', in John E. Joseph and Talbot J. Taylor, eds., *Ideologies of language* (London, 1990), 79–93, p. 93.

[4] These issues are discussed with great clarity by Fairclough, *Language and power*, 17–42. My discussion is influenced also by Michel Foucault's essay 'The order of discourse' in Young, ed., *Untying the text*, 48–78, and Anthony Easthope, *Poetry as discourse* (London, 1983).

[5] See Balibar and Macherey, 'On Literature', 91; and Fowler, *Literature as social discourse*, 7, who notes that 'it is a mistake to regard literary texts as autonomous patterns of linguistic form cut off from social forces'.

family row are forms of social language practice. In the latter instances, the material form of language used is conditioned by social factors such as status and role, and by competence in producing and participating in available modes of linguistic behaviour within an environment which both frames linguistic transactions and conditions their performance and reception.[6] There is an internal and dialectical relationship between the formal features of language use and the social matrix within which language users engage in language practice.[7] To argue this of a letter produced by a firm of solicitors, or an argument between family members is hardly open to debate. The types of discourse for each event, for instance, in terms of vocabulary, pronouns, and syntax are immediately recognizable, and not readily interchangeable, unless a participant, say, in a domestic imbroglio, were to adopt an impersonal, hypotactic, and polysyllabic register for sarcastic effect. I think that it is also possible to translate this argument into literary texts, even those produced over 600 years or so before the word 'discourse' was used in its sociolinguistic sense.[8]

Some of the texts which I examine can be seen explicitly to make a connection between language use and the social construction of reality; most explicitly perhaps, in *The Manciple's Tale*, where Chaucer, through the mouthpiece of his narrator, gives us a lesson in how the use of vocabulary segments the world into socially and culturally relevant categories.[9] I examine this in Chapter 1 and show how Hoccleve approaches the question of the relationship of language and reality from a knowingly opposing perspective. In politically opportunistic poetry, Hoccleve deploys conservative notions of language use in an attempt to peg social behaviour to sets of linguistic paradigms which, in other works, he acknowledges to be much more contested and conflicted.

---

[6] Cf. Fowler, 7, 21, and 94; and discussion in Peter Trudgill, *Sociolinguistics* (Harmondsworth, 1983), rev. edn., 100–22.

[7] See Fairclough, *Language and power*, 23; and James and Lesley Milroy, *Authority in language* (London, 1985), 117–39.

[8] *MED* 'discors' n. 1. The faculty or process of reason, ratiocination; 2. The discharging of a scrofulus sore.

[9] Fowler discusses how vocabulary segments the world into culture-relevant categories and how language also classifies these objectifications by grouping into lexical sets, for example, kinship terminologies, or jargons of specific occupations, *Literature as social discourse*, 25. See also David Lee, *Competing discourses* (London, 1992), 1–23, where the account of classification and selection avoids attributing (as Fowler does) agency to vocabulary and to language, and ascribes agency instead to language users and institutionalized language practices.

The witting manipulation of literary resources for social commentary is evidenced also in Lydgate's *The Churl and the Bird*, and I have chosen to finish with a brief study of this poem as its literary materials reprise many of the formal literary phenomena I examine in this study, but are positioned differently in terms of their social inflection.

The language of social description is a recurring interest in each of the chapters.[10] It is an obvious locus, perhaps, within which to argue for the materiality of literary language given that the representation of role, occupation, communities, and their interaction is a 'social' subject. But what is less obvious, I hope, is the various means by which the language of social description takes material form. While Chaucer and Hoccleve may be seen to address the issue overtly, other writers may also be seen to be negotiating this topic, even while there is no explicit steer towards it in the text, precisely because the formal features of text are inescapably social. For example, the shifts in pronominal economy in *Pearl*, the dialectical use of register, and the coexistence of aristocratic and mercantile semantic fields[11] are instances of social practice even if the poet was consciously unaware of it. Similarly, *Wynnere and Wastoure* inscribes a conflictual view of social relations and roles as a result of scrambling horizons of literary expectations which are themselves part of social structures.[12]

Part of my argument in this book rests on the premiss that writers recognized orders of discourse and could mobilize them to produce

[10] On the language of social description and the changes it underwent in the late fourteenth century, see Paul Strohm, *Social Chaucer* (Cambridge, Mass., 1989), 2–10.

[11] Geoffrey Hughes, *Words in time* (Oxford, 1988), 18–19, offers a very clear account of semantic fields.

[12] Recognizable literary forms generate patterns of expectation which inform their reception. Robert Hodge and Gunther Kress argue that 'genres only exist in so far as a social group declares and enforces the rules that constitute them . . . each genre codes "particular" relationships among sets of social participants', *Social semiotics* (Cambridge, 1988), 7. To illustrate this point they compare a committee meeting with the rise of the novel. In Jocelyn Wogan-Browne, Nicholas Watson, Andrew Taylor, and Ruth Evans, eds., *The idea of the vernacular* (Exeter, 1999), 109, the term 'audience' is preferred to 'reader' as it embraces 'more of the range of participants in textual culture'. 'The attempt to recover medieval audiences and to consider what roles they played in producing, responding to, and using texts, and through what modes of textual address these processes occurred, is crucial for an understanding of the language politics of the period', p. 110. See also the following articles by Paul Strohm, 'Form and social statement in *Confessio Amantis* and *The Canterbury Tales*', *SAC* 1 (1979), 17–40; 'Chaucer's fifteenth century audience and the narrowing of the Chaucer tradition', *SAC* 4 (1982), 3–32; and 'Chaucer's audience(s): fictional, implied, intended, actual', *Chaucer Review*, 18 (1983), 137–64.

social commentary.[13] Rhetorical handbooks may be seen as one type of literary order of discourse in that they constitute a discipline within which poetry in the Middle Ages was written.[14] I argue in Chapter 5 that the absence of authorial and narrative fixity in *The Nun's Priest's Tale* produces rhetorical comparisons between animals and humans which resonate very differently from those constructed in accounts of the 1381 uprisings in texts written by Chaucer's contemporaries. Formal rhetorical schemes, themselves part of an order of discourse, are freighted with social commentary. Prophetic writing and the mobilization of heraldic badges for political comment were also socially recognizable modes of writing. Gower tells us so in his explicit commentary on the subject in the side-notes to his *Tripartite Chronicle*. In Chapter 3, I explore how Gower and the anonymous writer of *Richard the Redeless* intervene in these orders of discourse and contest Ricardian sign-fashioning for the purposes of writing Lancastrian verse.

Language use in literary texts can also be seen as a material form of social practice in the way that writers deploy marked vocabulary whose significance would have been apprehended by audiences who belonged to a similar social matrix.[15] I argue in Chapter 6 that the anonymous writers of Wycliffite texts produce a distinctive vision of social community through their use of repeated tropes and marked vocabulary[16] to

---

[13] Wogan-Browne *et al.*, *The idea of the vernacular*, pp. xiv–xv, and 3–4 discusses authors' awareness of orders of discourse in terms of inherited Latin traditions and the significance of writing in English. A well-known acknowledgement of 'generic' diversity is the refusal of Chaucer's Parson to tell a 'fable' and his claim that as a 'southren man', he 'kan nat geeste rum, ram ruf, by lettre', *The Parson's Prologue*, 42–4. This, and all subsequent references to Chaucer's works, are taken from *The Riverside Chaucer*, ed. L. D. Benson *et al.* (Oxford, 1988).

[14] Foucault uses the term 'discipline' to describe a procedure for controlling and regulating discourse. 'A discipline is defined by a domain of objects, a set of methods, a corpus of propositions considered to be true, a play of rules and definitions, of techniques and instruments', 'The order of discourse', 59. He discusses how medicine is not constituted by the total of what can truthfully be said about illness; botany cannot be defined by the sum of all truths concerning plants, p. 60. Osbern Bokenham's refusal of working within the 'procedyng artificyal' exemplified by Geoffrey of Vinsauf, may be seen as an example of a writer's awareness of how literary writing inheres in orders of discourse which regulate what may be written, but also how a writer may choose to intervene in that process by commenting on it; see Wogan-Browne *et al.*, *The idea of the vernacular*, 67/83–98.

[15] On the relationship between narrative positioning, addresses, and audiences, see ibid. 109–16.

[16] F. R. Palmer, in *Semantics* (Cambridge, 1981), 2nd edn., 95–6, uses the terms 'marked' and 'unmarked' in his discussion of antonymy. For instance, in the phrase 'it is three feet

describe members of the second estate in relation to the third, and through their reregistration of available peasant and anti-peasant discourses. I argue in Chapter 7 that the narrative strategies and diction of *Mum and the Sothsegger* and *The Book of Cupide* bear religious commentary because they form part of a language code whose social significance would have been registered by audiences familiar with the ways that religious discussion was framed. The diction of Chaucer's *Prologue to the Legend of Good Women* inheres in the same kinds of semantic fields as those found in contemporaneous religious and political controversies. The discussion in the poem of the production and control of literary materials is simultaneously a discussion of production and control in the spheres of religion and politics. I argue in Chapter 4 that the *Prologue* shows us that representation, whether in linguistic form or outward signs such as dress, is a socially material practice; there is no gap between 'reality' and its staging. One may recover, however, how the staging of reality is socially anchored by attending to the narrative position from which utterances are produced, and by tracing the regulatory procedures which police orders of discourse.

Material language practice also involves writers making choices, whether of diction, modality, figure, verse form, or genre.[17] These choices mark out social positions and produce social interaction between other language users, and the orders of discourse within which they operate.[18] In late medieval England a crucial linguistic choice is that of language.[19] To write in English rather than in Latin and/or French means to take up a social position within available discourses and the resultant text is necessarily a product of that social matrix and an instance of its practices.[20] The relationships between Latin, French, and English inhere

high', 'high' is the unmarked term because it is that which is conventionally used, while 'low' used in the same phrase is an example of a 'marked' term because it is a specialized use of the word. This distinction between 'marked' and 'unmarked' can be translated into specifically cultural contexts in which a word may become 'marked' in a particular discourse. Cf. the discussion of keywords used in the expression of religious dissent between 1790 and 1830 in Diane Macdonell, *A theory of discourse* (Oxford, 1986), 24–7.

[17] See Nicholas Watson, 'The politics of Middle English writing' in Wogan-Browne *et al.*, *The idea of the vernacular*, 331.

[18] For discussion of this and illustration, see Fowler, *Literature as social discourse*, 80–95.

[19] With the proviso, of course, that some writers may not have had the choice of writing in either French or Latin.

[20] Many published studies address this issue. The texts and essays in Wogan-Browne *et al.*, *The idea of the vernacular* collect together important materials on this topic and trenchant discussion of the issues. Other important studies (not otherwise listed at more detailed dis-

in questions of institutional power and its contestation.[21] These are issues explicitly addressed by writers of this time,[22] and are also implicitly addressed through the social materiality of composition in whichever

cussion of this subject in the chapters which follow) include: Joyce Coleman, *Public reading and the reading public in late medieval England and France* (Cambridge, 1996); Rita Copeland, *Rhetoric, hermeneutics and translation in the later middle ages: academic traditions and vernacular texts* (Cambridge, 1991); Ralph Hanna III, 'Miscellaneity and vernacularity: conditions of literary production in late medieval England', in Stephen G. Nichols and Siegfried Wenzel, eds., *The whole book: cultural perspectives on the medieval miscellany* (Ann Arbor, 1996), 37–52; Tony Hunt, 'The trilingual glossary in MS London BL Sloane 146 ff. 69v–72r', *English Studies*, 70 (1989), 289–310; T. W. Machan, 'Language contact in *Piers Plowman*', *Speculum*, 69 (1994), 359–85; Alastair Minnis, *Medieval theory of authorship: scholastic literary attitudes in the later Middle Ages* (Aldershot, 1988), 2nd edn; Nicholas Orme, *Education and society in medieval and renaissance England* (Hambledon, 1989); M. B. Parkes, 'The literacy of the laity', in David Daiches and Anthony Thorlby, eds., *Literature and western civilisation* (London, 1973), ii. 555–78; William Rothwell, 'The trilingual England of Geoffrey Chaucer', *SAC* 16 (1994), 45–67; Thorlac Turville-Petre, *England the nation: language, literature and national identity, 1290–1340* (Oxford, 1996); Laura Wright, 'Macaronic writing in a London archive, 1380–1480', in Matti Rissanen *et al.*, eds., *History of Englishes: new methods and interpretations in historical linguistics* (Berlin, 1992), 582–91.

[21] While it is important not to essentialize relationships between Latin, French, and English, in many situations, the vernacular was a relatively less-powered form of linguistic practice because the languages of the important institutions of parliament, law, and Church were French or Latin, and because the ability to write in Latin and/or French depended on educational or social advantage. This does not mean, however, the vernacular could not be deployed by the powered as part of a political agenda; see especially John H. Fisher, 'A language policy for Lancastrian England', *PMLA* 107 (1992), 1168–80. Nor should it be assumed that the use of the vernacular always implies a dissident or extra-institutional writing position; the translation into the vernacular of texts of moral philosophy, for example, provide a notable exception.

[22] There are many examples included in Wogan-Browne *et al.*, *The idea of the vernacular*, see, for example, Robert Mannyng, *Chronicle*, 21–2/30–54; *The Northern Homily Cycle*, 127–8/35–44; 61–79; John Trevisa, *Dialogue between the lord and the clerk on translation*, 131–4; Thomas Usk, *The testament of love*: 'In Latyn and French hath many soverayne wyttes had gret delyte to endyte, and have many noble thynges fulfylde. But certes, ther ben some that spekyn their poysye-mater in Frenche, of which speche the Frenchemen have as good a fantasaye as we have in heryng of Frenchemennes Englysshe. And many termes ther ben in Englysshe whiche unneth we Englysshmen connen declare the knowlegynge. Howe shulde than a Frencheman borne such termes conne jumpere in this mater, but as the jay chatereth Englyssh? Right so, trewly, the understandyng of Englysshmen wol not stretche to the privy terms in Frenche, whatsoever we bosten of straunge langage. Let than clerkes endyten in Latyn, for they have the propirte of science, and the knowynge in that facultie; and lette Frenchmen in their Frenche also endyten their queynt termes, for it is kyndely to their mouthes; and let us shewe our fantasayes in suche wordes as we lerneden of our dames tonge', p. 30/19–29.

linguistic medium is used.[23] The use of one language rather than another, and also, importantly, the use of Latinate or French diction within English texts,[24] may be seen as a matter of style, in the sense of a manner, not just of writing or speaking, but of *doing*.[25] The 'style' of vernacularity, or Latin or French is indexical to variation in language use which marks out specific social agents and occasions within a broader language community.

Perhaps the strongest impetus which led to the writing of this book was to attempt to bypass the dichotomies 'literature and history', 'text and context', and 'form and content'.[26] These phrases force a binocular vision on literary texts which, in my view, distorts our apprehension both of literary practice and the social formations and processes of which

---

[23] This may be seen very readily from Gower's composing in all three languages and in his provision of Latin headnotes and glosses to his *Confessio Amantis*. The significance of Gower's trilingual output has been variously interpreted; see Siân Echard, 'With Carmen's help: Latin authorities in the *Confessio Amantis*', *Studies in Philology*, 95 (1998), 1–40; Derek Pearsall, 'Gower's Latin and the *Confessio Amantis*', in A. J. Minnis, ed., *Latin and vernacular: studies in late medieval texts* (Cambridge, 1989), 13–25; Winthrop Wetherbee, 'Latin structure and vernacular space: Gower, Chaucer and the Boethian tradition', in Robert Yeager, ed., *Chaucer and Gower: difference, mutuality, exchange* (Victoria, BC, 1991), 7–35, R. F. Yeager, 'Learning to speak in tongues: writing poetry for a trilingual culture', ibid. 115–29; id. 'English, Latin and the text as "other": the page as sign in the work of John Gower', *Text*, 3 (1987), 251–67; and id. *John Gower's poetic: the search for a new Arion* (Woodbridge, 1990), 7–12.

[24] I discuss the social resonances of the uses of Latinate or French diction within English in relationship to *The Manciple's Tale*, and *Pearl* in Chapters 2 and 3. For sustained discussion of these issues in relationship to Chaucer, see Christopher Cannon, *The making of Chaucer's English* (Cambridge, 1998).

[25] See Hodge and Kress, *Social Semiotics*, 80.

[26] Since I first planned this book, there has been a mushrooming of studies which have engaged with breaking down these distinctions and theorizing a relationship between literature and history which avoids binomes. Many of these are listed in the notes to the chapters which follow. While my own approach owes much to discussions on language which do not directly concern themselves with medieval literature, I have found the following studies especially fruitful in helping me to forge my own approach: Jeffrey N. Cox and Larry J. Reynolds, 'The historicist enterprise', in *New historical literary study: essays on reproducing texts, representing history* (Princeton, 1993), 3–38; L. Patterson, *Negotiating the past* (Madison, 1987), pp. ix–74; and the essays in Patterson, ed., *Literature and social change in Britain, 1380–1530* (Berkeley and Los Angeles, 1990); J. G. A. Pocock, 'Texts as events', in K. Sharpe and S. N. Zwicker, eds., *Politics of discourse: literature and history in seventeeth century England* (Berkeley, 1987), 21–34; B. Hanawalt and D. Wallace, eds., *Bodies and disciplines: intersections of literature and history in fifteenth century England* (Minneapolis, 1996), especially the essay by Paul Strohm, 'What happens at intersections?', 223–32.

they are part.[27] By engaging a concept of literature as social discourse and written texts as examples of socioliterary practice[28] I hope to have contributed to the pursuit of a mode of historical enquiry which deconstructs opposition between formalism and historicism but which does not simply replicate emergent critical strategies without intervention. While the legacy bequeathed to literary studies by practical criticism and new criticism has left a residue in which 'close reading' is associated with socially deracinated study,[29] I propose that the formal features of language used in literary texts are essentially freighted with social resonances and that to examine the literary language of texts in detail is simultaneously to examine the kinds of sociological work performed by literary texts. That said, I am not purposing to offer up a theoretical model of historical linguistic enquiry which will then serve as a template for the critical analysis of all late medieval writing. To essentialize any kind of linguistic relationships is to misrepresent linguistic behaviour as a mode of social activity because language is both socially determined and socially mobile. My choice of texts for analysis is purposefully eclectic, encompassing more and less canonical writing, Latin and English, prose and verse, and fourteenth and fifteenth centuries. My frameworks and tools of analysis are also purposefully eclectic because what interests me is how formal features of language have different social resonances in different kinds of texts. It would be fanciful and meretricious to expect to provide some over-arching socioliterary theory to provide an account of a social practice whose materiality is apprehensible—and yet

[27] When I first planned this project my aim was to provide a different conception of the relationships between 'literature' and 'history' from those I had encountered in the then influential (and still valuable) studies by V. J. Scattergood, *Politics and poetry in the fifteenth century* (London, 1971), and Janet Coleman, *English literature in history 1350–1400* (London, 1981), especially in light of Coleman's comment, 'My interest is primarily in the content, the message and the purpose of the verse and prose discussed, but I have also tried to say something about form. It is impossible to divorce form from content when speaking about a literature that consciously used its form and style to signal to its audience that the author was writing in a tradition or consciously breaking with it', p. 273.

[28] Stephen Knight, 'Chaucer and the sociology of literature', *SAC* 2 (1980), 15–51, is an example of a mode of enquiry concerned to locate literature and language within a sociological consciousness. His premises differ from mine in so far as I am more concerned with the linguistic detail of texts, and because I have wanted to avoid Marxist-specific vocabulary (hence the absence of cited engagement with Pierre Bourdieu, *Language and symbolic power*, ed. John B. Thompson (Cambridge, 1991)), even though I have found his discussion insightful and provocative.

[29] On this see especially Cox and Reynolds, *New historical literary study*; and Patterson, *Negotiating the past*.

protean, defined—and yet open to infinite variation. Instead, I have attempted to ground readings of a variety of texts in their linguistic detail in order to try not to impose a prior ideological interpretation of texts 'from above' (though inevitably my own reading position is ideologically invested in proposing the materiality of language practice), but to tease out ideological work and positions traced in their weft and warp.[30] While in some ways, my premiss in this book is consistent with a 'turn to history'[31] it is a 'turn' which returns also to the philology of text.[32]

---

[30] I use the term 'ideology' not in the sense of a 'false consciousness' but to refer to a complex of distinctive practices and social relations which are characteristic of any society and which are inscribed through its language and other material practices; a working definition heavily influenced by Louis Althusser, 'Ideology and ideological state apparatuses', in *Lenin and philosophy*, trans. Ben Brewster (London, 1971), 121–73.

[31] For the phrase, see Cox and Reynolds, *New historical literary study*, 6.

[32] The echo of Paul de Man, 'The Return to Philology', in *The resistance to theory* (Manchester, 1987) is deliberate.

CHAPTER ONE

Constructing Social Realities: *Wynnere and Wastoure*, Hoccleve, and Chaucer

THE LANGUAGE OF social description is a material form of social con-sciousness. Its nomenclature and classifications project versions of com-munity and community relationships which are open to validation and contestation. In contemporary Britain, contested quantifications of social relationships, which are indexical to the growth and prestige of statistical discourses, coexist with a residual stratification of social group-ings into upper, middle, and lower classes, terminology which has survived from an age of lesser social and geographical mobility. Neither version gives us a transparent account of the 'facts'.[1] The vocabulary and schemes used of social groupings and organization do not map out an existent demographic reality; rather they construct versions of com-munal relations from invested positions. In the late twentieth/early twenty-first centuries, single items of vocabulary, for example 'family', are terms in a social contest to establish, challenge, or to decry norms of social behaviour.[2]

In the late fourteenth/early fifteenth centuries, the language of social description is similarly contested. The written materials which survive demonstrate a broad consciousness of society as a network of communal relationships organized by the three estates: those who fight, those who work, and those who pray.[3] It is also clear that this residual version of

[1] See Ivan Reid, *Social class differences in Britain* (Glasgow, 1989) 3rd edn., 3. The statistical variables range from e.g. gross weekly earnings, life expectancy, to the age of mothers at the birth of their first child.

[2] These issues are discussed with eloquence and insight by Jan Zita Grover, 'AIDS: Keywords', in Christopher Ricks and Leonard Michaels, eds., *The state of the language:1990s edition* (London, 1990), 142–62. Her discussion of the word 'family' is on pp. 151–2.

[3] For literary discussions of the three estates see Ruth Mohl, *The three estates in medieval and renaissance literature* (New York, 1933). A fifteenth-century sermon on the conservative three estates model is edited by Alan. J. Fletcher in *Preaching and politics in late medieval England* (Dublin, 1998), 145–69.

social community was placed under strain by changes in the agrarian economy after the outbreaks of plague and by the emergence of professional classes.[4] In this chapter, I explore how a variety of texts deploy the language of social description in ways which either acknowledge changes in social demography, or conveniently ignore them for polemically political purposes.[5] To engage and mobilize the language of social description involves a participation in social practice, and in the poetry that I consider, it is the formal features of literary poetics which articulate this social commentary.

To illustrate these claims, I want to show how the social poetics of the alliterative poem *Wynner and Wastoure* articulates contemporary demographic shifts in the categorization of people, occupation, and rank. By deploying, and yet defamiliarizing, conventional literary horizons, the poet creates an implied audience[6] for his poem which is very different from assemblies created through the use of normative language of social description. This could hardly contrast more starkly with Hoccleve's practice in his poem *To Sir John Oldcastle*, where, through mobilizing a series of interconnecting dominant discourses, Hoccleve attempts to reassert a powerful connection between literary decorum and social hierarchy. Hoccleve can be seen knowingly to disregard what he must have

[4] The changes in agrarian economy and the challenge to feudal hierarchy posed by labour shortages following the plague are discussed in M. M. Postan, 'Medieval agrarian society in its prime: England', in *The Cambridge economic history of medieval England*, vol. i: *The agrarian life of the Middle Ages* (Cambridge, 1966), esp. pp. 604–10; R. H. Hilton, *The decline of serfdom in medieval England* (London, 1983), 28–44; id., *Class conflict and the crisis of feudalism* (London, 1985); J. L. Bolton, *The medieval English economy 1150–1500* (Totowa, NJ, 1980); R. H. Hilton and T. H. Aston, eds., *The English rising of 1381* (Cambridge, 1984).

[5] Strohm, *Social Chaucer*, 3–10. Strohm draws his evidence from a sermon of Thomas Brinton's in 1375 which divides society into four classes, not the traditional three, together with sumptuary laws, and poll tax returns to show how the expansion of the middle grouping of society, especially merchants, but also craftsmen, is reflected in a change in the language of social description. For the effect on Chaucer's *General Prologue* on the expansion of the professional classes, see Jill Mann, *Chaucer and medieval estates satire* (Cambridge, 1973), 1–16, esp. p. 5 and 12–14. See also Lee Patterson, *Chaucer and the subject of history* (London, 1991), 27–32.

[6] I use the term 'implied audience' to suggest the audience which the text expects or anticipates. Umberto Eco uses the term 'model reader' in his discussion of how, in order for an author to make his text communicative, he 'has to assume that the ensemble of codes he relies upon is the same as that shared by his possible reader (hereafter the Model Reader) supposedly able to deal interpretatively with the expressions in the same way as the author deals generatively with them'; *The role of the reader: explorations in the semiotics of texts* (London, 1981), 7.

learnt from Chaucer's social poetics. Chaucer's handling of voice and his treatment of semantics create a social turbulence. His treatment of ventriloquism and understanding of social semiotics reproduces late fourteenth-century cultural cross-currents in linguistic descriptions of society.

Wynner and Wastoure is not only a poem about contest, it is a site of contestation for editors and critics, each fighting over the property of the text from deeply invested positions.[7] The scholarly debate has generated almost as much disagreement as the poem itself dramatizes. For a comparatively brief poem, the measure of dissent has been striking.[8] But that, however, is not altogether surprising. The single text is incomplete and hence lacks the formal closure that might have supplied a focal point of interpretation.[9] At other points the text is clearly corrupt and readers are dependent upon editorial intervention for reconstruction of sense.[10] It may also be the case that the poem has been the subject of interpolation or that parts have been omitted during its transmission. Winner's army is described at length, while Waster's merits only four lines. Did a scribe interpolate the lines on Winner's army, or was the description of Waster's forces accidentally left out?[11]

I think, however, that to adduce textual corruption to explain the imbalance of structure within the poem may be beside the point. Nor do I think that the competing interpretations of the poem would be any

---

[7] The political investment in editing the text is well drawn out by Stephanie Trigg, 'Israel Gollancz's *Wynnere and Wastoure*: political satire or editorial politics?', in Gregory Kratzmann and James Simpson, eds., *Medieval English religious and ethical literature: essays in honour of G. H. Russell* (Cambridge, 1986), 115–27.

[8] See *Wynnere and Wastoure*, ed. Stephanie Trigg (EETS OS 297 1990), pp. xlii–xlvii, for a review of the critical history of the poem. All subsequent citations of the poem are to this text, though I have also consulted the edition by Thorlac Turville-Petre in his *Alliterative poetry of the later middle ages* (London, 1989), 38–66. Lois Roney, in '*Winner and Waster's* "wyse wordes": teaching economics and nationalism in fourteenth century England', *Speculum*, 69 (1994), 1070–100, reviews critical interpretations at pp. 1071–3.

[9] See *Wynnere and Wastoure*, ed. Trigg, pp. xiii–xviii and xlviii–xlix for an account of the text.

[10] For examples, see ll. 58; 79; 83; 91; 94; 121; 136; 176; 186; 266; 314; 337; 353–9; 400; 411; 420; 445; 454; 468–73; 485; 492; 494–500; and 502.

[11] Roney discusses this in '*Winner and Waster's* "wyse wordes"', 1093–8, and argues that there are two sets of blazons missing from the account of Waster's army. She attributes this to deletion somewhere along the transmission line by a copyist. T. H. Bestul argues that the disparity may be accounted for because there was no well-developed satiric tradition associated with Waster's position; see *Satire and allegory in* Wynnere and Wastoure (Lincoln, Nebr., 1974), 72.

the less clamorous were the end of the poem to have been preserved intact. For what strikes me as a reader of this poem is its discontinuities all the way through. The text is riddled with ambiguities and changes of temper, and raises more questions than it answers.[12] Some critics have imputed this to the incompetence of the poet.[13] And yet, the poem demonstrates great mastery of the formal features of alliterative metre and a sweeping command of genre and convention.[14] It seems to me that the inconsistencies are not incidental, nor accidental; they are an integral part of the design. The unexpected shifts and turns in the poem, the surprises and contradictions, articulate what I wish to call its social poetics. The poem's use of literary conventions and topoi, and registers of poetic diction, carry social resonance. It is a poem which is consistent, perhaps, in one thing only: its constant frustration of literary horizons of expectation.[15] To play, as the poet of *Wynner and Wastoure* does, with literary language and motif, is also to play with the social and cultural expectations that inhere in the formal properties of literary texts.[16] Such play has far-reaching consequences for reconstructing the putative audience of the poem.[17]

[12] This is well exemplified by Jerry D. James, 'The undercutting of conventions in *Wynnere and Wastoure*', *MLQ* 25 (1964), 243–58, 'from the fourth line of the poem, the reader has found himself time and again, coaxed into a convention only to have it drop straightaway from beneath him', p. 257. See also David V. Harrington, 'Indeterminacy in *Winner and Waster* and *The Parlement of the Thre Ages*', *Chaucer Review*, 3 (1986), 246–57, who notes that 'nearly every generic feature in these poems . . . encourages uncertainty rather than assurance', p. 247. In formalist terms, these articles offer a most acute account of the play with conventions. My interest is in reading these formal features materially.

[13] e.g. Constance B. Hieatt, '*Winner and Waster* and *The Parliament of the Three Ages*', *American Notes and Queries*, 4 (1966), 100–4; Dorothy Everett, *Essays on Middle English literature* (Oxford, 1955), 50; Nicolas Jacobs, 'The typology of debate and the interpretation of *Wynnere and Wastoure*', *RES* 36 (1985), 481–500, pp. 486 and 495.

[14] See e.g. R. W. V. Elliott, 'The topography of *Wynnere and Wastoure*', *English Studies*, 48 (1967), 1–7, p. 1; Derek Pearsall, *Old and Middle English poetry* (London, 1977), 160; and Thorlac Turville-Petre, *The alliterative revival* (Cambridge, 1977), 4.

[15] The term 'horizon of expectations' is from H. R. Jauss, 'Literary history as a challenge to literary theory', *New Literary History*, 2 (1970), 11–19.

[16] Bestul observes that the poem is a 'composite of a number of well-known and widely used medieval genres', *Satire and allegory*, 24.

[17] One of the most contested issues in the criticism of *Wynnere and Wastoure* has been that of date. Trigg provides an account of the debate, *Wynnere and Wastoure*, pp. xxii–xxvii. In 1920 Israel Gollancz dated the poem to 1352, *A good short debate between Winner and Waster: an alliterative poem on social and economic problems in England in the year 1352 with modern English rendering* (Select Early English Poems, 3, 1920). Gollancz's conclusions were found wanting in Elisabeth Salter's essay, 'The timeliness of *Wynnere and Wastoure*', *Medium Aevum*, 47

The prologue to the poem is full of conflicting generic signals.[18] From the reference to Brutus's legendary founding of Britain, the poem moves to address matters of provincial anxiety: division between west and south being registered as generational difference between father and son (ll. 7–9).[19] There follows a mini-catalogue of the signs of judgement and a section of apocalyptic prophecy which uses the world-upside-down topos, which in turn yields to a passage which has been read as a lament for the decline of true 'makers'.[20]

> Whylome were lordes in londe þat loued in thaire hertes
> To here makers of myrthes þat matirs couthe fynde
> And now es no frenchipe in fere but fayntnesse of hert
> Wyse wordes withinn þat wroghte were neuer
> Ne redde in no romance þat euer renke herde.
> Bot now a childe appon chere withowtten chyn-wedys
> Þat neuer wroghte thurgh witt thies wordes togedire
> Fro he can jangle als a jaye and japes telle
> He schall be lenede and louede and lett of a while
> Wele more þan þe man that made it hymseluen.
> Bot neuer þe lattere at the laste when ledys ben knawen;
> Werke witnesse will bere who wirche kane beste.   (19–30)[21]

(1978), 40–65. In the same year that Thorlac Turville-Petre argued for *Wynnere and Wastoure* as 'the earliest dateable poem of the Alliterative Revival', *Alliterative revival*, p. 1, David Lawton suggested that *Wynnere and Wastoure* was influenced by *Piers Plowman*, 'The date of two middle English alliterative poems', *Parergon*, 18 (1977), 17–25. Trigg, 'Israel Gollancz's *Wynnere and Wastoure*', suggests a date 1352–1370; cf. David Lawton, 'Middle English alliterative poetry: an introduction', in id., ed., *Middle English alliterative poetry and its literary background* (Cambridge, 1982), 3. It seems to me that while we can establish 1352 as a *terminus a quo*, there is nothing in the poem which precludes a date of composition in the later rather than middle fourteenth century. The sophisticated handling of literary convention suggests an audience which was familiar with generic conventions, though I am aware that the argument could be turned around to suggest that the poet was ignorant of them and therefore used them cack-handedly. I hope that the following discussion will show that the latter hypothesis is unlikely.

[18] Everett, *Essays*, 50, calls the opening reference to Brutus the Trojan and his founding of the kingdom of Britain 'pointless'. Turville-Petre, in 'The Prologue to *Wynnere and Wastoure*', *LSE* 18 (1987), 19–29, sees the Prologue to be organized around three roughly equal sections concerning the siege of Troy, the signs of Doomsday, and the nature of true poets, p. 23.

[19] James argues that in the opening the poet unexpectedly explodes stock elements. The Troy convention becomes absurd as Troy and the past vanish and the grand style sags, 'The undercutting of conventions', 246.

[20] e.g. Bestul, *Satire and allegory*, 60; Jacobs, 'The typology of debate', 498; Turville-Petre, *Alliterative revival*, 1, and 'The Prologue to *Wynnere and Wastoure*', 27.

[21] Turville-Petre, *Alliterative poetry*, punctuates this passage differently, see especially ll.

Trigg reads this passage to be concerned, not so much about oral poetry and its decline, as registering the narrator's concern to establish his narrative voice as that of an authoritative, prophetic truth-teller.[22] Both Trigg and Turville-Petre point out that the complaint that true poets were neglected, together with ritual abuse of more popular entertainers, were familiar medieval conventions.[23] Indeed, the passage blends a number of different topoi: the harking back to a former age to point up the ills of the present; the contrast between the wisdom of age and the callowness of youth; and the revelation of those who have done best at the Last Judgement.[24] But, apart from drawing a contrast between what is considered to be good and bad literature, to my mind, it is deeply unclear what kind of literary work the narrator is describing here.

Line 20 mentions 'myrthes' which lords were glad to hear, but then in l. 22, there is a shift to 'wyse wordes'. Courtly entertainment, of course, could contain 'wyse wordes',[25] but the slightly odd juxtaposition ('wyse wordes' suggests something more morally serious than 'myrthes') is fore-grounded by the use of the word 'romance' in l. 23. Other literary texts often associate romance with lightweight entertainment, as in, for exam-ple, *The Crowned King*,[26] *The Nun's Priest's Tale*, or *Troilus and Criseyde*. Both the Chaucer works align romance with literature favoured by women.[27] Further, l. 23 has an internal confusion: 'Ne redde in no

29–30, and differs in treatment of emendation, see 'thre' for 'thies' (25) and 'neuer-þe-lattere' (29).

[22] *Wynnere and Wastoure*, ed. Trigg, 18–19. Cf. Stephanie Trigg, 'The rhetoric of excess in *Winner and Waster*', YLS 3 (1989), 91–108, repr. in *Medieval English poetry* (London, 1993), 186–99. She notes that the authoritative speaking voice of the Prologue is but one of the many voices and rhetorical traditions woven into the poem, p. 199. Cf. Turville-Petre, 'The prologue to *Wynnere and Wastoure*', 26, who interprets the narrator as 'the prophet, the inheritor of the wisdom of Solomon who has the visionary experience recounted in his dream poem'.

[23] *Wynnere and Wastoure*, ed. Trigg, 19; Turville-Petre, 'The prologue to *Wynnere and Wastoure*', 23–6.

[24] These are discussed by Turville-Petre, ibid. 20–4. Bestul notes borrowings from exist-ing prophetic materials, *Satire and allegory*, 59–61.

[25] Geoffrey Shepherd, 'The nature of alliterative poetry in late medieval England', PBA 56 (1970), 57–76, argues that for all the courtliness of some alliterative poetry there is still a sus-tained concern with moral seriousness.

[26] *The Crowned King*, l. 22, collocates reading romances with 'reuelyng', text cited from *The Piers Plowman tradition*, ed. Helen Barr (London 1993).

[27] *Troilus and Criseyde*, II. 99–112 where Criseyde and her women read the romance of Thebes, and Pandarus trumps their literary knowledge by claiming to know Statius's *Thebaid*. In *The Nun's Priest's Tale* the narrator claims that his story is as true as the book of Lancelot de Lake 'that wommen holde in ful greet reverence' (VII. 3211–13).

romance þat euer renke herde'. To read a romance which previously has been orally composed is entirely consonant with how such works could have been received at the time,[28] but within the context of the passage as a whole, it contributes to an unstable sense of the kinds of literature that the narrator is discussing. The line reminds me of the 'advice' given in *The Canterbury Tales* that if we do not wish to *hear* a particular tale, then we can turn over the *leaf* and choose another one.[29] In *Wynner and Wastoure* we do not know whether the romance is oral or written, or whether it is orally composed or orally performed. Further, is it gravely moral, or courtly diversion? Despite the deployment of recognizable topoi in this passage, modes of literary texts are scrambled. It is clear that the narrator disapproves of janglers who tell simply 'japes', but what kind of literature he would wish to see instead remains unspecified.

This is important because it unsettles the audience's expectations in a fashion which is continuous with the medley of generic signals right at the start of the poem. Turville-Petre comments on this passage that while traditional poetry may begin by defining its listeners and their relationship with the reciting poet, in *Wynnere and Wastoure*, 'we are presented with a non-audience'.[30] This is a very important observation; we can often project the composition of the audience of a text through the social affiliations of its language and genre.[31] It is extraordinarily difficult to do this with *Wynnere and Wastoure* because of the discontinuities and conflicting literary signals. To my mind, the passage may be read as a self-reflexive observation of the way that the poem's own literary modes and affiliations are not kept distinct, and the passage functions as a proleptic announcement of how the entire poem will play with different literary modes and conventions.[32]

One aspect of this play is the characterization of the narrator. Trigg

---

[28] Ruth Finnegan observes that there are three ways in which a poem may be called oral: composition; mode of transmission; performance. She notes that some oral poetry has all three characteristics, some only two, *Oral poetry: its nature, significance and social context* (Cambridge, 1977), 16. Jacobs sees the line to refer to 'those who could improvise rather than learn their lines from another poet or from books', 'The typology of debate', 498.

[29] *The Miller's Prologue*, I. 3176–7.

[30] Turville-Petre, 'The prologue to *Wynnere and Wastoure*', 27. He goes on to remark that the 'lordes in londe' no longer listen and true poetry is disregarded. As a result of this aversion to truth, the world is in a degenerate state, p. 27.

[31] See references cited in Introduction, nn. 17–24.

[32] Harrington notes that 'nearly every generic feature in these poems—the irresponsible narrator, dream visions, debate, personification allegory—encourages uncertainty rather than assurance', 'Indeterminacy in *Winner and Waster*', 247.

notes how the narratorial guise of the prophetic truthteller in the prologue to the poem is not maintained.[33] For a start, the narrator practi-
cally disappears from view as an explicit presence once the poem has got
underway. We are reminded of his presence on two occasions. The first
is:

> The kynge waytted one wyde and the wyne askes,
> Beryns broghte it anone in bolles of siluere.
> Me thoghte I sowpped so sadly it sowrede bothe myn eghne
> And he that wilnes of this werke to wete any forthire,
> Full freschely and faste, for here a fitt endes.   (213–18)

For all that he has declared in the Prologue that courtly entertainers are
no longer fostered, in these lines the narrator casts himself as one. In the
Prologue, he distances himself from courtly 'myrthes', but here presents
himself as drinking the king's wine, and so deeply that it blurs his vision.
A drunken court minstrel is hardly consonant with the stance of a
wise truth-telling poet. It is also striking that the narrator constructs the
audience as belonging to the same milieu—fill up your cups fast, for
here a fitt ends. It is a very short fitt, and the jollity sits somewhat oddly
with the serious tone of the preceding portion of the poem.[34]

   The reintroduction of the narrative voice in the next fitt is just as
puzzling. This fitt is even shorter, and it concludes with exactly the
same words:

> And he þat wilnes of þis werke for to wete forthe,
> Full freschely and faste, for here a fit endes.   (366–7)

That the phrase is a topos is shown by its repetition, but its use here is
startling. Winner has just been enumerating the excesses of Waster's
feasts in extremely judgemental terms. There is no break between this
account and the injunction to the audience to replenish their glasses.
The audience and the narrator are thus co-opted into exactly the kind
of courtly occasion which Winner has just been satirizing. It creates a
split narrator and a split audience; both distanced from, and complicit in,
the court feasting and entertainment that has just been criticized. Far

---

[33] Trigg, *Medieval English poetry*, 199. Turville-Petre, 'The prologue to *Wynnere and
Wastoure*', notes that the narrator is at the centre of any dream vision and that it is striking that
the assurance that we are going to hear of the narrator's experience is delayed until the first
line after the Prologue (31), p. 26.

[34] James notes that ending the first fitt with a call to drink plays a joke 'on the much-
battered dream convention' and the audience both within and outside the poem, 'The
undercutting of conventions', 247.

from being an authoritative figure at this point in the poem, the narrator is fractured, and the relationship of the audience to the poem one
that is fissured. The audience is offered no secure focal point from
which to respond to the poem. And from this point onwards, the narrator as mediating consciousness between the audience and the matter of
the poem slips entirely from view. Narrative authority is enveloped in a
play of voices which the poem has already staged, and which now takes
over entirely.[35] Narrative boundaries and delimitations are abandoned
and the audience is left to pick their way through the literary free-for-
all that follows.[36]

   This unanchoring of the audience, and the dissolution of easily
identifiable and stable constituency is intensified by the provisionality
of the poem's literary affiliations at numerous points in the poem. The
treatment of the dream vision setting for the poem is a very telling
example:

> Bot I schall tell ȝow a tale þat me bytyde me ones,
> Als I went in the weste wandrynge myn one.
> Bi a bonke of a bourne, bryghte was the sonne
> Vndir a worthiliche wodde by a wale medewe
> Fele floures gan folde ther my fote steppede.
> I layde myn hede one ane hill ane hawthorne besyde
> The throstills full throly they threpen togedire
> Hipped vp heghwalles fro heselis tyll othire
> Bernacles with thayre billes one barkes þay roungen
> Þe jay janglede one heghe, jarmede the foles.
> Þe bourne full bremly rane þe bankes bytwene.
> So ruyde were þe roughe stremys and raughten so heghe
> That it was neghand nyghte or I nappe myghte
> For dyn of the depe watir and dadillyng of fewllys.
> Bot als I laye at the laste þan lowked myn eghne
> And I was swythe in a sweuen sweped belyue.   (31–46)

This passage deploys the literary convention of the 'locus amoenus'.
This is a topos that appears in a variety of Middle English texts to frame
a number of different dream settings: from the garden of earthly paradise

---

[35] Trigg, *Medieval English poetry*, traces the play of voices in the poem.

[36] James observes that from the fourth line of the poem, 'the reader has found himself [*sic*]
time and time again, coaxed into a convention only to have it drop straightaway from
beneath him. If the convention is gulled, so too is the precipitate reader', 'The undercutting
of conventions', 257. James draws the conclusion that the play with conventions shows that
the poet sides with Waster.

in *Pearl*[37] to the glut of possibilities offered to a poacher in *The Parlement of the Thre Ages*.[38] But whatever the local spin on the topos, one characteristic is usually stable; the 'locus amoenus' is pleasant; the prelude to the dream vision describes an idealized landscape, even if poets then go on from this to contrast it with a more disturbing reality, or to challenge its terms of reference.[39] The treatment in *Wynnere and Wastoure*, however, does not conform to this expectation.

Many key features of the topoi are present in the account: a profusion of birds and flowers, birdsong, and a river.[40] There are parallels between this account and those of other poems, especially between *Wynner and Wastoure*, and *The Parlement of the Thre Ages*. Indeed, one line is reproduced almost verbatim: 'The throstills full throly they threpen togedire' (38).[41] What is strikingly absent from this 'locus amoenus' in *Wynner and Wastoure*, however, is pleasure. In contrast to the rejuvenation of narrators in other poems which use this convention, and their expressed charm with the landscape in which they find themselves,[42] the narrator here derives no comfort from his setting. Rather, it is either a source of irritation to him, or he spoils it. Instead of bright, fresh flowers with sweet scents, we learn that the narrator crushes the flowers between his feet (35).[43] Instead of charming birdsong, we get noise: barnacle geese

[37] The convention and its history is examined in detail in relation to *Pearl* by Pamela Gradon, *Form and style in early English literature* (London, 1971), 197–206. Bestul compares the spring setting of *Wynnere and Wastoure* with that of twelfth-century Latin and French debate poems, *Satire and allegory*, 33–4.

[38] *The Parlement of the Thre Ages*, ed. M. Y. Offord (EETS OS 246 1959), ll. 1–103.

[39] For instance, the narrator in Chaucer's *The Parlement of Foules* compares the songs of the birds to angels (191–2) and states that there is more joy in the landscape than could be told (208–9). In the enumeration of the birds which follow, however, rather more unsavoury aspects of the natural world are not suppressed, e.g. the treacherous lapwing (347), the swallow, murderer of bees (353), and the drake which destroys its own kind (360).

[40] These are all present in Matthew of Vendôme's template for scene setting in his *Ars Versificatoria*, in E. Faral, ed., *Les arts poétiques du xiie et du xiiie siècle* (Paris, 1924), 149.

[41] Cf. *The Parlement of the Thre Ages*, 'And the throstills full throly threpen in the bankes' (14).

[42] e.g. *The Prologue to the Legend of Good Women* F. 175–8; *Pearl*, ed. E. V. Gordon (Oxford, 1953), ll. 45–6; *Piers Plowman: a parallel text edition of the A, B, C and Z versions*, ed. A. V. C. Schmidt (London, 1995), B. Prol., 10; (all subsequent references to *Piers* are to this edition; *Mum and the Sothsegger*, in *The Piers Plowman tradition*, ed. Barr, 940–42; *Death and Liffe*, ed. J. P. Donatelli (Cambridge, Mass., 1989), 29; and *The Parlement of Foules*, 10–12; 100–2, though the narrator does remark that he has to stay still for so long in order to stalk his deer that gnats gnawed at his eyes (50).

[43] Roney notes this and other discordant details. She argues that the poet depicts 'a realistic natural world of interaction and unintentional abrasion', which is an 'objective

champing at the shells of nuts, or as Turville-Petre reads the line, clattering on the barks of trees with their beaks (39). Unusually, there are jays present, which jangle (40).[44] In the same line, 'jarmede þe foules' is obscure. Turville-Petre glosses it as 'the birds twittered', but Trigg associates 'jarmede' with words which have the sense of 'bleating' or 'yammering'. The latter seems very plausible given that the narrator complains of being kept awake by the 'dadillyng of fewylls'—a phrase which suggests commotion or tumult. He is also prevented from sleeping by the fierce roar of the river. To use diction such as 'bremely' (41), 'ruyde', 'roughe', 'raughten' (42), and 'dyn' (44) of a river in a 'locus amoenus' transfigures the convention. In *Wynnere and Wastoure*, the framing topos is jangled by lexical choices which build up a picture of anti-pleasure and disharmony within a convention which usually stresses the opposite. But the genre is not simply undermined: there are also details which conform to how a 'locus amoenus' should work. In addition to the inclusion of staple features, the narrator does eventually fall asleep and wakes in a 'loueliche lande' (48).

What he sees and hears when he wakes is no less stable than what has gone before. Although he witnesses what is ostensibly an argument between the respective merits of the familiar opposition between avarice and prodigality,[45] as Trigg explains, the poem

constantly alter[s] the representations of its two personifications, attempting to flesh out a formal opposition in contemporary social terms. At different times, Waster is the leader of a mercenary army, a knight of the king's household, a disaffected aristocrat who squanders his inheritance, a laborer who refuses to

correlative to the economic world he will posit in the coming vision', *Winner and Waster's* "wyse wordes"', 1099.

[44] Which echoes the description of inept minstrels as jays which jangle and tell japes, l. 26. James notes the jangling of the birds as an undercutting of dream convention and observes how many an overwrought discussion progresses from debating (thrushes) to banging (woodpeckers) and finally to jangling (jays), 'The undercutting of conventions', 249.

[45] Bestul explores this in detail, *Satire and allegory*, 1–23. But as with most aspects of this poem, what the two characters represent has been disputed. John Speirs, *Medieval English poetry: the non-Chaucerian tradition* (London, 1957), 277, reads the two characters as representing two opposing personalities, ways of life; A.C. Spearing, *Medieval dream poetry* (Cambridge, 1976), 131–2, as symbolical abstractions of the opposing economic principles of gathering and spending; Jacobs as representatives of the golden feudal past against the mercantile, individualistic present, 'Typology of debate', 496; and Roney sees them to be 'bad examples' of economic practice, a view which includes aspects of the earlier critical views, *Winner and Waster's* "wyse wordes"', 1089–92.

work, a wealthy man with due concern for the poor, a glutton, and a courtly lover.[46]

Winner is presented both as an old-style feudal landlord, concerned at the sale of aristocratic land, a leader of a mercenary army, a parsimonious miser, and a bourgeois merchant concerned only with personal profit. The social roles of Winner and Waster are discontinuous and contradictory. At the end of the poem, it seems that their identification as knights has been forgotten: the king says that he will take Winner with him when he goes to his French wars: 'I thynk to do it in ded and dub þe to knyghte' (499). But Winner, along with Waster, has already been cast as a knight earlier in the poem (203). Further, the king collapses any residual moral antithesis between the positions of Winner and Waster. He says to Winner: 'Þe more þou wastis þi wele þe better þe Wynner lykes' (495). In pronouncing his final judgement, the earlier pageantry and martial framing of Winner and Waster is also abandoned. The King accedes to Waster's request that the debate be abandoned because he cannot stand the sight of his opponent (hardly a very chivalrous denouement) and packs Winner off to live with the Pope, and Waster to dwell with the riff-raff of Cheapside (460–95). It is a judgement which completely scrambles the courtly and chivalrous staging of the debate (though we might have forgotten by this stage that at the start, Winner and Waster were at the head of two armies preparing to fight each other (50–4)). One knight is bidden to lodge with the head of the second estate (461), and the other, with some of the poorest of the third (476–85). The tripartite division of society into three estates, which conservative writers liked to pass off as a normative representation of society, is here disrupted.

In fact, such a vision has been disrupted at many earlier points during the poem as a result of the poet's narrative descriptions and lexical choices. The description of the opposing armies presents well-drilled aristocracy dressed in bright armour with noble crests (50–69). But yet, when the banners of the two armies are described, we learn that the armies are composed, not of knights, but of members of the second and third estates. Amongst those present are the Pope, lawyers and merchants, and the four orders of friars (142–92). These are not the social groups we might expect to be ranged as opposing aristocratic armies, squaring up for a fight. It makes for good social satire, of course, by mingling the religious with merchants and lawyers traditionally known

---

[46] Trigg, *Medieval English poetry*, 188.

for their acquisitiveness and sharp practice.[47] But there is a broader dimension too; the description of the banners articulates a more sweeping sense of social confusion than specifically targeted estates satire, a confusion which is achieved by the poet's play with literary language and the conventional associations of poetic diction. The fifth and sixth banners of Winner's army may be taken as representative examples. First, the Carmelites:

> And ȝitt es the fyfte appon þe felde þe faireste of þam alle,
> A brighte banere of blee whitte with three bore-hedis.   (174–5)

Although the friars belong to the second estate, the emblem on the banner is one associated either with the aristocracy or with the third estate. A boar's head was a respected heraldic symbol, for instance in *Sir Degarré*, Sir Degarré's father has a shield of azure with three boar's heads enamelled upon it.[48] Boar's heads were also served up at banquets, as in l. 332 of *Wynner and Wastoure*, and consequently were often used as tavern signs.[49] Within a single line, the poet has conflated an heraldic sign and a tavern symbol in order to describe how the friars flout social order. The banner of the sixth group marks out the Augustinian friars:

> The sexte es of sendell, and so are þay alle,
> Whitte als the whalles bone whoso the sothe tellys.   (180–1)

'Whitte als the whalles bone' is a simile usually used to describe the pale complexion of women.[50] Here, the poet has mobilized this figure away from its customary context in order to describe the feminized, pampered luxury of the friars. As in the description of the fifth banner, however, over and above the local anti-fraternal satire, reregistration

---

[47] Cf. the treatment in *Piers Plowman*, B. I. 211–15 and B. VII. 18–59, and Chaucer, *General Prologue*, 270–84 and 309–30. The treatment of lawyers and merchants in estates satire is discussed by Mann, *Medieval estates satire*, 86–91, and 99–103.

[48] See *Sir Degarré*, ll. 1005–8 in *Middle English romances*, ed. A. V. C. Schmidt and Nicolas Jacobs (London, 1980), Part Two. The shield carried by Sir Thopas also bears a boar's head, *The Tale of Sir Thopas*, VII. 2060.

[49] See *MED* bor 6, 'bor(es) hed' (c). A boar's head is served up at the feast in *The Alliterative Morte Arthure*, see *King Arthur's Death*, ed. Larry D. Benson (Exeter, 1986), l. 177.

[50] e.g. *The Harley Lyrics*, ed. G. L. Brook (Manchester, 1956), no. 7/40; no. 9/1. See Derek Brewer, 'The ideal of feminine beauty in medieval literature, especially *The Harley Lyrics*, Chaucer, and some Elizabethans', *MLR* 50 (1955), 257–69, p. 260. Chaucer also reregisters the convention, describing the male eagle in Criseyde's dream as 'fethered whit as bon', *Troilus and Criseyde*, II. 296. Cf. discussion of this simile in *Pearl* in the following chapter.

of the simile from its usual context requires the audience to realign its customary identifications of type of literary language.

This manoeuvre is one that is practised frequently in the poem. There is often abrupt slippage between registers. Viewed in the context of other alliterative poetry, the style of *Wynner and Wastoure* is distinctive. It has often been observed that alliterative poetry can be divided into two contrasting corpora: the formal, courtly style with elaborate diction and a high density of alliterative vocabulary, as exemplified, for example, by *Sir Gawain and the Green Knight*, and that which is written predominantly in a much plainer style, with fewer instances of alliterative diction and a more pragmatic tone. *Piers Plowman* and the poems in the *Piers Plowman* tradition are representative of this latter mode of alliterative verse.[51] *Wynnere and Wastoure*, however, exemplifies both kinds of writing. There are passages in the poem which are insistently courtly and poetic, for instance the description of the king's costume (90–8), to which we might compare the elaborate dress of the Green Knight in *Gawain*.[52] There is also use of standard alliterative conventions such as the arming of the knight (108–18).[53]

Such rich writing also coexists with much plainer passages, for instance, the herald's speech which outlines the penalties for treason (124–35).[54] And even within passages, the affiliations of the alliterative diction are varied. One example must suffice. Winner's account of

[51] See Hoyt Duggan, 'Langland's meter', *YLS* 1 (1987), 41–71; David Lawton, 'Alliterative style', in J. A. Alford, ed., *A Companion to* Piers Plowman (Berkeley, 1988), 223–49; Pearsall, *Old and Middle English poetry*, 150–8; Turville-Petre, *The alliterative revival*, 31–2; Elisabeth Salter, '*Piers Plowman* and *The Simonie*', *Archiv*, 203 (1967), 241–54; ead., 'Langland and the contexts of *Piers Plowman*', *Essays and Studies*, 32 (1979), 19–25; and James Simpson, *Piers Plowman: An introduction to the B text* (London, 1990), 9.

[52] *Sir Gawain and the Green Knight*, ed. J. R. R. Tolkien and E. V. Gordon (Oxford, 1967), 2nd edn. rev. Norman Davis, 151–202. All subsequent line references are to this edition.

[53] James notes a subversive twist in the ritual arming of the champion in that the knight sits down for a while in order to pull on his armour, 'The undercutting of conventions', 251. Chaucer also plays with this convention in *Sir Thopas*, where the eponymous hero arms himself after the meeting with the giant, and puts on his underclothes (2047–73). In *Gawain*, the convention is used without burlesque, 566–639; cf. also *The Alliterative Morte Arthure*, 902–19.

[54] The syntax is hypotactic; there are only three adjectives—and these are functional. There is an even distribution of nouns and verbs, and the only distinctive vocabulary is 'beryn' (126 and 131). The plain style may be the result of the poet's echo of legislation passed to prevent the practice of leading armed bands of men, see *Wynnere and Wastoure*, ed. Trigg, 25–6. The speech at ll. 190–201 is also free of ornament and embellishment, and the king's concluding judgement, 456 ff., contrasts with the more ornate style of the rest of the poem.

Waster's feast is, in some ways, very similar to the courtly sumptuous-ness which is found in other alliterative poems, providing an occasion to indulge in one of the standard conventions of alliterative poetry: exten-sive cataloguing for displays of verbal pyrotechnics.[55] The description of the feast in *Wynnere and Wastoure* displays many signs of affinity with these traditions and could be placed alongside descriptions of feasts in other alliterative poems quite happily,[56] but for the fact that the social affiliations of the feast are not insistently courtly. The social register of the passage shifts—often alarmingly—as in the following:

> To see þe borde ouerbrade with blasande disches
> Als it were a rayled rode with rynges and stones.   (342–3)

Right in the middle of a description of an aristocratic feast the poet inserts an image of a precious crucifix. The decoration is consonant with the signs of courtliness which the feast celebrates, but the simile is one which belongs to clerical discourse and creates an abrupt shift of register within the passage. Line 356 comments on the extravagant cost of the dishes: '[Ich]e a mese at a merke bytwen twa men'. While extravagance is often a feature of courtly feasts, as in the detail in *Sir Gawain and the Green Knight* that there were so many dishes it was hard to find room to set the cutlery (124–5), it is unusual, and discordant, to have aristocratic plenty described in cash terms. The courtly register of the verse is disrupted by the mercantile connotations of the word 'merke'.[57] Like-wise, the inclusion of trumpets is often a constituent feature of literary feasts, but while in *Gawain* the sound of the trumpets is joyously har-monious with the courtly proceedings of the feast (116–17), in *Wynnere and Wastoure*, the trumpets are described as 'gouling' (359). The lexical choice here has connotations of disorderly yelling that is more in keeping with rebellious crowds than aristocratic music-making.[58]

---

[55] The use of the catalogue in alliterative poetry is discussed by Shepherd, 'The nature of alliterative poetry', 60.

[56] e.g. *Alliterative Morte Arthure*, 176–219; *Gawain and the Green Knight*, 884–900.

[57] In *Mum and the Sothsegger*, the narrator describes a feast given by a mayor and by punning on 'merke' in the sense of 'to observe' (*MED* merken 8(a)) and 'coin' (*MED* merke (n)2(a)), comments on the cost of the feast (834). The wordplay points up corruption in an urban context of feasting; a very different context from that in *Wynnere and Wastoure*.

[58] Additionally, the use of the words 'mawes' (355), and 'bowells' (357) are hardly con-sonant with a courtly register, referring as they do to bodily ingestion and digestion. It reminds me of the moment in *The Knight's Tale*, where, for all the strenuous sublimation of physicality in the description of love in the story, when Arcite is on the point of death, the knight betrays himself into mentioning 'venym and corrupcioun'; 'vomyt' and 'laxatif' (A. 2754 and 2756).

The concluding lines of this passage are a complete medley of social registers:

> 3e hafe no myster of þe helpe of þe heuen-kyng.
> Þus are 3e scorned by skyll and schathed þeraftir
> Þat rechen for a repaste a rawnsom of siluer.
> Bot ones I herd in a haule of a herdsmans tong,
> 'Better were meles many þan a mery nyghte'.　　(361–5)

Line 361 belongs to a theological register as Winner accuses Wastoure of one of the sins against the Holy Spirit; namely despair, while l. 362 deploys legal diction in 'skyll' and 'schathed' to remind Waster that he has been outwitted in argument, as in a legal disputation.[59] The diction of l. 363 scrambles vocabulary from two different lexical fields: a 'repaste' is a meal, but the ransom of silver suggests the thirty silver coins which Judas received for his betrayal of Christ. And finally, the aristocratic feast concludes with a proverb spoken by a herdsman—a labourer.

The description of the feast captures in miniature the persistent literary and social discontinuities of the whole poem. The audience is offered no fixed social point of reference from which to read the significance of the literary conventions, motifs, and diction. The audience is constantly wrong-footed, as the register, diction, and generic affiliations of the poem are juggled and redefined. The social significance of this—often abruptly—variegated texture is twofold. The poem as artefact cannot be accommodated within any one neat and tidy social setting. It cannot be seen to be the product of any one discrete ensemble of social practices. Rather, it inheres in several, which often compete with each other in sections of the poem where the generic signals create expectations of a more homogenous choice of register, alliterative style, and diction. Secondly, the scrambling of horizons of expectation creates an implied audience whose social identity is unstable; the poem does not offer any consistent position of social identity. I would argue that this is an index of the mobility of social position, and the changing language of social description current at the time when the poem was written.[60] While the tripartite division of society into those who fight,

---

[59] 'Skyll' has the sense of a legal argument, see *MED* 'skile' 5. In its legal sense 'scathe' means damages, wrongdoing, or theft, 'scathe' n.1(d).

[60] In this respect, the project of the poem bears similarities to the work of the contemporary poet Tony Harrison, where, for instance, in 'Me Tarzan', a poem which discusses the fracturing of Northern working-class masculine identity because of educational advantage,

those who pray, and those who work was a model frequently written about, it was a model increasingly inadequate to accommodate contemporary social formations.[61] To define the aristocracy as those who fight is archaic, given that the nobility were more concerned with administering either their own estates, or attending to political and bureaucratic duties. Boundaries between the three estates were frequently blurred, and the formulation offers no room, either, for the expanding professional classes such as merchants or lawyers, or aspirant artisans.[62]

The stylistic heterogeneity of *Wynnere and Wastoure* articulates a process of social reconfiguration. Although the poem preserves a sense of traditional hierarchy through the inclusion of the figure of the king and appeals to his law, the shifts and transitions in register and diction are signs of how such a vertical ordering of society is under strain. In its play with decorum, the poem lacks any authoritative focus or structure, and again, I would argue, this is indexical to the social situation which produced it. While it is more often to Chaucer's *General Prologue* that one turns for an example of the redefinition of social relationships and affinities in the late fourteenth century,[63] I would argue that the less familiar alliterative poem *Wynnere and Wastoure* accomplishes a similar project, and with great literary subtlety.

The ideological work performed by the formal features of this poem could hardly contrast more starkly with that in Hoccleve's *Poem to Sir*

the diction and metrical scheme projects a fully competent audience only if they have knowledge of Latin, literary heritage, Leeds dialect words, and popular culture. The formal features of the poem create an implied reader who is fully competent to understand the poem only by reassembling all the fractured points of social identity which the heterogeneity of the diction demands; see *Continuous* (London, 1981), 5.

[61] See discussion in Strohm, *Social Chaucer*, 2–10.

[62] The tension between conservative descriptions of society and the pressures on that language are well exemplified in the sermon preached by Bishop Stafford at the opening of the parliament of 1433, *Rot. Parl*, iv. 419. Stafford interprets his text: 'Let the mountains bear peace to the people, and the hills justice' (Psalm 72: 3), as representing 'the threefold estate of the realm'. His description of the members of the threefold estate does not correspond, however, to a conservative formation. The mountains represent prelates, nobles, and magnates; the hills the knights, esquires, and merchants; and the people, the peasants, artisans, and lower orders. (I am grateful to John Watts for a translation of this address.)

[63] See J. V. Cunningham. 'The literary form of the Prologue to the *Canterbury Tales*', *Modern Philology*, 49 (1952), 172–81 (an article especially germane to my argument as it discusses Chaucer's reregistration of dream vision materials to fashion an array of pilgrims commensurate with demographic changes). See also H. Marshall Leicester, 'The art of impersonation: a General Prologue to the *Canterbury Tales*', *PMLA* 95 (1980), 213–24; Mann, *Medieval estates satire* and Patterson, *Chaucer and the subject of history*, 26–32.

John Oldcastle.[64] The poem was written after the rebellion in 1413 which
the Lollard knight Oldcastle was reputed to have organized. Paul Strohm
has recently argued that Oldcastle was framed by the Lancastrian regime
as a threat to social order and that the revolt in 1413 was fathered upon
him as part of an attempt to bolster Lancastrian rule. Dogged by the
shadow of usurpation following the deposition of Richard II in 1399,
Henry IV and his advisers needed to find ways to construct the new
regime as one that was legitimate. By casting Lollards in general, and
Oldcastle in particular, as a menace to the realm, the Lancastrian regime
could deflect scrutiny about its own legitimacy by projecting questions
of order, threat, and stability onto perceived heretics. Oldcastle was use-
ful for the Lancastrians as a figure of insurgence. Through being seen as
defenders of the security of the realm, and punishing anyone who threat-
ened social stability, the Lancastrian regime authorized its right to rule.[65]

Hoccleve's poem is entirely complicit in this Lancastrian framing of
Oldcastle. Ostensibly, the poem is an appeal to the knight to recant his
heretical views. The terms in which it does so re-creates the Lancastrian
project to present Henry's rule as God-given and sanctioned, while
Lollardy is seen as evil perfidy. The narrator calls on Oldcastle to quench
his 'pryde' and 'presumpcioun', diction which frames Oldcastle as a
Lucifer figure.[66] Mercy, however, is still available to the errant knight:
'it renneth al in brede' (70). A well of mercy is a figure familiar from
religious lyrics[67] which Hoccleve here reregisters to present the
Lancastrian regime as one that is ever merciful, willing to take even their
Luciferian son back into their bosom.[68]

Hoccleve also mobilizes the diction of Christian knighthood in order
to effect an opposition between Oldcastle's disobedience and the God-
sanctioned chivalry of the Lancastrian regime. The narrator calls on

[64] The substance of the poem is discussed by Jerome Mitchell, Thomas Hoccleve: a study in
early fifteenth century English poetic (Urbana, Ill., 1968), 31–2.

[65] Paul Strohm, England's empty throne: usurpation and the language of legitimation (New
Haven, 1998), 65–86.

[66] To Sir John Oldcastle, in Hoccleve's works: the minor poems, ed. F. J. Furnivall and I.
Gollancz rev. Jerome Mitchell and A. I. Doyle (EETS ES 67, 73 1970), l. 66. In the play of
Lucifer in The Chester Mystery Cycle, ed. R. M. Lumiansky and David Mills (EETS SS 3 1974),
Lucifer declares himself to be 'pearlesse and prince of pride' (184); 'pearlesse' figures his revolt
socially as well as theologically.

[67] e.g. Douglas Gray, ed., A selection of religious lyrics (Oxford, 1975), nos. 35 and 42.

[68] Cf. Hoccleve's Regement of Princes, ed. F. J. Furnivall (EETS ES 72 1987), where the
beggar states that Henry, as prince of Wales, was present at John Badby's burning and begged
him to recant his heretical views to avoid punishment, ll. 295–322.

Oldcastle to be Christ's champion. (69) This is a deeply resonant image. The poem was written as Henry V was embarking on a voyage to wage war against the French, and the conclusion of the poem implores Oldcastle to resume his knightly ways; to join the king in the war (509–12). Hoccleve legitimizes the military campaign against the French by framing Oldcastle, a figure who is cast as a threat to God-given social order, as one who ought to know his duty in joining the campaign, but who has preferred instead to abandon his rightful social duties. The narrator reminds Oldcastle that there was a time when if knighthood was being practised, then he would have been there (505–7). The lines explicitly yoke chivalry with 'manhode' (506), a quality which Oldcastle has abandoned because he has changed his 'gyse' (508) by aligning himself with the devil rather than the king. By deploying diction from a mixture of religious, chivalric, and gendered registers, the poem figures Oldcastle as unruly, feminine, and fiendish. All of this stands in stark contrast to the bold chivalry of the manly champion of Christ, Henry V, who is, as the poem states, 'our cristen Prince' (499). The first-person plural pronoun is important in constructing the writer and his audience as loyal to the king while Oldcastle stands outside this discourse of Christian allegiance.

The strategy of casting Oldcastle as an 'outsider', or as a threat to a benign and proper order is omnipresent. What is especially interesting about this poem is how these tropes of civil obedience are explicitly related to literary practice:

> Bewar Oldcastel & for Cristes sake
> Clymbe no more in holy writ so hie!
> Rede the storie of Lancelot de lake
> Or Vegece of the aart of Chiualrie
> The seege of Troie, or Thebes thee applie
> To thyng þat may to thordre of knyght longe!
> To thy correccioun now haaste and hie,
> For thow haast been out of ioynt al to longe.
>
> If thee list thyng rede of auctoritee,
> To thise stories sit it thee to goon:
> To Iudicum, Regum and Iosue,
> To Iudith & to Paralipomenon,
> And Machabe & as siker as stoon,
> If þat thee list in hem bayte thyn ye
> More autentike thing shalt thow fynde noon,
> Ne more pertinent to Chiualrie.　　　　　　　(193–208)

Social rectitude is explicitly aligned with appropriate reading matter. As a knight, Oldcastle has transgressed by reading Holy Writ.[69] The use of diction such as 'clymbe so hie', and 'correccioun' figures Oldcastle's reading activity as presumptuous, anti-hierarchical, and disobedient. These lines offer up a model of policed reading: Oldcastle should read only those parts of the Bible which pertain to Christian knighthood. Such matter will, of course, implicitly provide Oldcastle with a mirror of his own liege lord, the Christian soldier knight, King Henry, after whom he should fashion his own behaviour. Throughout the poem, civil upset is figured as dissident reading. An earlier passage in the poem proleptically aligns Oldcastle's transgressive reading with the unruly female body:[70]

> Some wommen eeke, thogh hir wit be thynne,
> Wole argumentes make in holy writ!
> Lewde calates! sittith doun and spynne,
> And kakele of sumwhat elles, for your wit
> Is al to feeble to despute of it!
> To Clerkes grete apparteneth þat aart
> The knowleche of þat, god hath fro yow shit;
> Stynte and leue of for right sclendre is your paart.
>
> Oure fadres olde and modres lyued wel,
> And taghte hir children as hemself taght were
> Of holy chirche and axid nat a del
> 'Why stant this word heere? And 'why this word there?'
> 'Why spake god thus and seith thus elles where?
> Why dide he this wyse and might han do thus?'
> Oure fadres medled no thing of swich gere:
> Þat oghte been a good mirror to vs.   (145–60)

The imperative and axiomatic tone of these stanzas is characteristic of the whole poem. There is little use of modality in the verbs used in this poem; and an absence of conditionality or possibility.[71] Hoccleve makes one propositional statement after another, which orders the conviction that society is set out unconditionally and immutably in a fixed pattern

---

[69] Cf. *Against the Lollards* in *Historical poems of the XIVth and XVth centuries*, ed. R. H. Robbins (New York, 1959), 152–7, where it is stated that it is 'unkyndely for a kniȝt | þat shuld a kynges castel kepe, | To babel þe bibel day & niȝt', 25–8.

[70] Strohm (*England's empty throne*, 184–5) notes how Hoccleve's accusation that Oldcastle lacks manhood is reflected in his reading practice.

[71] Fowler analyses modality as an aspect of social discourse, *Literature as social discourse*, 89–91.

which it is dissident to alter. Subjects must unquestioningly obey according to social rank; they should not meddle.

In these stanzas, women are characteristically seen as lacking the intellect to argue points of Christian doctrine. It is noteworthy that Hoccleve attributes direct speech to them, emphasizing their orality rather than their literacy. And their orality is animalistic; like hens, they cackle.[72] No reading matter is allocated to women, in contrast to the chivalric syllabus enjoined on Oldcastle. Rather, they must clothe the menfolk and the children. They must sit (a verb which emphasizes keeping very firmly in their place), and spin.[73] Reading and intellectual argument is not for them. For a woman to open a book is to contravene God's authority and to usurp the learned discourse of the clerics.

Lines 152–60 picture a social vignette of correct reading practice in which a stable society nourishes infantilized reading. Hoccleve mobilizes the conventional trope of an idealized past as a foil against the corruptions of the present[74] to describe how good-living parents taught children as they themselves were taught. Socially correct reading is figured as an activity in which no questions are asked. There is no swerving from axiomatic truth and no interrogation of narrative order or interpretation. To query the arrangement of words or tensions of meaning between different passages is to unfix social and ecclesiastical order.

Rather, the meaning of a text is passed on in a kind of patrilinear succession. The family provides a stable frame to secure unmediated interpretation. While it is initially both fathers and mothers who teach their children, the ultimate exemplary figures are fathers: good mirrors to sons. Any construction of individuality or subjectivity is repressed. When a child looks into a mirror, what it sees is not its own reflection, but the authority of the father. In developing this model, texts are seen as property which is to be passed on to father and son:

> If land to thee be falle of heritage,
> Which þat thy fadir heelde in reste & pees,
> With title iust and treewe in al his age,

[72] The relationship between orality and animality is discussed more fully in Chapter 5.

[73] Cf. *The Book of Margery Kempe*, ed. S. B. Meech and H. E. Allen (EETS OS 212 1940), p. 129/35–6, where the people of Beverley tell Kempe to go and 'spynne & card as oþer women don'.

[74] Thomas J. Elliott discusses this conventional topos in 'Middle English complaints against the times: to contemn the world or to reform it?', *Annuale Medievale*, 14 (1973), 22–35, p. 23. See also Scattergood, *Politics and poetry*, 309–10.

And his father before him brygelees,
And his and his, & so foorth, doutelees,
I am ful seur, whoso wolde it reue,
Thow woldest thee deffende & putte in prees;
Thy right thow woldest nat, thy thankes, leue.   (161–8)

In these lines, Hoccleve selects diction from legal discourse: 'title . . . treewe'; 'his and his'; 'deffend'; 'right', and 'reue'[75] to argue that to disturb patrilinear succession is to break the law. To intervene in a patrilineal practice of interpretation is figured as a kind of 'breaking and entering'; an act of theft. A society which is a model of rectitude requires an unbroken succession of fathers all concerned to defend the sacred text of the Bible from violent appropriation by criminals. Hoccleve is on dangerous ground here. For, of course, the violation of patrilinear descent was exactly what the Lancastrians were anxious to deny they had committed in succeeding to the throne after Richard's deposition. By projecting such an act onto Oldcastle, Hoccleve exculpates the contemporary regime from such a charge and indicts a conveniently constructed menace with the crime instead.[76]

The correct use of literary texts envisaged in this poem is one that endorses normative social hierarchy. The third estate is excluded from access to authoritative texts; if a bailiff, a man of craft, or a reeve try to prove Christian faith by reason, they 'dote or raue' (144). To usurp social position in attempting to question what is beyond interrogation is seen to be an act of madness. Yet again, Hoccleve mobilizes an oppositional discourse; here, one which separates the mad from the sane, the unruly from the civilized.[77] There are no grey areas in this poem: dissident conduct is set at odds with an immutably proper civil order.

Throughout this poem Hoccleve images an unbendingly fixed picture of social relationships which are rooted in obedience to the Christian king and are organized around a rigid model of decorous reading practices. Several discourses are mobilized to endorse quietistic consumption of literary texts. In order to demonize (quite literally) unauthorized readings of the Bible, Hoccleve deploys figurative diction

[75] See *MED* 'treue-title' 13(e); 'his' pron (2); 1(a); 'defenden' 5(b); 'right'(n) 5(a); 'reven' 1(a).

[76] This is discussed by Strohm, *England's empty throne*, 183–4.

[77] Michel Foucault discusses how the division between reason and madness is one of the procedures for regulating discourse, 'The order of discourse', 53–4, a subject he treats at length in *Madness and reason: a history of insanity in the age of reason*, trans. Richard Howard (New York, 1965).

and analogies which yoke together discourses of patrilinear descent, transfer of property, legal ownership, land law, the normative model of the three estates, and conservative relations between men and women. These discourses of social rectitude are reinforced by a series of binary oppositions: Christ and Lucifer; past and present; reason and madness; high and low; movement and stillness; and obedience and disorder. The sheer number of normative discourses used, and their accretive inter-layering, is a measure of the force of the threat that Hoccleve seeks to neutralize. This, together with the insistent use of propositional statements, and absence of modality, creates a style that is so over-determined and obstinate that the very strenuousness of the assertions bespeak a high level of anxiety. There is rather too much protestation which points, ironically enough, not to the naturalness of the model of civic order which Hoccleve presents, but to its constructedness. Hoccleve's over-assertion of his message, and the inflexibility of the reading he permits, expose how his normative language of social description is under pressure from contemporary processes and practices. The picture which he presents has a material reality, but it is forged from literary motifs whose dominance had already been effectively challenged by newly emergent civil and religious discourses. The sheer conservatism of Hoccleve's imagery and diction is an index of how besieged a position he adopts politically. For all the discursive manoeuvres to bridle unruliness which the poem performs, both the strident inflexibility of its literary materials and the evident anxiety about unpoliced reading, show that Hoccleve is closing the stable door after the horse has bolted.

When viewed alongside some of Hoccleve's other writings, the positionality of the stern moralizing in *Oldcastle* seems almost comic. From the *Oldcastle* poem, we are led to believe that the only socially obedient reading which Hoccleve sanctions is that which is undigested, unruminative, unexamined, and uninterpreted. But Hoccleve knew only too well, of course, that reading matter passed from fathers to sons was not ingested open-mouthed and swallowed wholesale. In *Regement of Princes* he creates for himself a literary persona which explicitly models himself as the son of Chaucer, and the ways that Hoccleve plays with the father–son poetic legacy[78] show only too clearly that the infantilized reading figured in *Oldcastle* is a piece of political opportunism:

---

[78] Strohm discusses the Lancastrian implications of these lines in *England's empty throne*, 147–8 and 182. See also Derek Pearsall, 'Hoccleve's *Regement of Princes*: the poetics of royal self-representation', *Speculum*, 69 (1994), 386–410, pp. 403–4.

> O maister deere, and fadir reuerent!
> Mi maister Chaucer, flour of eloquence,
> Mirour of fructuous entendement
> O, vniversal fadir in science!   (1961–4)

It is noteworthy that the image of the mirror which Hoccleve uses to suggest Oldcastle fashion himself after King Harry is here deployed to create a flattering image of Hoccleve's own poetic skills.[79] Hoccleve selects just those qualities about Chaucer's writing which can be seen to legitimize his own poetic project: learnedness, eloquence, knowledge. This is a highly selective and sanitized view. There is no mention of anything which might compromise the moral seriousness of this universal father. But Hoccleve was clearly aware of such elements in Chaucer's poetry. In lamenting Chaucer's death Hoccleve writes:

> Mi dere maistir—god his soule quyte!
> And fadir, Chaucer, fayn wolde han me taght;
> But I was dul and lernéd lite or naght.   (2077–9)

The last line shows very clearly one thing that Hoccleve learnt from his illustrious father, the construction of a naive and ingenuous persona as narrator.[80] While the joke is ostensibly on Hoccleve himself, and his dull-wittedness, there are broader implications for reading the social poetics of Hoccleve's writing. Awareness of narrative positionality has potentially radical implications. To place an unreliable narrator at the heart of a work is to render its propositionality provisional and unstable. Such a narrative consciousness invites exactly the kind of readerly intervention in the text that Hoccleve is so anxious to deplore in *Oldcastle*. Far from the narrator telling the reader exactly what to think (even if ultimately, the constructedness of that position is self-evident), a self-effacing narratorial presence points, not to fixed statements, but to the arbitrariness of utterance. And once arbitrariness is placed at the centre

[79] Hoccleve uses the image of the mirror at several points in his poems; James Simpson analyses its use in the *Series* poems, 'Madness and texts: Hoccleve's *Series*' in Julia Boffey and Janet Cowen, eds., *Chaucer and fifteenth century poetry* (London, 1991), 15–26 as part of Hoccleve's exploration into ways of establishing himself as a figure of authority, pp. 24–5.

[80] See T. W. Machan, 'Textual authority and the works of Hoccleve, Lydgate and Henryson', *Viator*, 23 (1992), 281–99, repr. in Daniel Pinti, ed., *Writing after Chaucer: essential readings in Chaucer and the fifteenth century* (New York and London, 1998), 177–96, p. 178, where he observes that the numerous autobiographical passages show an awareness—perhaps learnt from Chaucer—of a narrator's rhetorical presence in his own narration. See also D. C. Greetham, 'Self-referential artefacts: Hoccleve's persona as a literary device', *Modern Philology*, 86 (1989), 242–51.

of textuality, then social relations and processes are placed in the melting pot. As I have argued of *Wynnere and Wastoure*, because language is itself a social process, to play with textuality is to play with social paradigms.

None of this, of course, appears in the 'official' list of qualities which Hoccleve the son praises in father Chaucer. But there is a hint of it in the narrative disclaimer after lamenting Chaucer's death. And elsewhere, Hoccleve shows a very fully developed understanding of the implications of narrative provisionality and playfulness that he learnt from Chaucer, for instance, the highly self-reflexive poem *Dialogue to a Friend*.[81] Here, in a reprise of Chaucer's *Prologue to the Legend of Good Women*, the friend in the poem accuses the Hoccleve persona of abusing women in his poem *Epistle of Cupid*, and warns him that they are on the warpath.[82] Hoccleve replies:

> ffreend, doutelees sumwhat ther is ther-in
> þat sowneth but right smal to hir honour;
> But as to þat now, for your fadir kyn,
> Considereth therof was I noon Auctour;
> I was in þat cas but a reportour
> Of folkes tales as they seide I wroot:
> I nat affermed it on hem god woot!
>
> Who so þat shal reherce a mannes sawe,
> As þat he seith moot he seyn & nat varie,
> ffor, and he do, he dooth ageyn the lawe
> Of trouthe he may tho wordes nat contrarie.
> Who-so þat seith I am hir Aduersarie,
> And dispreise hir condicions and port,
> ffor that I hade of him swich a report.   (757–70)

This is a tissue of playful narrative disclaimers. The passage shows, in contrast to what Hoccleve asserts in *Oldcastle*, that he is keenly aware that interpretation is not stable. Hoccleve claims that in transcribing tales, one must not act against the law of truth, but the passage shows all too well the writer's knowledge that 'trouthe' in narrative is not a fixed

---

[81] J. A. Burrow writes that the *Series* poem sequence is 'to an unusual degree preoccupied with the business of its own composition', 'Hoccleve's *Series*: experience and books', in R. F. Yeager, ed., *Fifteenth century studies: recent readings* (Hamden, Conn., 1984), 260.

[82] I discuss this moment in *The Prologue to the Legend of Good Women* in Chapter 4. On the relationship of Chaucer, Christine, and Hoccleve, see Roger Ellis, 'Chaucer, Christine de Pizan and Hoccleve: *The Letter of Cupid*' in Catherine Batt, ed., *Essays on Thomas Hoccleve* (Brepols, 1996), 29–54.

point, but a construction. The claim to be a reporter rather than an author shuffles off responsibility, but also questions the whole basis of authority in a text because the model of language which the lines encode is one which depends on ventriloquism.[83] 'Trouthe' and 'tales' are brought into opposition in a fashion which begs the question of how one is determined from the other.[84] This passage points to the arbitrariness in language, how the relationship between words and things is conventional rather than given. It is a view of language which Hoccleve learnt directly from Chaucer; the lines in *Dialogue* are a direct echo of a passage in *The General Prologue*:

> Whoso shal telle a tale after a man,
> He moot reherce as ny as evere he kan
> Everich a word, if it be in his charge,
> Al speke he never so rudeliche and large,
> Or ellis he moot telle his tale untrewe,
> Or feyne thyng, or fynde wordes newe.
> He may nat spare, although he were his brother;
> He moot als wel seye o word as another.
> Crist spak hymself ful brode in hooly writ,
> And wel ye woot no vileynye is it.
> Eek Plato seith, whoso kan hym rede,
> The wordes moote be cosyn to the dede.
> Also I preye yow to foryeve it me,
> Al have I nat set folk in hir degree.   (731–44)

For all its overt attempt to invoke authenticity in narration, this apologia exposes the gap between, in Plato's formulation, words and deeds.[85] The relationship between word and deed is not equivalent; it is a cousin to it;

---

[83] Paul Strohm discusses Hoccleve's 'multivocality' in his attraction to multiple and alternative voices; see 'Hoccleve, Lydgate and the Lancastrian court', in *CHMEL* 640–61, pp. 650–1.

[84] Cf. the even more linguistically anarchic moment in *House of Fame* where a truth and a lie jostle for precedence in flying through a window. Ultimately, they fly out together; 'fals and soth compouned' (l. 2108).

[85] In *Chaucer's poetics and the modern reader* (Berkeley, 1987), 1–21, R. M. Jordan discusses Chaucer's investment in linguistic indeterminacy in relation both to modern theorists such as Saussure, Jacobson, and Genette, and also in relation to the dissolution of the Augustinian synthesis between words and the Word, 'which coincided with the fourteenth century's preoccupation with the divergent conditions of revealed truth and natural knowledge', p.11. See also Edmund Reiss, 'Ambiguous signs and authorial deceptions in fourteenth century fictions', in Julian Wasserman and Lois Roney, eds., *Sign, sentence and discourse* (New York, 1989), 113–37.

a relation, and not the thing itself. 'Trouthe', likewise is constructed as a matter of literary decorum. To tell a tale 'proprely' is to impersonate, to assume a voice.[86] While Hoccleve uses the same arguments in the *Dialogue* to attempt to wriggle out of the responsibility for penning misogyny, Chaucer's discussion of literary 'truth' and narrative voice has an explicitly social dimension. The last two lines of the passage might seem, at first sight, to be an aside which is tacked on rather haplessly to the foregoing discussion. I do not think that this is the case. The apposition between failing to set pilgrims according to their proper social rank and narrative impersonation makes a telling point about the social significance of literary language. The narrator is cast here as an orchestrator of a play of voices, and a heteroglossic play[87] which allows to be heard a social diversity which is not reducible to stable decorum. The role of the poet here is figured, not as one which imposes an order from above, but one which gives free reign to the difference and multiplicity which normative discourses of social description attempt to reduce to order and degree. If each tale is told after the fashion of the teller, then deeds are recounted from a position of fabricated subjectivity which plays havoc with notions of received social truth. The disclaimers in *The General Prologue* demonstrate that what is perceived to be true is pegged to social positionality. This is a far cry from the delimitation of literary activity that Hoccleve insists on in *Oldcastle*. And the conservative untenability of Hoccleve's socioliterary agenda is nowhere more graphically demonstrated than in *The Manciple's Tale*, where Chaucer returns to exactly the issues he has raised in the *Prologue*, and spells out their sociolinguistic implications without reservation:[88]

> The wise Plato seith, as ye may rede,
> The word moot nede accorde with the dede.
> If men shal telle proprely a thyng,
> The word moot cosyn be to the werkyng.

[86] This issue is discussed in relationship to the *General Prologue* by Marshall Leicester, 'The art of impersonation', whose views are expanded and qualified by Barbara Nolan, 'A poet ther was: Chaucer's voices in the General Prologue to *The Canterbury Tales*', *PMLA* 101 (1986), 154–69.

[87] A. C. Spearing writes that in *The Canterbury Tales* Chaucer relinquishes his own paternal authority and enters the text 'thereby produced, "that tissue of quotations" [Barthes]; only as a guest', 'Father Chaucer', in Pinti, ed., *Writing after Chaucer*, 145–66, p. 160.

[88] Britton J. Harwood argues that the subject of the tale is language and the relation between words and things, 'Language and the real: Chaucer's Manciple', *Chaucer Review*, 6 (1972), 268–79. See also Donald R. Howard, *The idea of The Canterbury Tales* (Berkeley, 1976), 300.

I am a boystous man, right thus seye I:
Ther nys no difference, trewely,
Bitwixe a wyf that is of heigh degree,
If of hir body dishonest she bee,
And a povre wenche, oother than this—
If it so be that they werke bothe amys—
But that the gentile in estaat above,
She shal be cleped his lady, as in love;
And for that oother is a povre womman,
She shal be cleped his wenche or his lemman.
And, God it woot, myne owene deere brother,
Men leyn that oon as low as lith that oother.
Right so bitwixe a titelees tiraunt
And an outlawe or a theef erraunt,
The same I seye: ther is no difference.
To Alisaundre was toold this sentence,
That, for the tirant is of gretter myght,
By force of meynee for to sleen dounright
And brennen hous and hoom, and make al playn,
Lo, therfore, is he cleped a capitayn;
And for the outlawe hath but smal meynee,
And may not doon so greet an harm as he,
Ne brynge a contree to so greet myscheef,
Men clepen hym an outlawe or a theef.
But for I am a man noght textueel
I wol noght telle of textes never a deel.

(*Manciple's Tale*, IX. 207–36)

Language does not disclose some anterior picture of social reality; it creates it.[89] As in the passage from the *Prologue*, the relationship between word and deed is seen to be that of 'cosyn'. If R. A. Shoaf is right in detecting a pun here on 'cosyn' in the sense of 'friend/relative' and the verb 'to cosyn', as in 'to cheat or to defraud',[90] then the relationship between word and thing that is described acknowledges that the social significance of an action lies not so much in the deed itself as in the language that is used to describe it.

[89] Jordan discusses this passage (*Chaucer's poetics*, 158–9) as part of his study of Chaucer's treatment of semantics in *The Manciple's Tale*, pp. 149–62. While there are some minor differences in emphasis between his account and my own, I am in broad agreement with Jordan's engaging analysis of this tale.

[90] R. A. Shoaf, 'The play of puns in late Middle English poetry: concerning juxtology', in Jonathan Culler, ed., *On puns* (Oxford, 1988), 44–61, p.56. Cf. David H. Abraham, '"Cosyn and cosynage": pun and structure in the *Shipman's Tale*', *Chaucer Review*,11 (1977), 319–27.

In the first example, the same act, namely adultery, has different social consequences depending on how the woman who commits it is described linguistically. If she be 'gentile' then she shall be called by the courtly term 'lady' and the social valency of her actions thereby determined. A woman of low social standing, however, shall be dubbed a 'wench' or 'lemman' and her actions interpreted accordingly. Irrespective of the fact that there is no physical difference between the act of adultery committed by a lady or a commoner, language, as Monique Wittig has observed in another context, 'casts sheaves of reality upon the social body'.[91] While the pronouns 'oon' and 'oother' in l. 22 show that there is no physical, or sexual, difference between the two women, that women, and their actions, are classified according to diction which correlates to social rank, creates a linguistic difference which encodes social morality. The conventionality, or social arbitrariness, of such diction is made abundantly clear from the perceived relationship between word and deed being not one of equivalence but 'cosinage'. Bodily transactions which are identical at the physical level are granted differential social significance through the conventional semantics of nomenclature.

So too, in the second example, the basic actions of a tyrant, or a thief or outlaw, are identical. But they are named differently according to the different social power or status of the actor. Because a tyrant can command a large army and cause more damage, he is called a 'capitayn'. A man with less power, and a smaller army, merits the title merely of thief or outlaw, which frames his actions as illegitimate simply because he does not wield the political clout to call names himself. However arbitrary such evaluations of action are revealed to be, what the Manciple's words advert to very clearly is that social distinctions and power are maintained through linguistic terminology that is passed off as normative and natural because those who might be disadvantaged by such naming do not possess the power, or the social position, to change the linguistic rules which enforce the status quo.[92] It is no surprise, really,

[91] Monique Wittig, 'The mark of gender', in *The straight mind* (Hemel Hempstead, 1992), 76–89, p. 78.

[92] This is a point made most forcefully and eloquently by Jan Zita Grover in her analysis of keywords and naming in the context of AIDS: 'If it is true that we understand our worlds largely through language, then we need to pay closer attention to the words with which we shape our understanding of AIDS. We must make connections, wherever and whenever possible, between the keywords of AIDS and the wider vocabulary of power struggles to which these words are linked', 'AIDS: Keywords', 161.

that Hoccleve offers up a selective politically opportunistic account of
the qualities of his revered father. There are few more trenchant
accounts of how social relationships are constructed through language,
and inequalities of power distributed and maintained, than in the
Manciple's excursus on the subject in *The Canterbury Tales*. Needless to
say, Chaucer foists this radical account of the construction of social
realities onto a projected voice, thereby avoiding narratorial responsibility for discussion which strikes a death blow to passing off normative
accounts of communities and communal relationships as natural and
given.

Chaucer shows us explicitly that literary language is a material form
of social practice. Choices of discourse, register, and diction construct
versions of social reality. In the hands of writers who adopt a conservative writing position, literary materials can be used to shape a normative
view of society which has material currency as a projection of archaic
formations upon a more unruly present. Such material currency may
still have power, however, as *The Manciple's Tale* shows us—to possess
the power of naming is to practise power—to authorize some meanings
at the expense of others. The social positionality of literary materials is
well exemplified by the flexible use of literary language in Hoccleve's
oeuvre and the reregistration of literary conventions in *Wynnere and
Wastoure*. In the latter poem, the version of social reality which the
poem constructs is recoverable as much from *how* the poem uses literary
language as from *what* it may be deemed to discuss. In their various
ways, the texts I have considered here illustrate the internal and dialectical relationship between language and society. As Chaucer's Manciple
explains so clearly, literary utterance, even in details as apparently 'small'
as the impersonal pronoun 'oon', is always already freighted with posi-
tional social significance.

CHAPTER TWO

Pearl—or 'The Jeweller's Tale'

IN THE LAST CHAPTER, I examined literary texts which explicitly concern themselves with social issues, and have, as a result, generated critical histories attentive to their social significance, even if the formal literary features of those texts have not always been studied as an integral part of their social resonances. In this chapter, I turn my attention to *Pearl*, and turn purposefully to a work which might seem to pose a much greater challenge to exploring a literary text as an example of socioliterary practice. For most of its critical history, *Pearl* has been discussed transhistorically, seen as a beautiful artefact, a gem, within whose carefully wrought form, flawed human understanding about loss and death is challenged by theological instruction and vision.[1] Many studies map out a relationship between the Dreamer and the Maiden which is grounded in an antagonistic polarity between the earthly and the heavenly, and between what is literal and what is figurative.[2] The Dreamer's understanding is seen to be rooted in an earth-bound perception of temporal phenomena, taking at literal value events, signs, and language which he ought to comprehend in a figurative and transcendent sense.[3] His errors are exposed as such by the spiritual teachings of the Maiden.[4] The relationship between the literal and the figurative is

---

[1] Surveys of the state of *Pearl* criticism are in Lawrence Eldredge, 'The state of *Pearl* studies since 1933', *Viator*, 6 (1975), 171–94; and Robert J. Blanch, 'The current state of *Pearl* criticism', *Chaucer Yearbook*, 3 (1996), 21–33.

[2] e.g. Ian Bishop, *Pearl in its setting* (Oxford, 1968), 90; Gradon, *Form and style*, 199–211; Vendell Stacy Johnson, 'The imagery and diction of *The Pearl*: toward an interpretation', *ELH* 20 (1953), 161–80; P. M. Kean, The Pearl: *an interpretation* (London, 1967), 4–10; Sandra Pierson Prior, *The* Pearl-*Poet revisited* (New York, 1994), 28; A. C. Spearing, *The* Gawain-*poet: a critical study* (Cambridge, 1970), 148.

[3] e.g. Robert J. Blanch and Julian N. Wasserman, *From* Pearl *to* Gawain: '*Forme to fynisment*' (Gainesville, Fl., 1995), 56; Charlotte Gross, 'Courtly language in *Pearl*', in Robert J. Blanch, Miriam Youngerman, and Julian N. Wasserman, eds., *Text and matter: new critical perspectives on the* Pearl-*poet* (New York, 1991), 79–91, p. 79; James Milroy, '*Pearl*': the verbal texture and the linguistic theme', *Neophilologus*, 55 (1971), 195–208, p. 201; Spearing, *The* Gawain-*poet*, 152.

[4] e.g. Kean, *The Pearl*, 137; Catherine S. Cox, '*Pearl*'s "precios pere": gender, language

read as a movement from blinkered temporality to effulgent perman-
ence; the literal must be discarded as broken shell, damaged and misleading, in order to arrive at the kernel of true comprehension of the
divine which is offered through figure, symbol, and allegory.[5]

As John Watkins observes, until recently, this consensus in the reading of allegory has resulted in a closed system of critical reception:
'*Pearl*'s concern with the transition from time into eternity has encouraged critics to accept its theology at face value as part of a closed
hermeneutic system.'[6] In this chapter, I wish to continue recent moves
to break out of a closed hermeneutic system of juxtaposing the heavenly and the earthly, the literal and the figurative, and the aesthetic and the
cultural, to show how the narrative strategies and verbal texture of *Pearl*
can be seen as examples of late fourteenth-century social concerns and
practices just as much as *Wynnere and Wastoure* and works by Hoccleve
and Chaucer.[7] There are three key areas in which I shall examine the

and difference', *Chaucer Review*, 32 (1998), 377–90, p. 381; R. A. Shoaf, '*Purgatorio* and *Pearl*:
transgression and transcendence', *Texas Studies in Language and Literature*, 82 (1990), 152–68,
p. 162.

   [5] See Louis Blenkner, 'The theological structure of *Pearl*', in John Conley, ed., *The Middle
English Pearl* (Notre Dame, Ind., 1970), 220–71, esp. 228–36; and in the same volume, A. C.
Spearing, 'Symbolic and dramatic development in *Pearl*', 122–48, esp. 146–8; Jane Chance,
'Allegory and structure in *Pearl*: the four senses of the "Ars Praedicandi" and fourteenth
century homiletic poetry', in Blanch, Youngerman, and Wasserman, *Text and matter*, 31–59,
p. 40; W. A. Davenport, *The art of the* Gawain-*poet* (London, 1978), 50–4; Charles Moorman,
'The role of the narrator in *Pearl*', *Modern Philology*, 53 (1955), 73–81, pp. 79–81; Sarah
Stanbury, *Seeing the* Gawain-*poet: description and the act of perception* (Philadelphia, 1991), 15;
Nikki Stiller, 'The transformation of the physical in the Middle English *Pearl*', *English Studies*,
63 (1982), 402–9; Ad Putter, *An introduction to the* Gawain-*Poet* (London, 1996), 175, takes a
more nuanced view: 'To dismiss the Dreamer's problem as one of misinterpretation, or as
"literalism", is to miss the point that the figurative meaning of the maiden's talk of "courts",
"queens" or heavenly "marriages", is not a matter of fact . . . but a matter of faith. As the
Dreamer's reasoned approach to the Pearl-maiden's revelations shows, they cannot be made
to yield meaning by trying to turn them into logical propositions, with which they are
incompatible'.

   [6] John Watkins, '"Sengeley in synglere": *Pearl* and late medieval individualism', *Chaucer
Yearbook*, 2 (1995), 117–36, p. 117.

   [7] Important recent cultural or historical studies include David Aers, 'The self mourning:
reflections on *Pearl*', *Speculum*, 68 (1993), 54–73; Michael J. Bennett, 'The historical background', in Derek Brewer and Jonathan Gibson, eds., *A companion to the* Gawain-*poet*
(Cambridge, 1997), 71–90; id., *Community, class and careerism: Cheshire and Lancashire society in
the age of* Sir Gawain and the Green Knight (Cambridge, 1983); id., 'The court of Richard II
and the promotion of literature', in Barbara Hanawalt, ed., *Chaucer's England: literature in
historical context* (Minneapolis, 1992), 3–20; two essays by John M. Bowers, 'The politics of

rich social resonances of *Pearl*: the social status of the Dreamer and his relationship with the Pearl-maiden; the social implications of the figurative language used to describe the corporateness of heaven, and how references to time in the poem resonate with contemporaneous reconfigurations of the measurement of time in other cultural spheres of production and practices.

First, the Dreamer. The Dreamer, the narrator, is our guide in the poem, through whose mind and eyes we witness the events and the dialogue of the poem.[8] What happens when we see him, not solely as a 'pernicious, tainted literalist',[9] a representative of fallen humanity, but as a representative of a newly emergent social group? If we attend to the literal sense of the opening of the poem, then the Dreamer's social position is clear: he is a 'juelere' (252).[10] As Felicity Riddy has pointed out, the word 'jeweller' was used of someone who works with, or trades in, precious stones and gems. Jewellers were urban because they depended on the wealthy clientele that a large centre of trade could supply. And it is important that, while jewellers thus had transactions with the aristocracy, they were not themselves members of that social group; jewellers were either goldsmiths or merchants trading in luxury goods for their social superiors.[11] Jewellers were most likely to be retailers, or merchants, though the term sometimes also refers to craftsmen who

Pearl', *Exemplaria*, 7 (1995), 419–41; and '*Pearl* in its royal setting: Ricardian poetry revisited', *SAC* 17 (1995), 111–55. (Bowers's full-length study, *The politics of Pearl: court poetry in the age of Richard II* (Cambridge, 2001), was published after this current chapter was complete). Felicity Riddy, 'Jewels in *Pearl*', in D. Brewer and J. Gibson, eds., *A companion to the* Gawain-*poet* (Cambridge, 1997), 143–55; Watkins, ' "Sengeley in Synglere" ', and Nicholas Watson, 'The *Gawain*-poet as a vernacular theologian', in Brewer and Gibson, *A Companion to the* Gawain-*poet*, 293–314.

[8] Moorman, 'The role of the narrator in *Pearl*', 74: 'In the words of Henry James, the narrator-poet is the "central intelligence"; in those of Brooks and Warren, the poem is the "narrator's story" . . . we are forced by the point of view which the poet adopts to accept the experience of the vision only in terms of its relationship to him'. Stanbury, *Seeing the* Gawain-*poet*, 4, observes that 'the description in *Pearl*, carefully focalised by the dreamer, becomes not simply a precisely realized scene but also a perceptual frame that marks and signifies the fictional viewer's epistemological horizon'.

[9] Jane Chance, 'Allegory and structure', 43.

[10] All quotations are taken from *Pearl*, ed. E. V. Gordon (Oxford, 1953). Bowers asks why the casting of the dreamer as a jeweller has generated so little enquiry, '*Pearl* in its royal setting', 139, n. 98.

[11] Riddy, 'Jewels in *Pearl*', 149; and in n. 22 she observes that Mede is characterized as a 'jueler' in the A text of *Piers Plowman* (Passus II, 87), ref. from *MED* 'jeueler' n.

made or set the stones.[12] The Dreamer is established as a jeweller, 'not only explicitly in the first stanza, but explicitly at ll. 252, 264, 265, 276, 288, and 289'.[13] It is an identification whose social resonance has often been attenuated. For example, Andrew and Waldron comment:

The concatenation word 'jueler' is rich in potential significance. In [line] 7 the Dreamer has presented himself as a judge of gems; the varied use of the word in the present section, however, draws attention to the contrast between earthly and heavenly values—a distinction which he has yet to learn. The use of the word in 730 and 734 further identifies the true 'jeweller' with the merchant of the parable of the Pearl of Price (*Matt.* 13: 45–6).[14]

Here is the classic switch from the literal and social to the figurative and spiritual. I should like to argue, however, that the materiality of the vehicle in metaphorical language does not undergo some kind of transubstantiation into tenor. I take a much more Wycliffite view of figurative diction: there are no substances without accidents. In figurative diction the materiality of the vehicle does not somehow vanish. Or, as Susan Handelman puts it: 'Metaphor does not discard the particular, the letter, on the way to the universal; instead, metaphor exists within the tension of identity and difference, and metaphorical resemblance is at bottom, a unity of resemblance and difference.'[15]

One of the reasons why the particular of the literal is not disregarded in *Pearl* is that in casting the Dreamer as a jeweller, the poet establishes a material consciousness right at the heart of the poem. By trade, a jeweller deals in gems, and the narrator is hence cast as a mercantile figure concerned with the market value of luxury commodities. The social mobility of merchants and their challenge to existing hierarchies is an issue frequently raised in the literature of the period. Their ambiguous social position has been well documented by Paul Strohm.[16] Merchants do not come out well in medieval literary representations of

[12] See Marian Campbell, 'Gold, silver and precious stones' in John Blair and Nigel Ramsay, eds., *English Medieval industries: craftsmen, techniques, products* (London, 1991), 107–66, esp. 151 where she observes that the medieval understanding of the term 'jeweller' is problematic in that it seems to mean variously: a retailer of goldsmiths' work (including jewellery); a retailer of gem-stones; an appraiser of gem-stones, and only sometimes the craftsman who worked or set the stones.

[13] Riddy, 'Jewels in *Pearl*', 145; cf. Watkins, '"Sengeley in Synglere"', 126.

[14] *The poems of the Pearl manuscript*, ed. Malcolm Andrew and Ronald Waldron, rev. edn. (Exeter, 1987), 65–6.

[15] Susan Handelman, *The slayer of Moses: the emergence of rabbinic interpretation in modern literary theory* (New York, 1982), 23.

[16] Strohm, *Social Chaucer*, 3–10. And cf. discussion in Chapter 1.

their role in society: for instance they are left out of the pardon in *Piers Plowman*,[17] and are the targets of satire in a number of other literary works.[18] A key factor is that, in their capacity to earn money, merchants could become rich enough to compete with the wealth of the aristocracy, thereby blurring the distinction between wealth and power acquired through birth, and money and prestige obtained by trade.[19] Chaucer illustrates the mercantile disturbance of social boundaries, not just in the Merchant's coarse handling of aristocratic courtly love conventions in his tale, but also in some tiny lexical competition in his portrait in *The General Prologue*. We are told that no one knew he was in debt:

> So estatly was he of his governaunce
> With his bargaynes and with his chevyssaunce.   (A. 281–2)

'Estatly' and 'governaunce' are words from a noble register whose resonances are contested (partly through rhyme, partly through proximity) by the financial senses of 'bargaynes' and 'chevyssaunce'. The mercantile challenge to conservative social boundaries is marked by the abrupt jolt in register between the lines.[20]

A jewel merchant presents an even greater challenge to social boundaries because, although his business marks him as non-aristocratic, the very nature of his trade necessitates his dealing with the aristocracy.[21] He is both inside and outside aristocratic culture. That the mediating consciousness of *Pearl* is a persona of such ambivalent status creates some

[17] *Piers Plowman*, B. Passus VII. 18–19: 'Marchaunt3 in þe margyne hadde manye yeres, | Ac noon *a pena et a culpa* þe Pope nolde hem graunte'.

[18] e.g. Gower, who associates them with guile, cunning, and pride, *Miroir de L'Homme*, 25237 ff.; in *The complete works of John Gower: the French works*, ed. G. C. Macaulay (Oxford, 1899); *Vox Clamantis*, V. 706; 765–8 in *Complete works: the Latin works* (Oxford, 1902); cf. *Wynnere and Wastoure*, 401.

[19] See Strohm, *Social Chaucer*, 10–11; and Sylvia Thrupp, *The merchant class of medieval London* (Ann Arbor, 1962; repr. of 1948). The author of *The Anonimalle Chronicle* records a conversation between the king and Mayor Walworth after the meeting with the rebels in the field at Mile End, June 1381, in which Richard tells Walworth that he is to be knighted for his service and Walworth is given the reply: 'that he was not worthy, nor able to have or maintain a knight's estate, for he was only a merchant and had to live by trade' quoted in R. B. Dobson, ed., *The peasants' revolt of 1381* (London, 1983), 167. The king knights him anyway but the scripting of Walworth's reply may be seen to represent the social anxiety generated by the liminal position of wealthy merchants.

[20] For the treatment of the figure of the Merchant in *The General Prologue*, see Mann, *Medieval estates satire*, 99–103, and notes to the *Riverside Chaucer*, 809.

[21] The dreamer in *Pearl* also blurs the boundaries between an artisan or craftsman and a merchant. In so far as the dreamer is depicted as evaluating the value of gems, he is a mer-

very interesting social cross-currents in the poem. Right at the heart of a poem concerned with trying to understand the cruel anguish suffered by a parent whose child has incomprehensibly died in infancy, there is a narrative perspective which consistently defines social horizons of expectations for the audience.

The jeweller in *Pearl* is fascinated by wealth, and especially by the wealth of the aristocracy. His descriptions bespeak a concern with adornment and decoration, the signs of courtliness. The landscape of the earthly paradise is figured in terms of 'adubbement' (adornment), which is the link word for section II. The gleaming glory of the rich rocks is said to surpass the decoration of tapestries woven by human beings (69–71). The leaves slide over each other like 'bornyst syluer' (77); the steep slopes of the river-bank are like fine gold thread 'fyldor fyn' (106), and the pebbles in the river glow and glint like beams of light through glass (114–20).[22] There is a focus on exquisite craftsmanship and skill that is comparable to the fascination with courtly accomplishments in *Sir Gawain and the Green Knight*, and as in *Gawain*, a focus on courtliness mediated through the discourse of commodification.[23]

When the dreamer lovingly recounts the details of maiden's dress, his gaze is resolutely focused on courtly embellishment:[24]

chant, but in so far as his narrative voice in the poem creates the jewelled form and texture of the poem, he is a master-craftsman. Riddy, 'Jewels in *Pearl*', 150, notes: '*Pearl* is positioned at the meeting point between aristocratic and urban values which sanction acquisitiveness: the desire to own beautiful things, the taste to recognise them, the money to buy them, the skill, training and capital to make them. The poem reminds us that the court is not separate from the merchant or the artificer: and in the Book of Revelation the place of gold and jewels is not a court but a city'. Cf. Spearing, *The* Gawain-*poet*, 97–8.

[22] Kean's comparisons of sources to this passage, The Pearl: *an interpretation*, 105–7, serve to bring out the distinctive mercantile consciousness of the description. In contrast to the analogues she cites, there is, in *Pearl*, a distinctive emphasis on jewel, glitter, and value. Theodore Bogdanos in Pearl: *image of the ineffable* (University Park, Pa., and London, 1983), 48, stresses the insistent presence of comparisons to sumptuous works of art in this sequence: the burnished silver that could frame a diptych, the rich indigo of the tree trunks that could be found perhaps in a decorated initial of a psalter page, the rivers like gold leaf threads tooled into an interlace relief design, the opulent tapestry, the mosaic-like pebbles and the stained-glass transparency of the stream.

[23] See Jill Mann, 'Price and value in *Sir Gawain and the Green Knight*', repr. from *Essays in Criticism*, 36 (1986), 294–318 in Stephanie Trigg, ed. and intro., *Medieval English poetry* (London, 1993), 119–37.

[24] The narrator's 'gaze' is studied from a feminist perspective in Sarah Stanbury, 'Feminist masterplots: the gaze on the body of *Pearl*'s dead girl', in Linda Lomperis and Sarah Stanbury, eds., *Feminist approaches to the body in medieval literature* (Philadelphia, 1993), 96–115.

Perle3 py3te of ryal prys
Þer mo3t mon by grace haf sene,
Quen þat frech as flor-de lys
Doun þe bonke con bo3e bydene.
Al blysnande whyt wat3 hir beau biys,
Vpon at syde3, and bounden bene
Wyth þe myryeste margarys, at my deuyse,
Þat euer I se3 3et with myn ene;
Wyth lappe3 large, I wot and I wene;
Dubbed with double perle and dy3te;
Her cortel of self sute schene,
With precios perle3 al vmbepy3te.   (193–204)

Several details here show that we are looking at a woman through the
gaze of a merchant. The Maiden is seen first as a setting of pearls of royal
value, 'perlez py3te of ryal prys' (193), and the pearls which trim her
garment are the loveliest that the Dreamer has ever set eyes on, 'at his
deuyse' (199), in his judgement—a phrase which recalls his evaluation of
the worth of his pearl at the start of the poem. The Maiden's garments
are clearly those of an aristocratic woman: her 'biys', and her 'curtel'
with its fashionably long sleeves;[25] and there is a cluster of vocabulary
concerned with courtly fashioning, and with craft: 'pi3t'; 'bounden';
'dubbed'; 'dy3te'; and 'vmbepy3te'.

This mercantile fascination with the trappings of the aristocracy continues in the next stanza:

A py3t coroune 3et wer þat gyrle
Of mariorys and non oþer ston,
Hi3e pynakled of cler quyt perle.
Wyth flurted flowrez perfet vpon.
To hed hade ho non oþer werle;
Her here-leke al hyr vmbegon;
Her semblaunt sade for doc oþer erle,
He ble more bla3t þen whalle3 bon.
As schorne golde schyr her fax þenne schon,
On schyldere3 þat leghe vnlapped ly3te.
Her depe colour 3et wonted non
Of precios perle in porfyl py3te.   (205–16)

Once again, there is a clustering of courtly detail. The crown is elabo-
rately decorated, and, as John Bowers has shown, resembles the most

---

[25] Bishop notes how the maiden wears contemporary dress, Pearl *in its Setting*, 104.

finely wrought of crowns owned by the aristocracy at this time.[26] The
conventional comparison between the white complexion of a woman
and a whale's bone,[27] is given a mercantile spin. The mention of ivory is
juxtaposed with social evaluation: the Maiden's face is grave enough for
an earl or duke;[28] her hair is compared to bright cut gold, and her complexion to a precious pearl set in an embroidered border. Even the
speech of the Maiden is compared to jewels in ll. 276–7.

The Dreamer's reaction to the various landscapes and settings of the
poem also show him to be fascinated by aristocratic wealth, but from the
position of an impressionable outsider. After listening to the Maiden's
description of the inhabitants of the city of the heavenly Jerusalem, the
Dreamer's first concern is for what kind of buildings they inhabit. He
asks: have you no dwelling place with castle-wall, no manor where you
may meet and live (917–18)? As Gordon observes, the Dreamer visual-
izes the heavenly city in terms of a medieval town with a castle and
houses within a perimeter wall.[29] His anxiety that the Maiden, together
with the other pearls, may be forced to sleep rough, 'ly3 þeroute' (930),
shows that he is concerned that they might get spoilt by being left outside, their value tarnished. There is also more than a hint of class
voyeurism; such beautiful buildings must exist and he wants to be taken
to see them:

> If þou hat3 oþer bygynge3 stoute,
> Now tech me to þat myry mote.   (935–6)

---

[26] Bowers, 'Pearl in its royal setting', 139; cf. Riddy, 'Jewel in Pearl', 144.

[27] Cf. discussion in Chapter 1 of the reregistration of the whale-bone simile in Wynnere
and Wastoure. Prior, in The fayre formez, compares the description of the maiden to the framing of women as jewels in love lyrics, pp. 164–5.

[28] In a number of places, Spearing draws attention to the social consciousness of the
encounter between the dreamer and the maiden, although he does not develop these
comments into a continuous argument. He says of the dreamer: 'It would not be a great
exaggeration to think of him as something of a snob; he has at least a keen sense of social
status, a tendency to see reality in terms of social differences (one of his first thoughts on seeing the Maiden in her new state was that her face was 'sade for doc or erle' (211)', The
Gawain-poet, 156.

[29] Pearl, p. 77, note to l. 917: 'the dreamer thinks of the Heavenly City as a feudal town,
consisting of a castle with a cluster of buildings set within a castle wall. Later he actually sees
the City as such a castle: he describes it as a "manayre" in 1029, meaning a castle and its
precinct, and in 1083 as a "bayle", meaning a walled castle. The illustration in the MS
medievalizes the City even more completely.' Bishop notes how the comparison of the
Vision of the New Jerusalem to a medieval city represents a substantial change to the biblical
source, Pearl in its setting, 89.

At this point the Dreamer appears like a socially aspirant National Trust visitor, anxious to get a glimpse inside the houses of the great and the good![30]

This is not the first time that the jeweller is figured as a slightly nervous visitor to aristocratic property that does not belong to him. He thinks that the river in the earthly paradise is part of a device to mark out the divisions in pleasure gardens laid out beside pools (139–44),[31] and assumes that the sculptured landscape must be part of the gardens of a great house. In ll. 151–3, he tries to find a ford to cross the river but is aware that such an enterprise is fraught with dangers:

> To fynde a forþe faste con I fonde,
> Bot woþeȝ mo iwysse þer ware,
> Þe fyrre I stalked by þe stronde;
> And euer me þoȝt I schulde not wonde
> For wo þer weleȝ so wynne wore.   (150–4)

As Andrew and Waldron observe in their note to these lines, 'woþeȝ' (151) and 'wo' (154) 'appear to connote the risk of discovery rather than physical danger. The Dreamer's state of mind is that of a social inferior trespassing in the grounds of a castle.'[32] The anxiety around his position in a courtly setting registers the jeweller's sense of social precariousness.

Issues of social class are frequently highlighted in the exchanges between the Dreamer and the Maiden. For instance, the Maiden upbraids the Dreamer for his social presumption. She reminds him that he lacks 'gentyl' status (264), that he is 'no kynde jueler' (276), and in l. 303 she describes him as 'vncortoyse'.[33] The Dreamer acknowledges this social disparity:

> Þaȝ cortaysly ȝe carp con,
> I am bot mol and manereȝ mysse   (381–2)

> I am bot mokke and mul among,
> And þou so ryche a reken rose,
> And bydeȝ her by þys blysful bonc
> Þer lyueȝ lyste may neuer lose

> .   .   .   .   .

---

[30] Spearing notes, The Gawain-poet, 156, that the dreamer shows a 'powerful curiosity about how the great live in their heavenly world'.

[31] Putter notes the unresolvable pun in these lines: on the conduit joining pleasure gardens and a division between two kinds of mirth, earthly, and spiritual, Introduction, 156.

[32] Poems of the Pearl manuscript, ed. Andrew and Waldron, 61.

[33] Cf. Andrew and Waldron's note to these lines on p. 61.

And þaȝ I be bustwys as a blose
Let my bone vayl neuerþelese.   (905–12)

The Dreamer's troubled sense of social status is revealed by the fact that, when faced with what he hears as the resolute courtliness of the Maiden, he feels himself to be inferior to his own social class. He styles himself as a clod of earth, totally lacking manners, and as uncivilized as a peasant.

But the representation of the jeweller's speech is not that of an uncouth peasant totally fazed by confronting an aristocratic register of speech. While the register of the Maiden's speech is predominantly courtly, with a high density of French words, and a profusion of courtly reference, that is to be expected, given that she is concerned with explaining courtly or religious matters.[34] And, indeed, there are occasions when her speech is not insistently courtly:

'Now blysse, burne, mot þe bytyde,
Þen sayde þat lufsoum of lyth and lere,
'And welcum here to walk and byde,
For now þy speche is to me dere.
Maysterful mod and hyȝe pryde,
I hete þe, arn heterly hated here.
My Lorde loueȝ not for to chyde,
For meke arn alle þat wonez Hym nere;
And when in hys place þou schal apere,
Be dep deuote in hol mekenesse.
My Lorde þe Lamb loueȝ ay such chere,
Þat is þe grounde of alle my blysse'.   (397–408)

The only words here of French origin are 'apere' (405), 'deuote' (395), and 'place' (405). The register is predominantly vernacular. Arguably, this is because the Maiden has modified her sternness towards the Dreamer since he has tempered his rash claims. But there is more variation in the Maiden's register than the Dreamer's anxious comments about her 'cortayse carping' might lead us to think. In drawing attention to the courtliness of the Maiden's speech, the jeweller is not so much

---

[34] The French element of *Pearl* is discussed in *Pearl*, ed. Gordon, 101–6. He notes that 'there are more than 500 words of French origin in *Pearl*, about 800 in *Sir Gawain*, and about 650 in *Purity*. Pearl is closer to French poetic tradition than the others and less closely bound to the alliterative technique. There is about the same proportion of French words as in the works of Chaucer and Gower.' Charlotte Gross argues that the use of French is not synonymous with courtliness: in using courtly language as a metaphor for the ineffable, the *Pearl*-poet follows a well-established philosophical tradition, 'Courtly language in *Pearl*', 80–1.

describing linguistic fact, as revealing his own social anxiety.[35] It is true that the Dreamer sometimes employs vocabulary of a kind which the Maiden never uses: e.g. 'mokke', but he also shows an extensive command of courtly vocabulary in describing the Maiden and the settings in which he finds himself. Rather like the teller of Chaucer's *Merchant's Tale*, he has fully learnt and internalized the register of aristocratic language, even if there are moments where his mercantile accent shows through. This is seen most especially in the stanza quoted, starting at 905. Precisely at the point at which he declares himself to be 'mokke', the jeweller performs a courtly speech act in the last line by employing the French 'bone vayl' (912), to secure the maiden's favour. The mobility of the Dreamer's register is a sign of his ambivalent social position, and his comment about the gap between civilized and uncivilized speech marks his social insecurity.

Social uncertainty is also inscribed in the use of pronouns in the exchanges between the Dreamer and Maiden. In late fourteenth-century England, the decorum governing the use of the second-person pronoun reserved 'you' for polite usage, as between speakers in a formal encounter, or from an inferior to a superior, and 'thou' between intimates, or from a superior to an inferior.[36] The distribution of second-person pronouns between the Dreamer and the Maiden lacks this regularity. In so far as the Maiden is an aristocratic lady, and the Dreamer a jeweller, she holds the balance of power. But in so far as the Dreamer is her father, and she his daughter, then the power asymmetry is reversed. The Maiden generally addresses the Dreamer with the 'thou' pronoun, apart from her first address to him:

---

[35] Spearing observes on these lines that now that the Dreamer has grasped that there is an unbridgeable distance between himself and the Maiden, 'the Dreamer can see that distance only as it might be in this world: as a social distance . . . the distance between them is one of manners', *The* Gawain-*poet*, 154–5.

[36] Allan J. Metcalf, '*Gawain* and you', *Chaucer Review*, 5 (1971), 165–78. He outlines the rules on pp. 165–7. The choice of second-person pronoun is often crucial to an understanding of the power relations between speakers in Middle English texts. In *Troilus and Criseyde*, for instance, the only time when Troilus uses the 'thou' form to Criseyde is when Troilus addresses her when he thinks she is dead, and he is about to kill himself (IV. 1209). The pronoun distribution indicates the courtliness of the relationship. Cf. my discussion of second person pronouns in *The Churl and the Bird* and *The Manciple's Tale* in Chapter 7. The social significance of the second-person pronoun is discussed more generally in R. Brown and A. Gilman, 'The pronouns of power and solidarity' in Piero Paolo Giglioli, ed., *Language and social context* (Harmondsworth, 1982), 252–82.

Sir, ȝe haf *your* tale mysetente
To say *your* perle is al awaye.　(257–8)

Bot, jueler gente, if þou schal lose
Þy ioy for a gemme þat þe watz lef.
(265–6; my emphasis)

In the first quotation, she uses the respectful pronoun, but the tone is cold and distant; for the Dreamer has been gazing at her as though she were his lost daughter brought back to life. It is a shock both to the Dreamer and to the reader to hear her speak with this chilling formality. When the Maiden addresses the Dreamer with the 'thou' pronoun, it is often deeply unclear whether this is as a superior talking to an inferior (which may be the case at 265–6), or whether the tone is intimate, as in ll. 397–400, when she tells the Dreamer that he is welcome to her now that he has modified his speech.[37]

The Dreamer's usage swings uncertainly between the two forms of the pronoun, often within the same stanza:

My blysse, my bale, ȝe han ben boþe,
Bot much þe bygger ȝet watz my mon;
Fro þou watȝ wroken fro vch a woþe.　(372–5)

The vacillation in the Dreamer's use of pronouns reflects his uncertainty over social positions. He appears unsure whether to address the Maiden with the formal pronoun, or with the intimate,[38] and in contrast to the pronominal shifts which Allan Metcalf has detailed in *Sir Gawain and the Green Knight*, the usage in *Pearl* reveals a historical uncertainty about the relationship of event and social position. The fluidity of literary practice is consistent with the protean nature of social relationships in the late fourteenth century. The choice of the interpersonal pronouns is not governed by the social status of the participants fixed and determined in advance; rather it is negotiated between the speakers as the occasion arises. As the Dreamer's usage shows, recognition of what is socially apposite may not be clear-cut.

---

[37] Bishop argues that when we reach the very heart of the poem we find that the Maiden is even more particularly concerned with the Dreamer's own spiritual welfare and continues to employ the familiar, singular form of the second-person pronoun, Pearl *in its setting*, 44. There are some other occasions when the Maiden uses 'you', e.g. 305–6 and 905, but I think that these are plurals addressed not just to the Dreamer, but to the human community.

[38] Further instances of vacillation are at: 280–7; 371–87; 470–80; 913–35.

As can often happen when individuals on the fringes of cultivated life find themselves in situations where the rules of etiquette are unclear, the dreamer frequently demonstrates a hyper-correct attitude to issues concerning social class. He is anxious that the maiden's 'astate' be 'worþen to worschyp' (394); when he learns that she leads a 'blysful lyf', he wants to know the 'stage' of her position (410). He demands to know her 'offys' in heaven (755), and with what 'reiateʒ' (royal dignities) she has been invested (770). When he receives her replies, he is, of course, outraged at what he sees as her transgression of social order and rank. He is most indignant to learn that she has been crowned as a queen:[39]

> Þou lyfed not two ʒer in oure þede;
> Þou cowþeʒ neuer God nauþer plese ne pray,
> Ne neuer nawþer Pater ne Crede—
> And quen mad on þe fyrst day!
> I may not traw, so God me spede,
> Þat God wolde wyrþe so wrange away.
> Of countes, damysel, par ma fay,
> Wer fayr in heuen to halde asstate,
> Oþer elleʒ a lady of lasse aray;
> Bot a quene! Hit is to dere a date.   (483–92)

Were the Maiden to have been created a countess or a lady of lesser rank, the jeweller could just about have accepted it, but a queen is too 'dere a date'. This is an interesting phrase. It means 'too exalted a rank' but 'date' also suggests a concern with notions of fixed positions,[40] and 'dere' suggests cost. Her reward is more expensive than she has earned from her work. Complaint about inequitable trade-off is exactly what we might expect from a figure whose employment would necessitate him getting the best price for the goods he has either crafted, or has undertaken to sell.

And for all the Maiden's attempts to explain how the court of heaven operates, the Dreamer's understanding remains insistently mercantile:

---

[39] Spearing comments: 'The tone of his remarks is roughly that of a bourgeois father's astonished admiration at his daughter's unexpected marriage with the royal family's most eligible bachelor', *The Gawain-poet*, 163. Cf. the bourgeois Clement's incomprehension of the 'gentil' behaviour of Florent in *Octovian*, ed. F. M. McSparran, EETS OS 289 (London, 1986), 638–756.

[40] *MED* does not list this precise sense of fixed position; the closest is 'date' (3) n. 6c) 'limit' or 'end'.

Quat kyn þyng may be þat Lambe
Þat þe wolde wedde vnto hys vyf?
Ouer all oþer so hyȝ þou clambe
To lede wyth hym so ladyly lyf

.   .   .   .   .

And þou con alle þo dere out dryf,
And fro þat maryag al oþer depres,
Al only þyself so stout and styf,
A makeleȝ may and maskelleȝ.   (771–80)

The violent physicality of the diction is testimony to the jeweller's sense
that worshipful hierarchy has been violated. He thinks in terms of
exclusive possession and competition. The honour granted to the
Maiden, must, by necessity, deprive more deserving candidates, especially the Virgin Mary, of rank. The Dreamer's understanding is driven
by a fierce belief in individual merit within a hyper-correct understanding of social hierarchy. Such a mind-set is commensurate with his
liminal social position as a jeweller: one who must evaluate what is most
valuable for the aristocracy to own, but whose social location in the
market-place or the craftman's workshop sets him apart by birth from
those on whom his trade relies.[41]

In answer to the Dreamer's individualistic conception of honour, the
Maiden is anxious to stress how heaven is organized around the principle of commonality. She attempts to explain how the workings of
heaven are very different from those on earth. But the diction she uses
in this explanation is freighted with social resonance, with reference
both to contemporary practices of lordship and government, and to the
disturbance of conservative views on the hierarchical organization of
society. The Maiden refers several times to the company of the blessed
as the Lord's 'meyny' (892; 899), and in 960, to 'þe meyny þat is
wythouten mote'. 'Meyny' has a very specific sense: that of a lord's
retinue. The practice of retaining involved a noble recruiting followers
who acted for his interests. He often gave them food and lodging and a
livery badge to show they were in his service. This badge usually bore
the heraldic device of the noble concerned. An idealized practice of
noble retaining, the 'meyny' that is without 'mote', clearly organizes the

---

[41] Putter notes that the Dreamer's problem is not that he interprets her words unreason-
ably—for he takes her words to mean exactly what they say—but that he interprets them too
rationally, *Introduction*, 166. This seems to me an acute observation; and a rationality on the
part of the Dreamer which stems most naturally from interpreting what he hears according
to his social position.

Maiden's explication of the society of the blessed.[42] Even when she is attempting to correct the Dreamer's earthbound perceptions of merit and reward, her explication still inheres in contemporary cultural practices. *Pearl* is not distinctive in using images of livery and maintenance to describe spiritual purity: the Lollard text, 'Of Ministris in þe Chirche', describes the pure Church as one presided over by a good 'head' which 'doþ counfort to þe meyne of þis heed'. The Pope is the converse; a bad head, which discomfits its retinue. As in *Pearl*, theological discussion is fused with reference to earthly social organization.[43]

In the Dreamer's description of the procession of the chosen in the city of the Heavenly Jerusalem, aristocratic livery and maintenance becomes confused with civic and mercantile social practices:

> So sodanly on a wonder wyse
> I watȝ war of a prosessyoun.
> Þis noble cité of ryche enpryse
> Watȝ sodanly ful, wythouten sommoun
> Of such vergyneȝ in þe same gyse
> Þat watȝ my blysful an-vunder croun:
> And coronde wern alle of þe same fasoun,
> Depaynt in perleȝ and wedeȝ qwyte.   (1095–102)[44]
>
> Hundreth þowsandeȝ I wot þer were,
> And alle in sute her liuréȝ wasse.   (1107–8)

---

[42] See Bowers, '*Pearl* in its royal setting', 136–67. He notes how in Richard II's reign the practice was controversial and attracted fierce contemporary criticism. A statute was finally passed in 1390 to curb some of the excesses, *Statutes of the realm* (London, 1810–28), ii. 74–5. While Bowers (and Watkins) date *Pearl* to the late 1380s/90s, there is an absence of critical consensus on the date of the works of the *Gawain*-poet; see Susanna Greer Fein, 'Twelve line stanza forms in Middle English and the date of *Pearl*', *Speculum*, 72 (1997), 367–98; and W. G. Cooke and D'A. J. D.Boulton, '*Sir Gawain and the Green Knight*: a poem for Henry of Grosmont?', *Medium Aevum*, 68 (1999), 42–51, who suggest a *terminus ad quem* of 1361 for *Gawain*.

[43] *English Wycliffite sermons*, ed. Pamela Gradon (Oxford, 1988), vol. ii., p. 333/131–2. Cf. the punning on white hart livery badges, clerical tonsures, and pure hearts in *The twelve conclusions of the Lollards* in *Selections from English Wycliffite writings*, ed. Anne Hudson (Cambridge, 1978), p. 25/23.

[44] As in the description of the Earthly Paradise, we see the Heavenly Jerusalem through the eyes of a merchant keen to observe jewels, courtliness, and aristocratic artistry; hence the long description of all the precious stones in ll. 989–1020. In contrast to the scriptural source there is a detailed focus on commodification. The materiality of the vision is commented on by Bogdanos, *Pearl: image of the ineffable*, 117; Spearing, *The Gawain-poet*, 101; and Stanbury, *Seeing the Gawain-poet*, 25. The mercantile consciousness of the narrative voice is continued even after the Dreamer has awoken and imagines his jewel set in a 'garlande gay' (1186).

> Þise aldermen, quen he aproched,
> Grouelyng to his fete þay felle.   (1119–20)

> To loue þe Lombe his meyny in melle
> Iwysse I la3t a gret delyt.   (1127–8)

Bowers compares the procession to aristocratic pageants, for instance, the pageant held to celebrate Richard II's reconciliation with the City of London in 1392 and recorded in Richard of Maidstone's *Concordia inter regem Ricardum Secundum et civitatem London*. The pageant was organized by the guildsmen, and in his poem Maidstone lists thirty-four guilds in separate groupings.[45] Bowers notes the resemblance of the heavenly procession in *Pearl* to liveried trade fraternities, but argues that the Maiden and her company 'are not sullied by association with mere craftsmen'.[46] The parallels to civic procession and trade guilds are persuasive, and, to my mind, provide further evidence of the mercantile consciousness which mediates the description in *Pearl*. That the blessed are in a procession wearing crowns and jewels suggests the portrayal of the nobility in an aristocratic pageant. But a civic element is also strongly foregrounded, both by the setting in a city, and by the use of the word 'aldermen' (1119). While the livery of pearls might suggest the aristocratic practice of maintenance, liveries also figure prominently in accounts of trade fraternities.[47] In *The General Prologue*, the guildsmen are 'clothed alle in o lyveree | Of a solempne and a greet fraternitee' (I. 363–4). Each is described as being fit to have been an alderman because they had sufficient 'catel and rente' (372–3). Their social pretensions are further hinted at in the description of their wives:

> It is ful fair to been ycleped 'madame',
> And goon to vigilies al bifore
> And have a mantel roialliche ybore.   (376–8)

Located within the context of a procession, the wives are seen to be keen on acquiring pre-eminence ('bifore'); status ('madame'); and even miming the behaviour of royalty ('roialliche'). The noble and the mercantile becomes blurred, just as it does, I would argue, in the procession described by the jeweller in *Pearl*. The Dreamer's vision of an

---

[45] Bowers, '*Pearl* in its royal setting', 146–67. Richard Maidstone, *Concordia inter regem Ricardum Secundum et civitatem London*, in *Political poems and songs*, ed. Thomas Wright (Rolls Series, London, 1859–61), ii. 282–300. For the thirty-four liveried guildsmen, see pp. 284–5.

[46] Bowers, '*Pearl* in its royal setting', 146.

[47] As noted by Bowers, ibid. 146.

aristocratic Heavenly Procession is also mediated through recall of urban display of the wealth and prestige of trade-guilds; the pearls a sign, perhaps, of the livery of a goldsmiths' fraternity. Even as the final vision of the poem presents to us something eternal and timeless, fourteenth-century mercantile practices are woven into its very fabric.

It would be tempting to read the social resonances of the poem schematically: to read the Maiden as representative of the courtly or aristocratic, and the Dreamer the mercantile. But *Pearl* does not resolve so easily into this oppositional polarity. For all that the Maiden is figured as an aristocratic lady, especially, of course, in the eyes of the jeweller, her diction also engages very precisely with the mercantile. Just as her register is not solely aristocratic, neither is her use of figurative diction insistently courtly. This social resonance is especially marked in her account of the commonality of heaven. In order to contest the Dreamer's outrage that she occupies too high a place in heaven, and indeed has dispossessed more worthy inhabitants, the Maiden turns to the well-used image of the body politic. Political writing often made recourse to the image of the body politic to figure a realm operating in mutual harmony and for common profit. Just as the human body works more efficiently if its organic parts function holistically, so too does the political state if all its component estates work together in a spirit of mutual co-operation and respect. There are a number of individual permutations on this image, depending on the agenda of the writer who uses it. Hoccleve, for instance, associates the hand with the 'peple' who must defend the king's body if he fall.[48] An extensive comparison between the body and the realm is sustained in one of the Digby poems. While there are the traditional associations made between the head as the king and the feet as labourers, the poet includes parts of the body and social groupings in much more detail than is found in other works.[49] So, for instance, the squires are likened to hands (36); the fingers to yeomen (37); and the thighs to merchants (49). The language of social description, which, as I argued in the previous chapter, is plastic and

    [48] Hoccleve, *The Regement of Princes,*, ll. 3928–34.
    [49] A review of the image of the body politic is in A. H. Chroust, 'The corporate idea and the body politic in the middle ages', *Review of Politics*, 9 (1947), 423–52. A classic formulation of this image is in John of Salisbury's *Policraticus*, V. 2; see edition by Markland Murray (New York, 1979), 60–1. For examples in closely contemporary works, see Thomas Brinton, Sermon of 1375 in *The sermons of Thomas Brinton, Bishop of Rochester*, ed. M. A. Devlin (Camden Society, London 4, ser. 3), i. 85; *Richard the Redeless*, II. 62–6 in *The Piers Plowman tradition*, ed. Barr; and Gower, *Vox Clamantis* VI. 497–8.

mobile, undergoes extensive expansion to create a body politic that represents the increasing prominence of social groupings not accommodated by the conservative tripartite division of the realm.[50]

When the body politic image is used by the *Pearl* Maiden, the contemporary tensions in the language of social description are pointed up in a very distinctive way:

> Of courtaysye, as sayt3 Saynt Poule,
> Al arn we membre3 of Jesu Kryst:
> As heued and arme and legg and naule
> Temen to hys body ful trwe and tryste,
> Ry3t so is vch a Krysten sawle
> A longande lym to þe Mayster of myste.
> Þenne loke: what hate oþer any gawle
> Is tached oþer ty3ed þy lymme3 bytwyste?
> Þy heued hatz nauþer greme ne gryste
> On arme oþer fynger þa3 þou ber by3e.
> So fare we alle wyth luf and lyste
> To kyng and quene by cortaysye. (457–67)

The scriptural source for the Maiden's image derives from 1 Corinthians 12: 14 ff. in which St Paul argues for the equality of all Christian individuals in the face of God, regardless of rank or sex. But how consistently, or insistently spiritually, can we read this model? Lines 465–6 incorporate a distinctive detail in the representations of body politic image to introduce a note of social tension. Your head, the Maiden argues, feels no anger or resentment because you wear a ring on your arm or finger, so: if the chief member of the body, the head, be not perturbed if a less powerful limb wear a precious ornament, then neither should any of the other parts of the body. The analogy offers a corrective to the way that the jeweller conceives of honour as inseparable from individual possession of wealth.[51] 'Cortaysye', so the Maiden would have it, has nothing intrinsically to do with obtaining and displaying its material signs. But, as in other instances where the Maiden uses social reference to illustrate her argument, the social resonance is

---

[50] Digby Poem 15 in J. Kail, ed., *Twenty six political and other poems*, EETS OS 124 (London, 1904).

[51] Bogdanos says: 'He [the poet] verges here on the hilarious, rustic grotesquerie at the possibility that the head would demand out of spite, or better, gall ("greme [or] gryste") to wear a ring just like the finger. The parody on the contending members to the body distracts from the sublimity of divine "cortaysye" which it is meant to incarnate', *Pearl: image of the ineffable*, 93.

rather unstable. Given that the head of the political body in social terms is the king, the analogy also implies that members of the aristocracy ought not to be troubled if the lesser limbs of the body politic aspire to courtly possessions. But the existence of sumptuary laws shows that the wearing of courtly ornaments by those who were not felt to be entitled to them caused a very great deal of trouble and resentment indeed. For instance, the 1363 Sumptuary Laws stipulated that 'no-one below the rank of a knight with an income of over one hundred pounds, or below a merchant or artisan with an income of over five hundred pounds, was allowed to wear jewellery of gold set with precious stones'.[52] At the very point at which the Maiden attempts to correct the Dreamer's mercantile understanding of courtliness, her diction disturbs conservative views on social stratification. While the Maiden is ostensibly drawing attention to the difference between the operations of heaven and earth, that oppositional difference is preserved only if we latch onto the tenor of her remarks and leave the vehicle behind. Whatever the intentions of either the Maiden, or indeed of the poet, the Maiden's remarks reproduce contemporaneous tensions in social practice.

When the Maiden turns to that difficult Parable of the Vineyard told by Matthew in chapter 20: 1–16, her configuration of social relations engages with some very turbulent contemporary issues. Allegorical interpretations of the vineyard parable read the labourers as virtuous Christians, and their varying times of entry to correspond to the different times of life at which they were converted; for instance, the eleventh hour is taken to represent the life of a baptized Christian in childhood.[53] But, as a number of critics have noted, the very choice of this parable, together with the way in which it is told, reinforces a sense of earthly social formations:

although the story is a parable, told to convey a meaning which is not part of its literal sense, it already possesses in the Gospel a fairly fully realized material

---

[52] *Statutes of the realm*, i. 380–1: 37, EdwIII, c.8–14., quoted by Riddy, 'Jewels in *Pearl*', 143–4. Riddy also gives an account of how Lady Mary Coucy, cousin to Richard II, was considered unfit to look after Isabella while the king was away on his Irish campaign in 1399 because of her expenditure in excess of her social position. See also discussion in Strohm, *Social Chaucer*, 5–7. In *Piers Plowman*, the alliterative richness of the figure of Mede, together with the enumeration of her jewels, suggests a woman dressed beyond her degree: *Piers Plowman*, Passus II.7–17, and discussion in Simpson, *Piers Plowman: an introduction*, 10–12.

[53] See Putter, *Introduction*, 173–4; Bishop, Pearl *in its setting*, 122–5; Robert W. Ackerman, 'The *Pearl*-maiden and the penny', in Conley, *The Middle English Pearl* (Notre Dame, Ind., 1970), 149–62.

setting and human content. It is a vivid and concrete story of everyday life, as applicable to the agricultural society of 14th-century England, as to that of 1st-century Palestine.[54]

There are significant changes from the biblical source which point up the contemporary and the social: a lord hires labourers, who work for a penny and who are paid by a reeve. Spearing noted some years ago that the labourer's speech of discontent about the inequitable wage structure, seemed to him 'to catch the authentic note of the 14th century equivalent of the trade unionist: the journeyman protesting, let us say, against an over-strict interpretation of the Statute of Labourers'.[55] More recently, in articles published simultaneously in 1995, John Bowers and John Watkins have argued that the vineyard parable engages precisely with the terms and significance of the 1388 Statute, and the hotly contested domain of the legitimate wages that labourers could earn.[56] While both these studies refuse to attenuate the social and economic significance of the vehicle of the parable, and bring out very forcibly the thoroughgoing nature of the poem's engagement with agrarian competition, I think that the parable also engages with concerns relevant to the mercantile challenge to social stratification dramatized by the figure of the jeweller.

Crucially: time. In analysing the specificity of the use of the link word 'date' in the parable, Lynn Staley Johnson has shown that there are two ways of telling time in the poem: the actual time of the day in the vineyard and also the sequence of the year.[57] Ad Putter notes how the passage of time 'appeals directly to the world of our senses as well as to our preconceptions about the way the world works . . . but the parable that keeps on harping on the importance of "date" ends up by shrugging off its relevance. All receive the same reward.'[58] I disagree about the social relevance here. The semantic contest over 'date' also, I would argue, relates to two other ways of reckoning time: Merchant's time and Church time. According to Jacques Le Goff, Merchant's time is the

<hr>

[54] Spearing, *The Gawain-poet*, 101; cf. Davenport, *The art of the Gawain-poet*, 45; Putter, *Introduction*, 171–3; Prior, *The Pearl-poet revisited*, 47–8.

[55] Spearing, *The Gawain-poet*, 102 (with reference to ll. 549–56).

[56] Bowers, 'The Politics of Pearl'; Watkins, ' "Sengeley in synglere" '. The vineyard parable is also used in a Lollard sermon in which the different activities in the vineyard are related to the three estates, *Lollard sermons*, ed. Gloria Cigman (EETS OS 294 1989), 86–9.

[57] Lynn Staley Johnson, 'The *Pearl* dreamer and the eleventh hour', in Blanch, Youngerman, and Wasserman, *Text and matter*, 3–15.

[58] Putter, *Introduction*, 171–2.

secularized basis of productive effort, providing the terms in which use and productivity can be measured. Church time is experienced in relation to eternity, from which it is provisionally borrowed, and its sole possession by God renders it unavailable for measurement, mortgage, or profitable use.[59] Whitrow argues that the development of the use of the mechanical clock, and the measuring of time by uniformly divisible units in contrast to liturgical ritual, was a movement which began in towns, fostered by the mercantile class and a money economy:

As long as power was concentrated in the ownership of land, time was felt to be plentiful and was primarily associated with the unchanging cycle of the soil. With the increased circulation of money and the organization of commercial networks, however, the emphasis was on mobility. Time was no longer associated just with cataclysms and festivals but rather with everyday life. It was soon realized by many of the middle class that 'time is money' and consequently must be carefully regulated and used economically.[60]

Prior to the invention of the mechanical clock, hiring by fixed hours or payment by the hour would have been a near-impossibility. If time belonged to God, then human beings could not claim to trade in it. With clock-time, however, secular hours, as distinct from canonical hours, could be bought and sold. The Maiden's telling of the parable of the Vineyard negotiates between the feudal, and the emergent mercantile, understanding of time. The parable starts with seasonal time: the time of year to gather the harvest:

> Of tyme of ȝere þe terme watȝ tyȝt,
> To labor vyne watȝ dere þe date.   (503–4)

Created time is also mentioned with the references to telling the time by the sun (519; 538). The lord hires the second group of workers according to liturgical time: at 'vnder' (513). But alongside these seasonal and liturgical calculations, the parable also records a sense of commercial time. The lord hires the last group of labourers at the time of evensong, one hour before the sun should set (529–30). In two lines, there are three systems of time-calculation: liturgical, mechanical, and created. When the lord addresses the first group of labourers, he asks them why they are standing idle: 'Ne knawe ȝe of þis day no date?' (516), a rebuke

[59] Jacques Le Goff, 'Merchant's time and church's time in the middle ages', in *Time, work, and culture in the Middle ages* (Chicago, 1980), 33; summary drawn from Strohm, *Social Chaucer*, 123.

[60] G. J. Whitrow, *Time in history* (Oxford, 1988), 110. The earliest mechanical clock that is known in England is that designed for the Abbey of St Albans *c.*1328, p. 104.

which suggests the measurement of time in accordance with how much work is done. And when the labourers complain about the inequitable pay structure, time is computed in hours:

> More haf we serued, vus þynk so,
> Þat suffred han þe daye3 hete,
> Þenn þyse þat wro3t not houre3 two.   (553–5)

The dispute arises because the initial agreement to work for a penny a day (created time) is challenged by calculating payment by the hour (mechanical time). The diction of the parable embeds a commercial outlook right at the heart of an explication of the feudal and the eternal.[61] The Maiden's explication of the doctrine of the salvation of the innocent also inscribes a period of transition in how time was perceived; her lexis is embedded in changes in social structure and practice.

I am not trying to argue that we should cease to think of *Pearl* as a poem which discusses a tricky point about salvation in a consummately aesthetic fashion. Nor would I want to suggest that in attending to the social resonances of the poem, we turn a deaf ear to the poem's searingly honest examination of how untimely death fails to make human sense.[62] Rather, I would claim that it is the poem's refusal to separate the spiritual and the emotional from the social that makes the exploration of these issues so supple and affective. Attending to the saturation of social reference in *Pearl* shows us that, in wrestling with issues of eternity, the poem continuously reattaches itself to the material world. For all the talk of opposition and correction, engagement with theology is inseparable from engagement with society. In this, *Pearl* is very much a product of its times: Christian doctrine is seen to be a matter of concern and dispute beyond the confines of the university schools. It is a subject for a vernacular poem as well as for a sermon delivered by a cleric from the pulpit. Salvation is a matter of argument for the laity as much as for the clergy. The casting of the Dreamer/narrator as a jeweller is pivotal in anchoring the discussion of spirituality in a socially recognizable material world. The material consciousness which thus permeates the

---

[61] Cf. 'In Auguste in hy3 seysoun, | Quen corne is coruen wyth crokez kene' (39–40), which is both the time when the crops must be gathered, and the feast of the Assumption. A Lollard Sermon for Septuagesima Sunday insistently computes the time of entry into the vineyard in hours, but then relates these times to the eight ages of men, see *English Wycliffite sermons* ed. Anne Hudson, vol. i (Oxford, 1983; repr. 1990), 378–83.

[62] A point established early on in the poem, when it is clear that the jeweller is well aware of the teaching offered by Christian comfort, but cannot square this with his feelings of distress (ll. 55–6).

poem prompts us to take notice of the social valency of the figurative diction in *Pearl*. To read figure in a fashion which winnows the chaff from the grain is to prise the poem away from the ensemble of social practices of which it is part.

CHAPTER THREE

Unfixing the King: Gower's *Cronica Tripertita* and *Richard the Redeless*

> In every society various techniques are developed to *fix* the
> floating chain of signifieds in such a way as to counter the terror of
> uncertain signs.[1]

In the following two chapters I discuss how some late fourteenth-
century texts expose the materiality of social representation and intervene in its processes of construction. Barthes's comment on the assemblage of social meaning, the attempt to anchor certain signifying systems
within an otherwise unregulated proliferation of signs, is an apt description of how Richard II attempted to control the representation of his
role as king. In order to preserve his position at the apex of the social
community of England, Richard strove to fix the signs of kingship.
From the evidence of texts such as *Richard the Redeless* and Gower's
Cronica Tripertita, the project was not lost on the very subjects he
attempted to subdue. While both these poems might be seen as part of
the ensemble of social practices because they explicitly comment on
contemporary events, they are also examples of social practice because
they reproduce and challenge contemporary sign systems, both linguistic and visual.

It is well known that Richard II was keen to blazon his kingship.[2]
Throughout his reign he cultivated a magnificent court culture in
which conspicuous consumption, largess, ritual, pageant, icons, and
consummate artistry acted as the visible signs of his earthly power.[3]

---

[1] Roland Barthes, 'Rhetoric of the image', in *Image, music, text*, trans. Stephen Heath
(Glasgow, 1977), 32–51, p. 39.

[2] See G. Mathew, *The court of Richard II* (London, 1968); and Patricia J. Eberle, 'The
politics of courtly style at the court of Richard II', in Glyn S. Burgess and Robert A. Taylor,
eds., *The spirit of the court* (Cambridge, 1985). Comprehensive coverage of Richard's image
making is given in the various essays in Dillian Gordon, Lisa Monnas, and Caroline Elam,
eds., *The regal image of Richard II and the Wilton Diptych* (London, 1997).

[3] Bowers, '*Pearl* in its royal setting', provides an extensive appraisal of these visible signs.

Ceremonies such as the 1392 royal entry into London,[4] symbolic arte-facts such as the Wilton Diptych,[5] and exquisite books such as the *Breviaire de Belleville*[6] survive as material demonstrations of his majesty. The chroniclers record the king's investment in spectacle and theatric-ality: to fuel Richard's interest in royal coronation ritual and its history, the Westminster monk Walter of Sudbury composed a short treatise on the regalia for him, tracing its history back to St Edmund and St Alfred.[7] According to the Westminster chronicler, Richard sought 'the deference properly due to his kingship' (ab omnibus prout regi decuit venerari),[8] and in 1386, took the king of Armenia to Westminster Abbey by candlelight in order to show him the king's regalia.[9] The king's sponsorship of art and ritual kept power on display.[10]

Central, as is also well known, to this ostentatious staging of regality was Richard's employment of his personal heraldic badge of the white hart. Richard appears to have adopted the hart from the cognizance of his mother, the countess of Kent,[11] and may originally have used it as

[4] This procession is described in a number of the chronicles, e.g. T. Walsingham, *Historia Anglicana*, ed. H. T. Riley (Rolls Series, 2 vols. 1863–4), ii. 210–11; H. Knighton, *Chronicon*, ed. J. R. Lumby (Rolls Series, 2 vols. 1889–95), ii. 319–21; and principally, Richard Maidstone, *Concordia inter regem Ricardum Secundum et civitatem London*, in *Political poems and songs*, ed. T. Wright, i. 282–300. The symbolism of this procession is examined by G. Kipling, 'Richard II's "sumptuous pageants" and the idea of civic triumph', in D. M. Bergeron, ed., *Pageantry in the Shakespearean theater* (Athens, Ga., 1985), 83–103. See also the account by Paul Strohm, *Hochon's arrow* (Princeton, 1992), 105–19.

[5] For discussion of its significance and techniques see Dillian Gordon, *Making and mean-ing: the Wilton Diptych* (London, 1993).

[6] Richard received this in 1396 as a gift from Philip the Bold, duke of Burgundy, see Jeanne E. Krochalis, 'The books and reading of Henry V and his circle', *Chaucer Review*, 23 (1988), 59–60. See also Michael J. Bennett, 'The court of Richard II and the promotion of literature'.

[7] See *The Westminster Chronicle 1381–1394*, ed. and trans. B. Harvey and L. C. Hector (Oxford, 1982), 206–9, 508–9; for Walter of Sudbury, see Richard of Cirencester, *Speculum Historiale*, ed. J. E. B. Mayor (Rolls Series 30 London 1863), 2 vols., ii. 26–39.

[8] *Westminster Chronicle*, 138–9.

[9] Ibid. 154–7.

[10] Richard's court culture is examined in V. J. Scattergood and J. W. Sherborne, eds., *English court culture in the later middle ages* (New York, 1983), see especially the essays by Sherborne and Scattergood. The king's patronage of Westminster Abbey is examined in Paul Binski, *Westminster Abbey and the Plantagenets* (New Haven and London, 1995). One of the most outrageous examples of Richard's display of power is the *Eulogium*'s account of how he set up a throne in the room where supper was eaten and commanded the assembled company to kneel to him, irrespective of rank, while he looked down in silence, *Eulogium Historiarium*, ed. F. S. Haydon (Rolls Series, 1863), iii. 378.

[11] See *Mum and the Sothsegger*, ed. M. Day and R. Steele (EETS OS 199 1936), 89.

a personal ornament: among the king's jewels in 1380 were three brooches of the white hart set with rubies.[12] In time, however, the hart became part of a public parade of regality.[13] In the copy of Roger Dymock's *Liber contra duodecim errores et hereses Lollardorum* (MS Trinity Hall, Cambridge, no. 17), possibly a presentation copy to Richard himself, there is a portrait of the enthroned king with two couchant chained harts at the bottom of the page.[14] The large representation of the chained white hart painted on the wall of the Muniment Room in Westminster Abbey may have been a gift from the king,[15] and the device also appears on the double tomb which Richard ordered to be made for himself and Queen Anne after her death in 1394. Both effigies can still be seen in Westminster Abbey; and the white hart is prominent amongst the very delicate heraldic pounce work.[16] Other showcases for the hart include the string moulding under the window of Westminster Hall,[17] a watching loft in St Albans Cathedral,[18] and a capital beside the south-east pier of the central crossing in York Minster. The York carving was an acknowledgement of Richard's patronage of York, exemplified in 1395 by a gift of 100 marks.[19] These artefacts show the king as a patron of the arts: 'a man of cultivated taste'.[20]

Crucial in Richard's promulgation of his personal sign of the white hart was its distribution in the form of livery badges to his retainers.[21] According to the Evesham chronicler, the livery of the white hart was first worn publicly as a royal emblem at the Smithfield tournament of 1390,[22] but the hart sign had already featured prominently in an earlier ceremonial context: in 1385, Richard ordered special robes with white harts embroidered in pearls for the Feast of the Purification of the

[12] Mathew, *The court of Richard II*, 27.

[13] Joan Evans, *A history of jewellery 1100–1870* (Boston, 1953), 64–7, traces the transformation of heraldic signs into political badges to the reign of Richard II.

[14] Roger Dymock, *Liber contra XII errores et hereses Lollardorum*, ed. H. S. Cronin (London, 1922). The illustration is reproduced in A. Steel, *Richard II* (Cambridge, 1941), facing p. vi.

[15] Mathew, *The court of Richard II*, 151.

[16] Lawrence E. Tanner, *The history and treasures of Westminster Abbey* (London, 1953), 44.

[17] Joan Evans, *English art 1307–1461* (Oxford, 1949), 62.

[18] M. D. Anderson, *The medieval carver* (Cambridge, 1935), 141.

[19] John H. Harvey, 'Richard II and York', in R. Du Boulay and C. Barron, eds., *The reign of Richard II* (London, 1971), 201. See illustrated plate on facing page.

[20] J. A. Burrow, *Ricardian Poetry*, (London, 1971), 2.

[21] See C. Given-Wilson, *The royal household and the king's affinity: service, politics and finance in England, 1350–1413* (London, 1986), 236–43.

[22] *Historia Vitae Ricardi Secundi*, ed. G. Stow (Philadelphia, 1977), 132.

Virgin.[23] What does appear to be the case, however, was that from October 1390 onwards, Richard intensified his reward of the white hart livery in order, it has been suggested, to build up a retinue comparable to those of his nobles.[24] This was an extravagant enterprise: the royal livery was also a royal maintenance, kept in being by a series of petitions and grants, and between November 1390 and September 1394, the expenditure of the great wardrobe, responsible for the granting of liveries, doubled spectacularly, as did the expense of the household.[25]

All the elements of the showcases for the white hart listed above, the opulence, the craftsmanship, the badges of loyalty, and the religious symbolism, cohere in the classic locus of Ricardian self-fashioning: the Wilton Diptych. Dating from the mid 1390s, the Diptych is a religious object, a portable altarpiece for private devotional use,[26] but it is clear from its compositional focus that its significance is also political.[27] The exterior right wing of the Diptych is dominated by a white hart with a crown and chain around its back. It may have been drawn after a living animal as it lacks the stiffness of an heraldic image; in 1393 Richard was given a white hart which he kept in the Forest of Windsor.[28] The white hart also features prolifically on the interior wings. The craftsman exploited the pun on Richard's name—'Richart' to the full. Richard's robe is richly patterned with harts pricked out in gold, while the white hart badge he wears on his chest is thickly painted in raised layers of lead, which grants it physical and symbolic prominence. This was an expensive painting technique imported from France and it creates a jewel-like, enamelled quality.[29] The costly technique and luxurious finish are significant in their own right as material signs of civilization and power.

On the right wing of the interior the Virgin and Child are sur-

---

[23] *Historia Vitae Ricardi Secundi*, ed. G.Stow, 156.

[24] R. L. Storey, 'Liveries and commissions of the peace 1388–90', in Du Boulay and Barron, *The reign of Richard II*, 151.

[25] J. A. Tuck, *Richard II and the English nobility* (London, 1973), 150.

[26] Gordon, *Making and meaning*, 21. Eleanor Scheifele suggests that the Diptych might have been commissioned for Richard's birthday in 1398 in glorification of Richard's renewed regal authority, which had been augured by his birthright on Epiphany 1367, confirmed ceremonially at his coronation in 1377, and restored in parliament in 1397, 'Richard II and the visual arts', in Anthony Goodman and James L. Gillespie, eds., *Richard II: the art of kingship* (Oxford, 1999), 255–71, p. 270.

[27] There is a fuller discussion of the symbolism of the diptych in the following chapter.

[28] Gordon, *Making and meaning*, 50.

[29] Ibid. 49.

rounded by eleven angels, perhaps in reference to Richard's age when he was crowned.[30] They all wear Richard's personal white hart badge on their robes to display the loyalty of the court of heaven to the king. There is punning in this scene which revolves around the Latin word for angels—'angelis' and English—'Angli', which suggests that the allegiance of the court of heaven and the loyalty of Richard's English subjects are equivalent. This bold correspondence yokes the temporal and political to the eternal and sacramental, and is a powerful example of how Richard used the white hart sign to construct an opulent display of sacral kingship in which the issue of loyalty figured prominently.[31]

The enterprise was not lost on his subjects. John Holland, duke of Exeter, possessed a livery of the white hart, set with three rubies and two sapphires.[32] The *Dieulacres* chronicler records that in August 1399, while Richard was at Carmarthen, he was attended by a bodyguard especially chosen from his Cheshire retinue, who wore on their shoulders 'the royal badge of the white hart resplendent'.[33] Three years after Richard's death, the Welsh volunteers who joined with Henry Percy at the battle of Shrewsbury turned up wearing Ricardian badges of the white hart.[34]

Richard's success in parading his sign, however, can also be determined by the attention it drew from his detractors. While the *Dieulacres* chronicler preserves a vignette of the badge as a sign of fidelity, a few lines further on, he relates the capture of Richard at Flint, and the subsequent march to London, in terms of the eclipse of the white hart:

Then indeed were those royal badges both of the hart and of the crown hidden away, so that some said that the esquires of the duke of Lancaster, wearing their collars, had been pre-ordained by a prophecy to subdue like greyhounds in this year the pride of that hated beast the white hart.[35]

---

[30] Richard must have been about 28 when the Diptych was made, but his youthful appearance has been attributed to the desire to present the king at the age of his coronation, ibid. 24, 58.

[31] Richard's determination to impress his majesty on his subjects in order to secure their obedience is examined by Nigel Saul, 'The kingship of Richard II', in Goodman and Gillespie, *The art of kingship*, 38–57, pp. 49–52.

[32] Mathew, *The court of Richard II*, 27.

[33] *The Dieulacres Chronicle*, ed. M. V. Clark and V. H. Galbraith, *Bulletin of the John Rylands Library*, 14 (1930), 164–81; translation from Chris Given-Wilson, ed., *Chronicles of the revolution* (Manchester, 1993), 154.   [34] *Eulogium*, iii. 396.

[35] Given-Wilson, *Chronicles*, 155.

This account resonates suggestively with a passage in Adam Usk's *Chronicle*, where, in the entry for the year 1399, Usk unravels a prophecy of Merlin concerning Henry Bolingbroke. Punning on the various heraldic badges sported by Henry, he says that he ought to be known as the dog: 'by reason of his badge of a collar of linked greyhounds, and because he came in the dog-days and because he utterly drove out from the kingdom the faithless harts, that is, the livery of king Richard which was the hart.'[36] So thoroughgoing was Richard in establishing his hart badge as a material sign of his regality that his opponents recorded its obliteration as equivalent to the downfall of the king himself.[37]

One of the more curious examples survives in an account of litigation arising from a land dispute compiled by John Catesby, a Warwickshire lawyer. Catesby includes in this account a bald summary of the itinerary of Bolingbroke's supporters from Ravenspur to London. Within what is essentially a list of names and places, Catesby summarizes the major incidents:

Then afterwards, about the quinzaine of the Nativity of St John, Henry duke of Lancaster and Hereford landed at Ravenspur in the country of York and began his march. In his company were the earl of Northumberland, the earl of Westmorland, Sir Henry Percy the son and heir of the said earl of Northumberland, Lord Willoughby, the son and heir of the earl of Arundel, Thomas Arundel archbishop of York, Philip abbot of Leicester, and many other knights and esquires. They advanced towards Pontefract, then on to Leicester, and from there, two days before the feast of St James, to Coventry, and on the vigil of St James (24 July) to Warwick; there, because Thomas Holand, earl of Kent—and, by creation of King Richard in his twenty-first year, duke of Surrey—had placed above the gates of Warwick castle a crowned hart of stone, which at that time was the said King Richard's livery, and a white hind which was at that Time the said duke's livery, the duke of Lancaster ordered them to be knocked down, which was done. From there they marched on to Bristol, where Sir William le Scrope earl of Wiltshire and treasurer of England, Sir John Bussy, and Sir Henry Green were beheaded; Sir John Russell escaped, for he had lost his mind. From there they marched on to Flint castle, where King Richard was, having landed at Milford and made his way to Conway castle; and there, through the mediation of the aforesaid

<hr/>

[36] Adam Usk, *Chronicon de Adae de Usk*, ed. and trans. E. Maunde Thompson (London, 1904), 2nd edn., 173.

[37] The Lancastrian efforts to efface Richard's material and symbolic enterprises are discussed in relation to the king's death and burial(s) by Paul Strohm, 'The trouble with Richard: the reburial of Richard II and Lancastrian symbolic strategy', *Speculum*, 71 (1996), 87–111; and more extensively in his *England's empty throne*, 1–31; 63–127.

archbishop and the earl of Northumberland, King Richard surrendered to the duke of Lancaster, whereupon the duke of Surrey and John earl of Salisbury were sent to the north in the custody of the earl of Westmorland, where the said John Catesby was unable to follow them.[38]

The account is orchestrated around three main events: the destruction of a stone hart at Warwick Castle, the beheading of three of Richard's most prominent supporters, and the capture of the king. An equivalence is set up between these events. Because Richard's adversaries attached such symbolic importance to the destruction of his material signs of power, smashing the stone hart is as powerful an action as imprisoning Richard and eliminating his supporters. The episode at Warwick Castle is of a piece with what appears to have been systematic Lancastrian effacement of the cultural artefacts Richard had been so keen to promote at his court, for instance, the covering over of the splendid portrait of the king in Westminster Abbey.[39]

A further example of this Lancastrian challenge is the treatment of the white hart in *Richard the Redeless*, an alliterative poem composed shortly after January 1399, by an anonymous author who had in-depth knowledge of Richard's reign and of his deposition.[40] Many lines of this poem intervene in Richard's symbolically regal discourse, not by obliterating but by revalorizing the key icon in his spectacle of sacral kingship: the white hart. While the Wilton Diptych parades a costly enamelling and aestheticization of the natural world in an ostentatious display of the civilizing power of human control over nature, the poet of *Richard the Redeless* demystifies the political artifice in order to foreground the lawless brutality of Richard's policies. In Passus II of the poem, the writer explicitly focuses on the disastrous consequences of Richard's granting of the white hart livery to his supporters and one of the principal means by which he effects this is to prise the white hart from its ceremonial and regal discourse and return it to its natural origins. Richard's retainers are figured as wild animals rampaging through the kingdom:

---

[38] Given-Wilson, *Chronicles*, 135–6.

[39] Bennett, 'The court of Richard II', 15–16. Paul Binski comments that the Westminster Abbey portrait 'represents an audacious icon of power; anxieties about improper objects of devotional adherence (which doubtless explain, in part, the widespread use of profile types for lay portraits in this period) are here contested and resolutely set aside'. The royal gaze connotes power, action and distance from the subject, *Westminster Abbey and the Plantagenets*, 204.

[40] Quotations from the poem are taken from *The Piers Plowman Tradition*, ed. Barr.

> But moche now me merueilith and well may I in sothe
> Of youre large leuerey to leodis aboughte,
> That ye so goodliche gaf but if gile letted.
> As hertis y-heedyd and hornyd of kynde,
> So ryff as they ronne youre rewme thoru-oute.   (II. 1–5)

The deer are rampant, not in the heraldic, but in the bestial ('hornyd of kynde') sense, of running wild through the kingdom, and oppressing the king's subjects. Further, the poem contests Richard's fashioning of the hart as an exquisitely crafted sign of allegiance:

> So, trouthe to telle, as toune-men said,
> For on that ye merkyd ye myssed ten schore
> Of homeliche hertis that the harme hente.
> Thane was it foly in feith, as me thynketh,
> To sette siluer in signes that of nought serued.   (II. 41–5)

These lines are rich in wordplay[41] and the puns serve to strip away the carefully manufactured regal veneer of the white hart badge. Far from securing loyalty, the harts destroy it. In distributing worthless badges, Richard failed to secure the true 'hertis' of his subjects. For all the 'siluer' employed, the action was costly in both senses of that word ('of nought serued'). And while in its regally commissioned settings, the hart is richly decorated and lavishly crafted, here, it is seen as a sign of disfigurement. The king 'merks' his subjects by providing them with badges, but also by striking and staining them.[42]

One might read the polysemy of these lines as a contestative strategy in its own right. In the Wilton Diptych the regal significance of the hart is established partly through punning,[43] but the wordplay of *Richard the Redeless* subjects the sign to competing interpretations, which, as well as registering criticism, foregrounds the very process of constructing political symbolism. Richard's excessive investment in materially symbolic *signs* of kingship is exposed as such, and Richard's faith in costly signification as a source and display of power is shown to be misplaced and naive.

The narrator also exposes Richard's folly by translating the hart from grand ceremonial contexts to proverbial asides. The narrator remarks that before the king distributed his white hart badge, the allegiance of his subjects was secure:

---

[41] For a full analysis of the wordplay in these lines, see Helen Barr, *Signes and sothe: language in the Piers Plowman tradition* (Cambridge, 1994), 73–4.

[42] See *MED* 'marken' 3(e); 4(b) and 10(a).

[43] There is fuller analysis of this in the following chapter.

Tyl ye, of youre dulnesse deseueraunce made
Thoru youre side signes that shente alle the browet,
And cast adoun the crokk the colys amyd.   (II. 50–2)

The homely idiom, together with the image of spilling the broth, the broken crock fizzing and spitting in the coals, takes us behind the scenes of Richard's ceremonial banquets, with their lavish display of exotic fine cuisine,[44] to the chaos in the kitchen. The 'signes' are no longer magnificent, but crooked ('side'). The king's attempt at regal self-fashioning goes badly awry as the signification of the hart exceeds his control; a situation which is pithily encapsulated in the narrator's comment that Richard was deceived by his 'hertis':

Thus were ye disceyued thoru youre duble hertis
That neuere weren to truste so God saue my soule!   (II. 111–12)

His faith in his white hart badge as a sign of the loyalty of his subjects is shown to be misplaced, for despite the king's attempt to govern the political valency of image-making, the signs are 'duble': capable of having more than one meaning, and untrustworthy.[45] In contrast to the John Catesby account in which the white hart is smashed, this poem contests the hart's regal significances by exposing, through the use of metalanguage and wordplay, the strategies which stage kingship. In laying bare the process of creating symbols and signs, Richard's regality is (post-eventfully) dismantled.

Gower's *Cronica Tripertita* also contests the regal symbolism of the white hart, but while this work shares a number of points of similarity with *Richard the Redeless*,[46] the attack on the material signs of regal power is differently inflected. Both works use the standard technique of political narration whereby persons in the narrative are referred to in coded form: the narrative is generated out of punning on the heraldic signs or badges of the key actors in the drama.[47]

---

[44] See the account in Mathew, *The court of Richard II*, 23–5. Richard's plate and cutlery is discussed by Marian Campbell, 'White harts and coronets: the jewellery and plate of Richard II', in Gordon *et al.*, *The regal image* , 95–114, pp. 97–9.

[45] The pun alludes to the excessive granting of livery badges: *MED* 'double' 3(a) 'twice as much; great' and to the disloyalty of the retainers: 6(a) 'false; deceitful'.

[46] Both works are written after Richard II's deposition; both are written from a Lancastrian perspective, and show particular sympathy for the plights of the Lords Appellant. In both poems, substantial stretches of the narrative depend on punning on the heraldic signs of the nobility.

[47] In the second preface to *The prophecy of John of Bridlington*, the writer lists ten ways of concealing topical references in verse. These range from numerical codes, rearranging letters,

Gower is explicit about explaining his use of code. In lamenting Richard's misrule, he writes:

> Tres namque tunc regni nobiles super hoc
> specialius moti, scilicet Thomas Dux Glouernie,
> qui vulgariter dictus est Cignus, Ricardus Comes
> Arundellie, qui dicitur Equs, Thomas Comes de
> Warrewyk, cuius nomen Vrsus.[48]

There were then three nobles of the realm who were especially disturbed about all this, namely Thomas Duke of Gloucester, who is commonly called the Swan; Richard Earl of Arundel, who is called the Horse; and Thomas Earl of Warwick, whose name is the Bear.[49]

Obviously, these cognomens were well known and yet, in keeping with the pseudo-prophetic nature of the entire work,[50] Gower asserts that his narrative is secret and needs to be teased out:

> Si non directe procerum cognomina recte,
> Hec tamen obscura referam, latitante figura:
> Scribere que tendo si mistica verba legendo
> Auribus apportant, verum tamen illa reportant.

> (*Cronica Tripertita*, I. 45–9)

If I do not refer directly to the right names of the nobles, I shall nevertheless report them disguisedly, in hidden form. Even if I tend to write words which convey mysteries to your ears in the reading of them, those words nonetheless report the truth. (p. 291)

Given that he reveals the identity of the persons to whom the heraldic signs belonged,[51] it is obvious that Gower is using these devices, not so

---

to referring to people by punning on some aspect of their coats of arms, e.g. grey lions for the earl of Hereford. See *Political poems and songs*, i. 123–215, pp. 126–7. There is a similar use of these devices in the poem *On King Richard's ministers*, in *Political poems and songs*, i. 363–6.

[48] Gower, *Explicit* to *Vox Clamantis*, ll. 9–13, quoted from *The Latin works*, ed. G. C. Macaulay.

[49] Gower, *The Tripartite Chronicle*, IV. 315. English quoted from *The major Latin works of John Gower*, ed. and trans. E. W. Stockton (Seattle, 1961), 288.

[50] For instance, Gower pretends that the chronicle antedates the events that he is writing about: 'With this book as witness, the chronicle was written beforehand; it was spoken at another time, but it did not pass unheeded by the ear', p. 290. The strategy of writing about the past as if the events are yet to unfold is a staple topos of prophecy writing, see discussion in Strohm, *England's empty throne*, 1–31.

[51] See his identification of Northumberland as the crescent moon, I. 55; the earl of Oxford as the boar, I. 65 and the running commentary to II. 53–105 in which the cognomens of the Lords Appellant are once again enumerated.

much to write in code, which only the initiated will be in a position to crack, but to use very well-known cognomens as a means to align himself with the authority of prophetic discourse, and as a consequence, to harness political authority to his work.[52]

What is so striking, however, is that in a text bursting at the seams with heraldic codifications, Richard's badge of the white hart is never mentioned. It is inconceivable that Gower was ignorant of it, given its widespread promulgation and contestation, and his in-depth knowledge of the heraldic signs of the nobility. Indeed, Gower knows of one of the king's other badges, that of the sun, which is how he refers to him briefly in the early part of Book One of the chronicle (I. 61 and 64).[53]

One must conclude, I think, that the omission of the white hart is deliberate. The text erases the regal symbolism of the badge in which the king so heavily invested. There are two strategies which run concurrently throughout the text which enact this effacement of the king's magnificent regalia. One is substitution: the king is coded with reference to a series of animals, often with rather unflattering allegorical, rather than heraldic, connotations. So, for instance, Richard is figured as a cunning or rapacious fox (II. 21 and 249); as a fierce wolf (II. 36); a falcon (II. 51); and as a wild beast (II. 283). In narrating the king's actions on Henry Bolingbroke's return, Gower remarks: 'Tunc rex Ricardus lepus est et non leopardus' (then Richard was a hare, and not a lion) (III. 160). The pun on 'lepus', meaning both 'hare' and 'leper' contrasts strongly with the Latin puns Gower constructs around the cognomens of the Lords Appellant.[54] Perhaps the most unflattering comparison is that of Richard to a mole, 'which ever spoils the land by digging it up' (Sicut humum fodit euertens talpa que rodit, III. 17).[55]

The second strategy used by Gower is silence. He simply refuses to

---

[52] Cf. the discussion of his claims for prophetic validity in *Vox Clamantis*, discussed in Chapter 5.

[53] Sunbursts form part of the decoration of Richard's double tomb in Westminster Abbey, along with harts, broom pods, and tree-stocks, Binski, *Westminster Abbey*, 202.

[54] For instance the 'Equs/Equus—Honourable/Horse' wordplay relating to Arundel (I. 49), and the 'Cygno/Cristes signo'—'Swan/Christ's banner' wordplay relating to Gloucester (I. 214). While one cannot surmise that Gower knew the Wilton Diptych, it is intriguing that he associates Christ's banner with Thomas Woodstock, given that the right interior panel shows the Christ child offering his banner to Richard.

[55] Stockton notes that the comparison is appropriate enough as a description of Richard's plotting against the liberties of the kingdom, 'but the comparison is perhaps chiefly intended to suggest that Richard, and not Henry, was the "talpa ore dei maledicta" of prophecy', *Major Latin works*, 479.

grant any textual space to the hart. In effect, he blots out the king's key material sign of power. Such a reading is endorsed by the conclusion to the work in which he recapitulates Richard's failings:

> Cronica Ricardi, qui sceptra tulit leopardi
> Vt patet, est dicta populo set non benedicta:
> Vt speculum mundi, quo lux nequit vlla refundi,
> Sic vacuus transit, sibi nil nisi culpa remansit.
> Vnde superbus erat, modo si preconia querat,
> Eius honor sordet, laus culpat, gloria mordet.
> Hoc concernentes caueant qui sunt sapientes,
> Nam male viuentes deus odit in orbe regentes:
> Est qui peccator, non esse potest dominator;
> Ricardo teste, finis probat hoc manifeste.   (III. 478–87)

This chronicle of Richard, who bore the sceptre of the lion, was uttered by the people, as is clear; but his chronicle has not been a blessed one. Like the mirror of the world, to which no reflection can be restored, he passed away a blank, with nothing but blame remaining for his portion. Because he was haughty his honor has grown tarnished, his praise has become blame, his glory has died away, even if he now were to seek approval. Let those who are wise beware as they look upon this, for God abominates rulers on earth who live evilly. He who is a sinner cannot be a ruler; as Richard is my witness, his end proves this clearly. (p. 326)

In so far as Richard is framed as a counter-exemplum of kingship, these lines conform to a conventional motif of 'advice to princes' literature.[56] Gower urges those who are wise ('sapientes') to beware as they look on Richard's crimes. The fall of Richard can also be seen to conform to a type of Isidorean tragedy as exemplified in the series of tales told by Chaucer's Monk.[57] Within these paradigms, however, Gower's conclusion effects a powerful effacement of Richard II. The comparison of the former king to a non-reflecting mirror reworks the trope of mirror as exemplum or counter-exemplum which is used both

---

[56] In Book V of the *Confessio Amantis*, for example, Gower re-retells the popular tale of Virgil's mirror as a counter-exemplum of kingship. Crassus, the Emperor of Rome, allows his greed for gold to destroy the mirror which Virgil had set up wherein all the movements of enemies of Rome within a compass of thirty miles might be seen. With the mirror destroyed, Hannibal of Carthage is able to capture the city, and the Romans punish Crassus by pouring molten gold down his throat. The mirror, in its ability to see clearly and defend against covert subterfuge, represents the clear-sighted political wisdom and power so lacking in Crassus, who represents the antithesis of good kingship.

[57] *The Riverside Chaucer*, 929, notes that the general plan of *The Monk's Tale* is due to Boccaccio's *De Casibus Virorum Illustrium*.

within individual 'speculum principis' texts and is also, as the Latin indicates, a controlling narrative scheme for the genre as a whole. Gower made frequent use of mirrors, both in the organizational schemes of his works, and in their narrative details.[58]

The simile of the non-reflecting mirror could hardly contrast more strongly with Richard II's zeal for political image-making, and this, I think, is precisely the point.[59] As is evident from the line: 'Sic vacuus transit, sibi nil nisi culpa remansit' (481), Gower is attempting to blank out Richard's kingship and assign the former monarch to an empty space. The first half of the hexameter plays on the well-known Latin tag 'Sic gloria transit', which was used at coronations.[60] To replace 'gloria' with 'vacuus' is a literary erasure of Richard's kingly munificence comparable to the covering up of his portrait in Westminster Hall.

What more powerful way of obliterating the majesty of the former king than by refusing textual space to the key icon of his kingship: the white hart? The absence at the centre of *Cronica Tripertita* corresponds to Gower's attempt at its conclusion to figure the king as a blank, an empty space. This is an iconoclastic contestation of the white hart and all its attendant regal symbolism, which may remind one of the destruction of the stone hart at the gates of Warwick Castle, but is effected with the subtlety characteristic of the revalorization of the hart in *Richard the Redeless*. Gower's blanking out of the white hart is a calculated snub, which itself reverses one of the powerful meanings which Richard attempted to annex to the sign—that of loyalty. Gower's narrative silence contests the strategic means of representation characteristic of Richard's concern to bolster his kingship through opulent, material display.

It is, in light of this, a sad irony, that one of the Latin hexameters which Richard commissioned for his tomb reads: 'The king [i.e. Richard] laid low those who violated regalia.'[61] The word 'regalia' has the senses both of the physical signs of power, and the intangible

---

[58] In *Mirour*, for instance, his summary of King David's exemplarity states that 'he was (so to speak) a mirror for other kings' (22883–4); Gower, *Mirour de L'Omme*, trans. William Burton Wilson (East Lansing, Mich., 1992), 299.

[59] It compares to the erasures in Fairfax MS of *Confessio Amantis* following the rededication of the *Confessio Amantis* from Richard to Henry Bolingbroke, see *The English works of John Gower*, ed. G. C. Macaulay (EETS ES 81 (1900)), pp. xxi–xxii.

[60] See Hans Walther, *Lateinische sprichworter und sentenzen des mittelalters under der frühen neuzeit* (Göttingen, 1986), 629, n. 697b.

[61] See Gordon, *Making and meaning*, 19.

prerogatives of royalty. As such, it is unsurprising that Richard was so concerned with 'regalia', nowhere more opulently than in the Wilton Diptych. So successful was his promulgation of this concept, however, that for his detractors, to oppose the king was to contest the material signs of his intangible royal prerogative, and, in the case of Gower, to obliterate the sign of the white hart.

It is tempting to use the term 'literary deposition' to describe the social and political significance of these acts of writing. But assessing the social positioning of these texts is fraught with complications. It could be argued that in contesting the sign of the white hart, none of these oppositional texts is radical. The obliteration or revalorization of the badge takes place in texts written after Richard's deposition. Moreover, none of these texts offers a new vision of a social polity. While the public tropes of Richard's kingship are negotiated there is no narrative alternative offered to the figuring of kingship, either as a concept, or as an institution. Even as they reverse or contest its terms the texts reproduce the conventional paradigms of social description without intervention. Their oppositional commentary focuses on the past as a counter-exemplum to guide the present. In their chronicles of past misrule, present configurations of government remain unchallenged.

Such a conclusion, however, while plausible, irons out some interesting problems. Two issues, in particular, place such a reading under strain: the articulation of pro-Wycliffite sentiment, and the internal time-schemes of the texts. The first issue pertains exclusively to Gower. In the closing passage of *Cronica Tripertita*, quoted above, Gower writes:

> Est qui peccator, non esse potest dominator   (III. 486)

As Anne Hudson observes, with this line Gower, 'doubtless unwitting . . . [enunciates] a view dangerously close'[62] to Wyclif's argument in *De Civili Dominio* that no one, secular or cleric, king or peasant, in a state of mortal sin, has true dominion over anything, whether inanimate objects, or animate nature.[63] This proposition was condemned as an error in Pope Gregory XI's bull against Wyclif in 1377, and in the 1382 Council of London's condemnation of Wyclif's teaching.[64] Gower's stated opposition to 'this newe Secte of Lollardie'[65] is well known, and it could be

---

[62] Anne Hudson, *The premature reformation* (Oxford, 1988), 410.

[63] Ibid. 359.

[64] Ibid. 359.

[65] *Confessio Amantis*, Prol. 349. Cf. V. 1807–24. Gower's relationship to Lollardy is discussed by Hudson, *Premature reformation*, 408–10.

argued that the coincidence of this line with pro-Wycliffite sentiment is to be explained as resulting from the staple narrative technique of advice to princes manuals which places the political focus of malaise on the moral failings of a ruler.[66] Especially in those mirrors for princes which derive from the *Secreta Secretorum* tradition, bad kingship results from being a disordered human being. Improper rule stems from personal vice or corruption. This view underwrites Book VII of Gower's own *Confessio Amantis*.[67] Ethical focus on kingship, which uses the macro/microcosm model of moral-political analysis allows for criticism of particular kings while leaving the orthodox political conception of kingship intact.

Gower's comment at the end of *Cronica Tripertita* does not fit so neatly into this scheme. First, the statement that 'he who is a sinner cannot be a ruler' is generic and axiomatic. It offers a model of kingship based on role, rather than individual name. The internal rhyme of the hexameter draws 'peccator' and 'dominator' parallel. The following line: 'Ricardo teste, finis probat hoc manifeste' (III. 487) uses Richard as a specific example to prove a general proposition. As a result, this comment could be seen to destabilize the orthodox view of the *office* of kingship. The line could be read to support the view that since a sinful ruler has no right to dominion, then a subject need owe no allegiance. Such a view completely undermines the sacral majesty of kingship ritualized in coronation procedures and regal iconography—and here, it is worth recalling that in blanking out the sign of the white hart, Gower obliterates a richly crafted sign of allegiance. Given Gower's manifest attempts to secure Henry IV's favour, he must presumably have been oblivious to how his comment could appear much more subversive than the almost routinely orthodox views on secular allegiance in Wycliffite texts.[68] Gower's blindness may not have been shared,

[66] See D. M. Bell, *L'idéal éthique de la royauté en France au moyen âge* (Paris, 1962) and L. K. Born, 'The perfect prince: a study in thirteenth and fourteenth century ideals', *Speculum*, 3 (1928), 470–504.

[67] See *Secreta Secretorum: nine English versions*, M. A. Manzalaoui, ed. (EETS OS 276 1977), introduction, pp. ix–xii, and xiv–xlvi. The moral framework may have been derived from Giles of Rome's *De Regimine Principum*; see H. C. Mainzer, 'A study of the sources of the Confessio Amantis of John Gower', D.Phil. thesis (Oxford University, 1967), 45–8. See also A. H. Gilbert, 'Notes on the influence of the *Secreta Secretorum*', *Speculum*, 3 (1928), 84–93; R. A. Peck, *Kingship and common profit in Gower's* Confessio Amantis (Carbondale, Ill., 1978); and Elizabeth Porter, 'Gower's ethical microcosm and political macrocosm' in A. J. Minnis, ed., *Gower's* Confessio Amantis: *responses and re-assessments* (Cambridge, 1983), 135–62.

[68] Wycliffite views on secular obedience are discussed in Chapter 6.

however; the line is omitted in Glasgow, Hunterian MS T.217, and as a result, any trace of heterodoxy is removed.[69]

The second issue, the internal time-scheme of the texts is relevant both to *Richard the Redeless* and to *Cronica Tripertita*. Both works post-date Richard's deposition in 1399. *Richard* refers to the 1400 Cirencester uprising in II. 17[70] and Gower refers to the return of Thomas Arundel (side-note to III. 121). Yet the declared internal time-scheme of the poems problematizes this chronology. In Passus I of *Richard* the narrator claims that he does not know whether Richard will be king again and writes him this book to 'wissen him better' (I. 31). Throughout, the time references are unclear and inconsistent. At no point does the narrator refer to Henry as king. Within the explicit narrative timescale, then, the narrator offers a revalorization and critique of the white hart ostensibly while Richard is still king. Within the declared time frame of the poem, the narrator dismantles kingly regalia even while Richard is still supposed to be invested with sacral majesty.

Similarly, within the internal time-scheme of his poem, Gower effaces the white hart during, not after, Richard's reign. He states explicitly that his chronicle was written ahead of the events it describes: 'With this book as witness, the chronicle was written beforehand; it was spoken at another time, but it did not pass unheeded by the ear' (p. 290). Obviously, this is simply part of the prophetic apparatus of the poem, but as in *Richard the Redeless*, the textuality of the poem *imagines* the dismantling of sacral kingship. To depose, even in imaginary terms, a present king, is a different matter entirely from a post-eventful account of a change of rule. As Paul Strohm has pointed out in his discussion of prophecy and gossip in the first few years of the new Lancastrian regime, the Statute of Treason passed in 1352 included as basis for conviction anyone who 'fait compasser ou ymaginer le mort notre Seigneur le Roi'. Strohm argues that 'to compass or imagine' the death of the king 'is to commit treason, whether or not a concrete action ensues, and the evidence of words spoken or written is subordinate to (although clearly contributory to) a determination'.[71] While *Richard* does not imagine the death of the apparently reigning king, the written words of *Cronica Tripertita* most certainly do, and both texts, within their declared temporality, imagine Richard's deposition and the dismantling of his

---

[69] Gower, *The Latin works*, ed. Macaulay, p.342.

[70] Helen Barr, 'The dates of *Richard the Redeless* and *Mum and the Sothsegger*', *Notes and Queries*, 235 (1990), 270–5.

[71] Strohm, *England's empty throne*, 26.

regal image. Taken on their own terms, they may be regarded as treasonous texts. Paradoxically, the use of evasion, and the forgery over date, permit a reading of the texts which enable them to be seen to reproduce treason, even as their authors are obviously writing from a position which endorses the new Lancastrian rule, and may even have been part of the Lancastrian aim of legitimation. In unfixing the signs of Richard's kingship, the poems intervene in one social practice of representation only to fetch up on the wrong side of another, the system of power which determines one set of meanings as legitimate, and another as treasonous.

CHAPTER FOUR

The Regal Image of Richard II and the *Prologue to the Legend of Good Women*

AS THE PREVIOUS CHAPTER has shown, Richard II invested heavily in a rich variety of symbolic practices to project a carefully fashioned image of sacral kingship.[1] In this chapter I wish to explore further the politics of that representation, and to argue that the *Prologue* to Chaucer's *Legend of Good Women* may be seen both to reproduce, and to intervene in, the process of image-making as a means of displaying power and maintaining political control.[2]

One of the most striking aspects of the construction of the regal image is its insistence and plenitude. This can be seen from the sheer range of symbolic practices employed: from the decoration of architectural space;[3] portraiture; the fashioning of cutlery[4] and dress[5] to pro-

---

[1] His obsession with image-making draws frequent, and hostile, comment in the chronicles, for instance, the *Eulogium* writer records a speech by Richard Arundel which accuses the king of despoiling his subjects and raising taxes in order to satisfy his pomp, iii. 382. Cf. the resentment towards Richard's extravagance in *The Westminster chronicle*, 161–3. The portrayal of Richard in the chronicles is studied by John Taylor, 'Richard II in the chronicles', in Goodman and Gillespie, *The art of kingship*, 15–35; and Louisa D. Duls, *Richard II in the early chronicles* (The Hague, 1975).

[2] Nigel Saul observes: 'Courtly life can be seen as a series of unfolding set-pieces or occasions: occasions at which visitors were received, business transacted, gifts bestowed and the splendour of the king's majesty revealed to his subjects,' *Richard II* (New Haven and London, 1997), 337. Scheifele ('Richard II and the visual arts', 256) comments that whether Richard were more or less extravagant than his predecessors in his cultivation of sign and symbol, he was personally invested in 'the selection of forms, symbols and physical sites for his commissions and . . . was keenly aware of their political potential to further his image of kingship'.

[3] See Christopher Wilson, 'Rulers, artificers and shoppers: Richard II's remodelling of Westminster Hall, 1393–99', in Gordon *et al.*, *The regal image*, 33–59, esp. 37–41 and 59.

[4] See Campbell, 'White harts and coronets', 95–114.

[5] See Kay Staniland, 'Extravagance or regal necessity: the clothing of Richard II', in Gordon *et al.*, *The regal image*, 85–94.

cession.[6] In all of these media, there is an intense interest, or as one critic has put it, myopic preoccupation, with regalia as material signs of power.[7] When Richard travelled round the realm he was in the habit of taking his regalia with him,[8] and one of the few literary works which can be said to have been commissioned by the king is a treatise on regalia by William Sudbury, a Benedictine monk of Westminster Abbey.[9] This treatise describes the regalia both as signs of the sacrament of the coronation and also the means by which the king takes on his royal dignity. This royal dignity is said to take first place above all the riches, pleasures, and honours of this world, supereminently, at the very highest point.[11]

The Westminster Abbey portrait makes this point very forcibly. Its sheer size is imposing; it measures over two metres by over one metre. Also, if the portrait were to have been hung above the king's pew in Westminster Abbey, as has been suggested, then the surrounds of the holy space of the abbey foregrounds the sacral regality of the king.[11] The iconic close-up of the face, with its frontal pose, parallels representations of Christ in majesty.[12] Further, Richard is depicted throned, replete with crown, orb, and sceptre.[13] The prominence of the regalia creates an

[6] I discuss the royal entry later in this chapter.

[7] Saul, 'The kingship of Richard II', 54.

[8] Michael J. Bennett, 'Richard II and the wider realm', in Goodman and Gillespie, *The art of kingship*, 187–204, p. 200.

[9] *De primis regalibus ornamentis regni Angliae*. The treatise circulated as part of the *Ricardi de Cirencestria Speculum Historiale*, ed. J. E. B. Mayor (London, Rolls Series, 1863–9), ii. 26–39.

[10] See Patricia J. Eberle, 'Richard II and the literary arts', in Goodman and Gillespie, *The art of kingship*, 231–53, p. 239, quoting: 'regiam . . . dignitatem, quae inter omnes et super omnes huius mundi divitias, delicias, et honores supereminenter in culmine residet principatus' from p. 30 of the treatise.

[11] See Saul, 'The kingship of Richard II', 51. Saul notes that the creation of a 'semi-deus' portrait of the king is consonant with Richard's cultivation of a new language of address which encouraged his subjects to refer to him as 'your majesty'.

[12] Simon Walker notes that '*imitatio Christi* was a mode of action routinely urged on late medieval rulers . . . but few of them seem to have adopted it so literally and personally as Richard II', 'Richard II's views on kingship', in Rowena E. Archer and Simon Walker, eds., *Rulers and ruled in late medieval England: essays presented to Gerald Harriss* (Hambledon, 1995), 48–63, p. 60.

[13] Pamela Tudor-Craig notes how the importance which Richard attached to the orb is seen by its inclusion in the Westminster Abbey portrait where, contrary to custom, he carries it in his right hand and the sceptre in his left, 'The Wilton Diptych in the context of contemporary English panel and wall painting', in Gordon *et al.*, *The regal image*, 207–22, p. 217.

image of omnipotence.[14] The details of the painting, together with its positioning, defy any challenge to regal authority.[15]

The Westminster portrait also shows how Richard exploited personal dress as a surface for political posturing.[16] His robe is decorated with the letter 'R'. The king was fond of using symbolic lettering on clothes; he wore outfits embellished with whole phrases, individual words, and letters.[17] Lettering also appears on commissioned artefacts: Richard had spoons made fashioned with a crowned 'R', girdles decorated with the letters 'A' and 'R'—the 'A' with reference to Richard's first queen, Anne of Bohemia.[18] The letters 'A' and 'R' also appear on the double tomb which Richard commissioned for himself and Anne in West-minster Abbey. This double tomb is rich in iconography and symbol-ism. In the tester above the tomb, Christ is depicted in majesty. The robes of Richard and Anne are delicately pounced with a profusion of heraldic signs; there is the deer, representing Richard's sign of the white hart, sunbursts, and broom pods, which pun on the botanical name *planta genista* and plantaganet.[19] Richard and Anne hold sceptres in their left hands, and this exceptional inclusion of regalia was a demonstration of Richard's royal prerogative.[20]

In constructing and maintaining an image of supreme power, Richard exploited to the full the imaginative possibilities of sign and symbol. This is seen at its most intense in the Wilton Diptych.[21] It is

[14] Jonathan J. G. Alexander notes how the iconic close-up marks a transitional moment in the depiction of subjectivity, but that it is as much an icon of kingship as a portrait of an indi-vidual king, 'The portrait of Richard II in Westminster Abbey', in Gordon *et al.*, *The regal image*, 197–206, p. 205.

[15] Saul notes that the construction of image-making was to distance the king from his subjects: 'Richard was seen in ritualistic terms as a sacred icon, supreme and all-powerful', *Richard II*, 239; cf. Goodman and Gillespie, *The art of kingship*, 49.

[16] Scheifele, 'Richard II and the visual arts', 257. According to the Evesham chronicler, *Historia Vitae Ricardi Secundi*, ii. 156, on one occasion he spent £20,000 on a robe lined with precious stones.

[17] See Lisa Monnas, 'Fit for a king: figured silks shown in the Wilton Diptych', in Gordon *et al.*, *The regal image*, 165–77, p. 172.

[18] See Caroline Barron, 'Introduction', in Gordon *et al.*, *The regal image*, 13.

[19] See Phillip Lindley, 'Absolutism and regal image in Ricardian sculpture', in Gordon *et al.*, *The regal image*, 61–83, pp. 62–74. The broom pods were also an adaption from the livery of King Charles VI of France, see Maurice Keen, 'The Wilton Diptych: the case for a crusading context', in Gordon *et al.*, *The regal image*, 189–96, p. 190.

[20] See Scheifele, 'Richard II and the visual arts', 263.

[21] The techniques of the Diptych are analysed by Ashok Roy, 'The technique of the Wilton Diptych', in Gordon *et al.*, *The regal image*, 125–35.

precisely because of the complexity of signs and symbolism in the work that its significance is still a subject of debate.[22] As on the double tomb, Richard's robe is heavily patterned with signs of the white hart and the broom pod. The Diptych as a whole is awash with symbolism. Not content with one significance, or one connection, multiple symbolism and many-layered narratives are woven together to create an accretive and prominent image of sacral majesty. An analogy may be drawn to the painting of the badge of the white hart on Richard's chest. The badge derives its enamelled, jewel-like quality from the thickness of the paint in raised layers of lead. The accumulation of the layers grants the badge physical and symbolic prominence in the Diptych.[23]

The brooch also inheres in a dense web of punning. The rich hart puns, of course, on Richard's own name—'Richart' and also alludes to his personal livery badge of the white deer. The Virgin and her eleven angels all wear this badge on their blue robes, establishing the fact that the court of heaven is loyal to the king. There is also a pun, as I mentioned in the previous chapter, on the word 'angel' and the Latin word for the English—'Angli', which creates a parallel between the loyalty of the court of heaven and the allegiance of Richard's English subjects.[24] Number symbolism is also used. The eleven angels may be a reference to Richard's age when he was crowned, thus suggesting a coronation context for the Diptych, a suggestion endorsed by Richard's youthful appearance. Certainly, the Diptych is full of coronation symbolism, especially crowns: Richard's own crown, the crowns of St Edmund and St Edward; Christ wears his Crown of Thorns and, rather than divine haloes, the angels sport coronas of red and white roses. Red and white are the colours of England.[25]

It has recently been argued that the number eleven and the coronation references may refer, not to Richard's actual coronation in 1377, but to a later event. Eleanor Scheifele has argued that an appropriate context would be Richard's victory over the Appellants in 1397. In the opening sermon to the parliament, Richard declared that he had restored the 'crown of his youth' which had been denied him by the Appellants at the Merciless Parliament in 1388.[26] At the close of the 1397

[22] See Barron, 'Introduction', 9.

[23] Gordon, *Making and meaning*, 49. Cf. discussion in Chapter 3 above.

[24] See Chapter 3.

[25] Campbell discusses the cost and appearance of Richard's crowns, including the 'bacynet du Roy' which, in 1384, was valued at £254 22d., 'White harts and coronets', 98.

[26] *Rot. Parl*, iii. 347–85, quoted in Scheifele, 'Richard II and the visual arts', 269.

parliament, Richard conferred eleven new titles, and those eleven nobles renewed their oaths of coronation fealty to the king at Westminster Abbey. These same eleven were then invested with the king's livery. Scheifele suggests that the significance of the banner in the Diptych is twofold. It symbolizes both Christ's resurrection, and also Richard's renewal and victory over the Appellants. Such a reading of the Diptych suggests how iconic representation was used to proclaim absolute power and control: a statement of royal triumph after the challenges to Richard's rule by the Appellants.[27]

A possible occasion for the commissioning of the Diptych, if this argument be followed, would have been for Richard's birthday on 6 January 1398. While any date for the Diptych is open to debate, this would fit the complex Epiphany symbolism of the work. In the interior panels, Richard holds centre stage; although the king kneels, the hands of St Edmund, St Edward the Confessor, and St John the Baptist point to him, as do those of Christ and the angels who surround the Virgin.[28] Recent photographic work has shown how the hand of the angel on the far right-hand side of the portrait originally pointed to the Virgin, but this was subsequently painted over, and now, she too, like all the rest, points to the boy-king.[29] There is no doubt who is the subject of the adoring gaze. The left-wing interior shows Richard being presented to the Virgin and Child by these saints.[30] Richard venerated John the

---

[27] *Rot. Parl*, iii. 347–85, quoted in Scheifele, 268–71. The king's zeal in blazoning victory against his opponents can be seen in the letter he sent to Emperor Manuel II in which he declared that in defeating his rebellious subjects, he had trodden on the necks of the proud and haughty. In language that recalls the words of the *Magnificat*: 'he hath put down the mighty from their seat', he describes how disobedience is founded on pride and parallel to the sin of Lucifer. Richard's reduction of his subjects to obedience is seen as the temporal counterpart of God's retributive justice, Walker, 'Richard's views', 53.

[28] Gordon, *Making and meaning*, 22 and fig. 29, p. 77. Cf. Lucy Freeman Sandler, 'The Wilton Diptych and images of devotion in illuminated manuscripts', in Gordon *et al.*, *The regal image*, 137–54, p. 148.

[29] Gordon, *Making and meaning*, 22 and fig. 29, p. 77.

[30] The symbolism of the three saints in the Diptych, and their relevance for Richard II is discussed ibid. 53–7. St Edmund was linked very strongly to Westminster Abbey, and especially the coronation service. The saint's slippers formed part of Richard's coronation regalia. Edward the Confessor was buried in Westminster Abbey and became regarded as its founder. After the death of his wife Anne in 1394, Richard took up the cult of Edward with great fervour. In 1395 he had the royal arms impaled with those of the saint and throughout his kingship, worshipped at the shrine of Edward in times of crisis. At his coronation he was said to have been clad in Edward's coat and wore his crown. Richard gave a ruby ring to the shrine of St Edward to be used in future coronations.

Baptist as his patron saint, possibly because he became king on the eve of the Nativity of St John, or, more probably because Richard was born on 6 January, the Feast of the Baptism of Christ.[31] John is the only one of the three saints who has physical contact with Richard in the Diptych; he touches him on the shoulder. John is also singled out for special devotion in the inscription around Richard's tomb in Westminster Abbey, where he is invoked as intercessor for the king.[32]

The imagery of the three kings adoring the Christ child further alludes to the Feast of the Epiphany, also on 6 January,[33] and hence, both the choice of kings, and their iconographic significance as a group, show Richard marshalling traditional religious imagery to his own personal circumstances.[34] Richard is inserted into this motif by becoming one of the three kings himself. This may show influence of the international cult of the three kings.[35] The Adoration of the Magi was a very popular subject in medieval art, and in the mid-fourteenth century a new

[31] Bowers, '*Pearl* in its royal setting', 123–30, discusses Richard's especial devotion to John the Baptist and notes on p. 126 that in 1389, the king presented Westminster Abbey with a chasuble in which John appears along with St Edmund and Edward the Confessor (information drawn from J. Wickham Legg, ed., 'On an inventory of the vestry of Westminster Abbey', *Archaeologia*, 52 (1890), 280). Bowers, '*Pearl* in its royal setting', 123. The importance of St John for Richard is discussed further in Gordon, *Making and meaning*, 55–6: in the epitaph to his will, Richard particularly singled out John the Baptist for protection, he is shown kneeling before the king in a stained glass window in Winchester College, and the royal entry for the king and queen in London in 1392 culminated with a tableau of John the Baptist in the wilderness. Richard acquired relics and bestowed gifts associated with the saint.

[32] *Royal commission on the ancient and historical monuments and constructions of England: London*, vol. I: *Westminster Abbey* (London, 1924), i. 31 'O clemens Christe—cui devotus fuit iste: Votis Baptiste—salve quem pretulit iste'. See Shelagh Mitchell, 'Richard II: kingship and the cult of the saints', in Gordon *et al.*, *The regal image*, 115–24, pp. 122–4.

[33] According to a contemporary chronicle, three kings were present when Richard was born in Bordeaux: those of Spain, Navarre, and Portugal. This probably apocryphal story is cited in Gordon, *Making and meaning*, 57, with reference to *Chronica W Thorn. mon. S. Augustini Cantuarie* in *Historia Anglicanae Scriptores X*, ed. Twysden (1652), col. 2142.

[34] The religious claims of Richard's royal propaganda are discussed in R. H. Jones, *The royal policy of Richard II* (Oxford, 1968); J. Taylor, 'Richard II's views on kingship', *Proceedings of the Leeds Philosophical Society*, 14 (1971), 189–205. The traditions of Christological kingship are examined in E. H. Kantorowicz, *The king's two bodies: a study in medieval political theology* (Princeton, 1957). The premises of Kantorowicz's interpretation of Shakespeare's *Richard II* have been re-evaluated by David Norbrook in '"A liberal tongue": language and rebellion in *Richard II*', in J. M. Mucciolo, ed., *Shakespeare's universe: renaissance ideas and conventions; essays in honour of W. R. Elton* (London, 1996), 37–51, esp. 38.

[35] See Olga Pujmanovà, 'Portraits of kings depicted as magi in Bohemian painting', in Gordon *et al.*, *The regal image*, 247–66, pp. 254–66.

political spin was placed on the topos. The practice grew up of identifying a contemporary living king with two other kings in Adoration
scenes. The practice was especially employed by Charles IV of Bohemia,
although he was not its originator. Given that Richard's first wife, Anne
of Bohemia, was daughter of Charles IV and sister of Wenceslas IV, this
Bohemian self-styling could well have been appropriated by Ricardian
image-making.

Such density and elaboration of regal coding is also apparent in the
Latin poem by Richard Maidstone, a Carmelite friar, written to cele-
brate the reconciliation of London with Richard II in 1392.[36] In its
description and framing of Richard, the poem reproduces this concern
with multiplex symbolism. There is a dazzling mix of iconographical
pageants within the procession, but the procession itself also inheres in
multiple iconographic schemes: London is cast in the role of the New
Jerusalem, with Richard figured as Christ at the Second Coming, entering his kingdom for the second time; the forgiving bridegroom of an
errant but penitent spouse (p. 283/8).[37] London is also figured as Troy
(p. 282/11), hence Richard is presented as the redeemer of this besieged
city, an ancient site of civilization more famous for its fall.[38] Literary
allusions are showered on Richard. He is scripted into a variety of roles
and assumes the dignity of a number of symbolically resonant personae.
In addition to the Christ parallels, he is compared to Caesar (p. 288/24),
described as more beautiful than Paris (p. 283/10), as becoming as
Absolom[39] or Troilus (p. 285/28), and most remarkably (in light of the
materials produced by his detractors), as possessing a wisdom akin to
Solomon's (p. 283/22). Eberle remarks that the pageant as a whole and
the poem that commemorates it 'echo and extend the kind of profession
of "ligeance" found in Gower's *Confessio Amantis* into a fully articulated
doctrine of obedience to a Solomonic (even Christ like) king'.[40]

What is conspicuous about the construction of Richard's regal image

[36] *Political poems and songs*, ed. Wright, i. 282–300. Eberle discusses this poem, 'Richard II
and the literary arts', 244–6; and cf. Strohm, *Hochon's arrow*, 105–19.

[37] Such parallels were made right from the start of Richard's reign. In Bishop Houghton's
address to parliament in January 1377, he said that Richard had been sent to England by God
in the same way that God had sent his Son into the world for the redemption of his people,
Rot. Parl, ii. 362.

[38] Cf. the account in Saul, *Richard II*, 343.

[39] Usk, at the beginning of his chronicle, also compares Richard II to Absolom, p. 1.

[40] Eberle ('Richard II and the literary arts', 246–7) discusses various attempts to associate
Richard with the figure of Solomon as part of his regal self-fashioning, including that made
by Roger Dymock in his *Duodecim hereses*.

is, not just the symbolism and features of its component parts, but its insistent accretion. The rich surfeit of signification might simply be thought of as an index of material opulence, but I think there is more to it than this. The excess of signification may also be seen as a sign of anxiety. So over-determined are the meanings and symbols of the Diptych or the Maidstone poem, so intense the task of rhetorical persuasion, that it causes one to wonder what the makers are so desperate to conceal, or to put it another way, what they are desperate to suture.

Suture describes a process of 'filling in', a stitching up, an attempt to close together what must not be seen: a gap or lack. But the very stitching must, by necessity, draw attention to what has been sewn closed. Laclau and Mouffe apply this concept of suture to society, especially to the ways that dominant power groups, in their attempts to hold absolute power, can be seen to be practising suture. But because the practice of suture inscribes both an act of filling in and the presence of what is sewn closed, a totally sutured society, they argue, can never exist:[41]

Hegemonic practices are suturing insofar as their field of operation is determined by the openness of the social, by the ultimately unfixed character of every signifier. This original lack is precisely what the hegemonic practices try to fill in. A *totally* sutured society would be one where this filling-in would have reached its ultimate consequences and would have, therefore, managed to identify itself with the transparency of a closed symbolic order. Such a closure of the social is, as we shall see, impossible.[42]

This account resonates very suggestively with the construction of Richard's image. The image-makers attempt to identify Richard's representation with what is given, and to permit no other account of majesty. Complex symbolism is used accretively and aggressively to promote one single meaning: the sacral majesty of Richard II. But, such closure of available representation, while striven for, is not achieved. The insistent emphasis on making, stitching, and fabrication in artefacts which produce Richard's regal image, the concern to layer, to say things

---

[41] Ernesto Laclau and Chantal Mouffe, *Hegemony and socialist strategy: towards a radical democratic politics*, trans. Winston Moore and Paul Cammack (London, 1985). They acknowledge their adoption of the concept of suture from psychoanalytic theory, p. 88, n. 1; see Jacques-Alain Miller, 'Suture elements of the logic of the signifier', *Screen*, 18 (1977/8), 23–34. 'Suture names the relation of the subject to the chain of its discourse . . . it figures there as the element which is lacking, in the form of a stand-in . . . Suture implies a filling in', p.88. (I am indebted to Paul Strohm for drawing my attention to this work.)

[42] Ibid. 88.

twice, to establish, not one connection, but two or more, inscribe anxiety, and expose the constructedness of the project.

The centre-stage positioning of the king in the Diptych is matched by the frontal pose in the Westminster portrait which presents Richard as the epitome of majesty. Iconographically, Richard is established as the source of power; all the excessive, multiple signification leads back to this single point. The compositional focus of Richard as originary point may be seen as another attempt at total suture, an attempt to stitch up anything that may challenge the primary status of Richard at the heart of a system of differential meanings. The regal iconography demands a system of signification which fixes Richard at its centre. In the terms used by Laclau and Mouffe, Richard becomes a nodal point in the discursive field of government. They argue that any discourse is constituted as an attempt to dominate the field of discursivity, to arrest the flow of differences and to construct a centre. This centre, or nodal point, is a privileged discursive point in the partial fixation of the discursive field.[43] This centre, or nodal point, however, is not a fixed locus, but a function. Its function is to arrest the flow of social difference. But, as Laclau and Mouffe argue, 'the partial character of this fixation proceeds from the openness of the social, a result, in its turn, of the constant overflowing of every discourse by the infinitude of the field of discursivity'.[44]

In Ricardian iconography, Richard is the nodal point, which determines in advance the meaning of kingship and tries to arrest any alternative representations. Rather as the hand of the eleventh Virgin in the Diptych was redirected to ensure uniformity of pointing, all signs point back to the power of the king. But, just as the redirection was not ultimately covered up, neither could Richard totally suture the flow of differences within the discursive field of kingship. As Simon Walker has argued, Richard's ideas, even his ideological and rhetorical postures, were already available within the frameworks of kingship. What the king and his supporters did was to emphasize certain features in response to counter-emphases on how kingship should function.[45] And it is helpful, I think, to read Richard's royal image, not as an expression of personal absolutism, but as inscribing a response to the fact that his rule

[43] Laclau and Mouffe borrow this term 'nodal point' from Lacanian theory and the concept of 'points de capiton'—privileged signifiers that fix the meaning of a signifying chain, ibid. 112.

[44] Ibid. 112–13, quotation from p. 113.

[45] Walker, 'Richard II's views', 62.

was characterized by a series of acts of defiance: his uncles, the lords in general, and the commons in parliament.[46] While the Diptych, and indeed the Westminster Abbey portrait, grant ceremonial majesty and sacral aura to the youthful king, these are gestures which attempt to suture the fact that the royal adolescence posed enormous political and constitutional problems for his subjects. As John Watts has written: 'how was a king who was clearly no longer a child to be guided and counselled?'[47] The emphasis in the regal iconography on Richard as centre overpaints the wider baronial picture and also the complexities of the relationship between Richard and his council.[48] By fixing Richard and his sacral majesty as the centre point in the representation of kingship, there is the attempt to edge out an institutional account of government.[49] But this filling in is predicated on something missing. For in terms of power, Richard required institutionalized support in the form of counsel, parliament, and baronial cooperation. The representation of majesty through carefully crafted letters, punning, costly regalia, and allegorical stagings of allegiance is predicated on a lack of unfractured support for his rule.[50]

How does this relate to Chaucer's *Prologue to the Legend of Good Women*? First, I wish to show how some of the descriptions in the poem appear to reproduce some of the symbolic materials deployed in the construction of Richard's regal image. The first passage is the entrance of Cupid and his queen, Alceste, into the poem:

And from afer com walkying in the mede
The god of Love, and in his hand a
    quene,

'I se' quod she, 'the myghty god of Love.
Lo! yond he cometh! I se his wynges
    sprede.'

[46] For the relationship between Richard II and parliament, see A. L. Brown, 'Parliament c.1377–1422', in R. G. Davies and J. H. Denton, eds., *The English parliament in the middle ages* (Manchester, 1981), 109–40; and for his relationship with the nobility, C. Given-Wilson, *The English nobility in the late middle ages: the fourteenth century political community* (London, 1987); A. Goodman, *The loyal conspiracy* (London, 1971); K. B. McFarlane, *The nobility of later medieval England* (Oxford, 1973); J. A. Tuck, *Richard II and the English nobility* (London, 1973).

[47] John Watts, 'Review of Nigel Saul, *Richard II*', *Notes and Queries*, 224 (1999), 91–3, p. 93.

[48] For relations between Richard and his council see Anthony Goodman, 'Richard II's councils', in Goodman and Gillespie, *The art of kingship*, 59–82.

[49] John Watts provides an institutional account of government in the later Middle Ages in *Henry VI and the politics of kingship* (Cambridge, 1996), 1–101.

[50] Lindley observes: 'fundamentally, though, Richard's position rested on military power and on the support of his nobility, not on an iconography of kingship', 'Absolutism and regal image', 83.

And she was clad in real habit grene.
A fret of gold she hadde next her
    heer,
And upon that a whit corowne she beer
With flourouns smale, and I shal nat lye;
For al the world, ryght as a dayesye
Ycorouned ys with white leves lyte,
So were the flowrouns of hire coroune white.
For of o perle fyn, oriental,
Hire white coroune was ymaked al;

For which the white coroune above the grene
Made hire lyk a daysie for to sene,
Considered eke hir fret of gold above.

Yclothed was this myghty god of Love
In silk, enbrouded ful of grene greves,
In-with a fret of rede rose-leves,
The fresshest syn the world was first bygonne.
His gilte heer was corowned with a sonne
Instede of gold, for hevynesse and wyghte.
Therwith me thoghte his face shoon so bryghte
That wel unnethes myghte I him beholde;
And in his hand me thoghte I saugh him
    holde
Twoo firy dartes as the gledes rede,
And aungelyke hys wynges saugh I sprede.

(F. 212–36)

Tho gan I loken endelong the mede
And saw hym come, and in his honde a
    quene
Clothed in real habyt al of grene.
A fret of goold she hadde next hyre her
And upon that a whit corone she ber
With many floures, and I shal nat lye;
For al the world, ryght as the dayesye
Ycorouned is with white leves lite,
Swiche were the floures of hire coroune
    white.
For of o perle fyn and oryental
Hyre white coroun was ymaked al;
For which the white coroun above the
    grene
Made hire lyk a dayesye for to sene,
Considered ek the fret of gold above.
Yclothed was this myghty god of Love
Of silk, ybrouded ful of grene greves,
A garlond on his hed of rose-leves
Stiked al with lylye floures newe.
But of his face I can not seyn the hewe,
For sikerly his face shon so bryghte
That with the glem astoned was the
    syghte;
A furlong-wey I myhte hym not beholde.
But at the laste in hande I saw hym holde
Two firy dartes as the gleedes rede,
And aungellych hys winges gan he sprede.

(G. 142–68)[51]

[51] *The Prologue* exists in two versions. The F text, named after one of the witnesses for that version—Oxford Bodleian Library MS Fairfax 16—is generally thought to date from about 1386; see J. L. Lowes, 'The Prologue to the *Legend of Good Women* as related to the French *Marguerite* poems and the *Filostrato*', *PMLA* 19 (1904), 593–683; and 'The Prologue to the *Legend of Good Women* considered in its chronological relations', *PMLA* 20 (1905), 749–864; Lisa Kiser, *Telling classical tales: Chaucer and the* Legend of Good Women (New York, 1983), 18, n. 2; George Kane, 'The text of the *Legend of Good Women* in CUL MS Gg.4.27' in D. Gray and E. G. Stanley, eds., *Middle English studies presented to Norman Davis in honour of his seventieth birthday* (Oxford, 1983), 39–58; and *The Legend of Good Women*, ed. J. Cowan and G. Kane (London, 1995), 124–39. The G version, found only in Cambridge University Library MS Gg.4.27, after which it is named, is thought to have been composed after the death of Queen Anne in 1394 on the basis that F. 496–7, 'And whan this book ys maad, yive it the quene | On my byhalf, at Eltham or at Sheene', is not present in G. After the death of Anne in 1394, Richard had the palace of Shene razed to the ground. Sheila Delany proposes that F is the later of the two texts, *The naked text: Chaucer's* Legend of Good Women (Berkeley, 1994), 34–43. My own view is that it is more likely that G is the later version

These lines reproduce key features of Ricardian regal iconography.[52] The mythological Cupid is presented as a king, scripting in reverse the way that Ricardian iconography displayed the king as a kind of semi-deus and inserted him into all kinds of symbolic narratives and schemes. Cupid is richly dressed in silk[53] and his robes embroidered with green sprays—a detail which reproduces the Ricardian practice of decorating clothing with signs and symbols. Green sprays were not originally one of Richard's badges, though he came to adopt the sprigs of rosemary used by Anne.[54] The F version has Cupid crowned with a sun, which carries the suggestion of a nimbus, but was also one of Richard's badges, seen especially on the double tomb. In G, Cupid wears a garland of roses and lilies. There is multiple symbolism at work here: the flowers symbolize martyrdom and purity, and passion and chastity in harmony.[55] Also, heraldically, the rose is the badge of England and the lily the badge of France. Further, the red and white colours of the flowers are the colours of England, seen, for example, in the banner in the Diptych which may represent St George.[56] Red and white were Richard's favourite colours in dress.[57]

The narrator's eyesight is dazzled by the radiance of Cupid. As Helen Phillipps observes in her note to these lines, faces which gleamed with

because of the removal of explicit references to Anne, and also a sharper pointing of political reference; see the later discussion in this chapter. As the presentation of iconography is not identical, I shall quote both versions, but I do not propose that the refraction of royal iconography undergoes any *significant* shift between the two versions. There are some minor changes of emphasis.

[52] A connection between Cupid and Richard II was first suggested by J. B. Bilderbeck, *Chaucer's* Legend of Good Women (London, 1902), 85–7.

[53] Monnas cites examples of Richard's rich clothes in 'Fit for a king', 165. The figure is partially modelled on Cupid in *The Romance of the Rose* but in Chaucer's translation of this text, there is the explicit comment that the god is not clad in silk: 'nought clad in silk was he', *Romaunt*, 890.

[54] See Celia Fisher, 'A study of the plants and flowers in the Wilton Diptych', in Gordon et al., *The regal image*, 155–63, pp. 161–2.

[55] As noted by Helen Phillipps in her note to these lines in *Chaucer's dream poetry*, ed. Helen Phillipps and Nick Haveley (London, 1997), 315.

[56] See Nigel Morgan, 'The signification of the banner in the Wilton Diptych', in Gordon et al., *The regal image*, 179–88, p. 180.

[57] Saul, *Richard II*, 258. In the negotiations between the king and Charles VI for peace, Richard is reported to have worn a long scarlet gown bearing the white hart, ibid. 230. In the Smithfield tournament of 1390 there was a procession of twenty knights and twenty ladies who all wore the red livery with the chained white hart, Eberle, 'Richard II and the literary arts', 257–8.

light, dazzling the sight, symbolize divinity or divine grace. Gilded faces
or masks were used in mystery plays to represent characters such as God,
Mary, and the angels.[58] Just as Richard strove to create an image of
kingship supported by divine grace by having himself painted in Christ-
like iconicity, or taking part in scriptural narrative, so here, Cupid's
radiant face suggests a king figure infused with divinity.[59] Moreover, the
abasement of the narrator before the king could be seen to reproduce
the characteristic Ricardian demand for unstinting allegiance to his
majesty.[60] The final comment that Cupid spreads his wings like an angel
resonates suggestively with the king's manipulation of symbolic practices: at Richard's coronation, an angel offered Richard a crown as he
processed towards Westminster;[61] there was a castle of angels mysteri-
ously suspended in mid-air in the 1392 reconciliation with London
(p. 291/16), and also, of course, there are the angels in the Diptych.

There is a further iconographical dimension to the regal representation of Cupid and Alceste. We learn that they are at the head of a procession and pageant. They are followed by a procession of nineteen
ladies, all dressed in royal array, who proceed to make a solemn act of
devotion. The description resembles a royal entry, especially as the
principle of fealty is inscribed so strongly in the passage.[62] Chaucer's
treatment of the symbol of the daisy reads like a literary displacement of

[58] *Chaucer's dream poetry*, 315.

[59] In Maidstone's poem, Anne's face dazzles the sight of onlookers, p. 286/13–14.

[60] Saul discusses this in relation to Richard's cultivation of a new language of address from
his subjects. He writes: 'the king was raised to a higher level and wrapped in mystique, while
his subjects were reminded of their inferiority to him. The lofty language complemented
such other expressions of deference as bowing or averting the gaze', *Richard II*, 341. Saul
notes examples of bowing from *The Westminster Chronicle*, pp. 112 and 226. Cf. the story told
by the *Eulogium* writer of Richard's setting up a throne in the room to which the court
retired after supper; see Chapter 3 n. 10. In 'The kingship of Richard II', 44, Saul discusses
how Richard was indebted to ideas drawn from Giles of Rome in elaborating his demand for
obedience from his subjects. At the September Parliament of 1397, Bishop Stafford preached
the opening sermon on the text from *Ezekiel*, 37: 22 'There shall be one king over them all'.
He singled out three things needed for the realm to be well governed: that the king should
be powerful enough to govern; that his law should be properly executed; and third, that his
subjects should be duly obedient, *Rot. Parl*, iii. 347.

[61] An event which is probably alluded to in *Piers Plowman*, Prol. 128.

[62] The company of lovers at the end of the *Confessio Amantis* also contains suggestion of a
royal pageant and the principle of allegiance. Some of the garlands are of the leaf, and some
of the flower (VIII. 2467–8). Gower mentions 'grete Perles' (2469) and the 'newe guise of
Beawme' (2470)—a reference to the Bohemian fashions of dress introduced to court by
Queen Anne and her entourage. The question of whether Chaucer influenced Gower, or
vice versa, or whether any influence can be proved either way, is probably unanswerable.

how Richard used his white hart badge to fashion allegiance to his sacral majesty. The comparison of the ornamental petals (flourons) on Alceste's crown to a daisy (F. 218; G. 150) reproduces the way that Ricardian iconography selected objects from the natural world: deer, and broom pods, for example, and wrought them into exquisite courtly artefacts. The daisy is an heraldic sign worked into sovereign regalia.[63] The whole person of Alceste, with her white crown and her green array, is also likened to a daisy (F. 224; G. 156).[64] With this line, Alceste is compared, not just to a flower, but to the sun.[65] Earlier in the Prologue, Chaucer has explicitly brought out the pun on 'daisy' and the 'day's eye':[66]

> But for to loke upon the dayesie,
> That wel by reson men it calle may
> The 'dayesye', or elles the 'ye of day',
> The emperice and flour of floures alle. (F. 182–5)[67]

The wordplay resembles the intense punning on the hart in the Wilton Diptych, where the rich hart plays on Richard's own name, and is further suggestive of regal heraldry, given that the sun was another of Richard's badges.[68] The yoking together of the daisy and the sun brings together a symbol of allegiance and a sign of majesty. While the pun is omitted in G, both versions of the Prologue invest this daisy with Marian iconography: 'flour of floures' in both texts, and 'emperice' in

[63] In addition to the harts and flowers in the Diptych, we might compare the golden altar cross, set with nearly 400 pearls, other gems, images of the Virgin, St John the Baptist, and white harts, all enamelled and weighing 74 oz; see Saul, *Richard II*, 355.

[64] Phillipps discusses Chaucer's indebtedness here to the fourteenth-century marguerite poems by Machaut, Froissart, and Deschamps, *Chaucer's dream poetry*, 286–7. See also *The riverside Chaucer*, 1061–63.

[65] See Donald Rowe, *Through nature to eternity: Chaucer's* Legend of Good Women (Lincoln, Nebr. and London, 1988), 21–7.

[66] The technique of punning on flowers is also used in the Diptych, see Fisher, 'Study of the plants', 155–64.

[67] The pun is omitted in G. The equivalent lines are: 'This dayesye, of alle floures flour, | Fulfyld of vertu and of alle honour' (55–6). Kiser argues that the treatment of the daisy draws attention to the mediating function of poetry and powers of representation as a result of the 'truly extraordinary' daisy's identity as metaphor, *Telling classical tales*, 46–7.

[68] In games on 5 January 1378, organized for the eve of his eleventh birthday, Richard took part in a dazzling display for which he wore the sun as his emblem. The clothes of his three knightly supporters were stamped with golden suns, and Richard himself was dressed in cloth of gold woven with golden suns, riding on a horse with trappings made of the same cloth; Monnas, 'Fit for a king', 167.

F.[69] The overlaying of symbolism parallels the co-opting of the white hart badge into a scene of heavenly allegiance in the Diptych, and the ways that Ricardian image-making strove to insert the figure of the king into scriptural narrative.[70] In the G version, when the ladies approach the daisy, they instantaneously kneel down to make obeisance to it in an act of homage:

> Now whether was that a wonder thyng or non,
> That ryght anon as that they gonne espye
> This flour, which that I clepe the dayesye,
> Ful sodeynly they stynten alle atones,
> And knelede adoun, as it were for the nones.
> And after that they wenten in compas,
> Daunsynge aboute this flour an esy pas,
> And songen, as it were in carole-wyse,
> This balade, which that I shal yow devyse.

> (G. 194–202)

The daisy commands instant worship and then inspires the creation of new aesthetic practices in its praise. One presumes that Richard would have died for such unstinting, elaborate display of allegiance. Sadly, for him, his death was in opposite circumstances.[71]

Whether or not there are parallels in these lines to specific objects within the Ricardian project to create an image of sacral majesty the passage reproduces many of the characteristic techniques of the art of kingship: schematic iconography, complex symbolism, and multiple signification. It would be tempting to read this reproduction of kingly endeavour as oblique flattery on Chaucer's part. If we examine the portrait of Cupid further, however, a rather more knowing picture emerges. Far from producing an unthinking investment in image-making, and succumbing to the rhetoric of iconicity, I think we can see that Chaucer was very well aware of the *politics* of representation.

[69] Cf. Chaucer's *ABC*, l. 4: 'Glorious virgine, of alle floures flour', and lyric no. 59 in Gray, ed., *A selection of religious lyrics*: 'O emperesse, the emperoure | Quem meruisti portare, | Of heven and erthe hath made the floure: | Regina celi, letare!' (1–4). Lyric 57, also addressed to the Virgin, includes the lines: 'To whome, evermore immaculate | The margarite is well appropriate' (55–6).

[70] Phillipps notes how Chaucer's representation of the daisy 'seems to inhabit several different discourses simultaneously: amatory, religious and national', *Chaucer's dream poetry*, 286.

[71] Cf. Usk, who wrote: 'how many thousand marks [Richard] spent on burial places of vainglory for himself and his wives among the kings at Westminster! But Fortune ordered it otherwise', *Chronicon*, 205.

There is a passage in the Prologue, which, as Helen Phillipps has shown, is suggestively close to the criticisms levelled against Richard, especially in the later years of his reign:[72]

This shoolde a ryghtwis lord have in his
    thoght,
	This shulde a ryghtwys lord han in his
	    thought,

And nat be lyk tirauntz of Lumbardye,	And not ben lyk tyraunts of Lumbardye,
That han no reward but at tyrannye.	That usen wilfulhed and tyrannye.
For he that kynge or lord ys naturel,	For he that kyng or lord is naturel,
Hym oghte nat be tiraunt ne crewel	Hym oughte nat be tyraunt and crewel
As is a fermour, to doon the harm he kan.	As is a fermour, to don the harm he can.
He moste thinke yt is his lige man,	He moste thynke it is his lige man,
And is his tresour and his gold in cofre.	And that hym oweth, of verray duetee,
This is the sentence of the Philosophre,	Shewen his peple pleyn benygnete,
A kyng to kepe his liges in justice;	And wel to heren here excusacyouns,
Withouten doute, that is his office.	And here compleyntes and petyciouns,
Al wol he kepe his lordes hire degree,	In duewe tyme, whan they shal it profre.
As it ys ryght and skilful that they bee	This is the sentence of the Philosophre,
Enhaunced and honoured, and most dere—	A kyng to kepe his lyges in justice;
For they ben half-goddes in this world here—	Withouten doute, that is his office.

Yit mot he doon bothe ryght, to poore and
    ryche,
	And thereto is a kyng ful depe
	    ysworn

Al be that hire estaat be nat yliche,	Ful many an hundred wynter herebeforn;
And han of poore folk compassyoun	And for to kepe his lordes hir degre,
. . . . .	As it is ryght and skylful that they be
For, syr, yt is no maistrye for a lord	Enhaunsed and honoured, and most dere—
	For they ben half-goddes in this world here—
To dampne a man without answere of word,	This shal he don bothe to pore and ryche,
And for a lord that is ful foul to use.	Al be that her estat be nat alyche,
And if so be he may hym nat excuse,	And han of pore folk compassioun
But asketh mercy with a dredful herte.	. . . . .
	For, sire, it is no maystrye for a lord
(F. 373–90, 400–4)	To dampne a man withoute answere or word,
	And, for a lord, that is ful foul to use.
	And if so be he may hym nat excuse,
	But axeth mercy with a sorweful herte.
	(G. 353–76, 386–90)

While Alceste's speech *may* be regarded as a series of advice to princes commonplaces—avoid tyranny, flattery, cherish your subjects, and mix justice with mercy—the remarks are particularly applicable to precise

---

[72] *Chaucer's dream poetry*, 294–300.

complaints brought against Richard.[73] Especially in the latter years of his
reign, the king was accused of tyrannical rule. The G version associates
'tyrannye' with 'wilfulhed', which may be an English version of the
accusation that Richard was rather too fond of his own 'voluntas' and
followed his will rather than listening to reason.[74] The warning in both
versions not to behave like a 'fermour'—or raiser of money—tallies
with contemporary criticisms against Richard for over-taxation of his
subjects, criticisms usually made with reference to his capricious
expenditure on pomp and ceremony,[75] but also in the latter years of his
rule, with reference to the way that he extracted pardons from those of
his subjects who had challenged his authority for which they had to
pay.[76] Both versions enjoin the king to maintain his magnates according
to their rank, and both versions describe these nobles as 'half-goddes'.
Baronial unrest and opposition proved to be an insurmountable challenge to Richard's authority. According to the chroniclers, Richard
either advanced unworthy favourites to positions of power beyond
their deserved rank, or he treated wise and venerable members of the
nobility with contempt.[77] Crucially, of course, in 1397, he executed

[73] Florence Percival places the speech in the context of mainstream *De regimine* writing,
seeing it as applying not specifically to Richard II, but as showing that Chaucer thought that
an advice to princes speech in English would have a broad appeal, *Chaucer's legendary good
women* (Cambridge, 1998), 113–29, p. 129.

[74] The accusations of tyranny against Richard began in the late 1380s, Given-Wilson,
Chronicles of the revolution, 4–5. Saul remarks that the answers to the questions Richard put to
the judges in 1387: 'comprise the most remarkable statement of the royal prerogative ever
made in England in the middle ages . . . establish[ing] that it was the king's prerogative to
choose his ministers; that those ministers were responsible to him and not to parliament; that
parliament was dependent on his will, and his will alone', *Richard II*, 174. The articles of
deposition drawn up in the 1399 parliament stress this wilfulness, especially the sixteenth,
where the king is accused of having claimed himself to be above the law because the laws of
the realm were in his breast and mouth; see Given-Wilson, *Chronicles of the revolution*, 177–8.
See also Caroline Barron, 'The tyranny of Richard II', *BIHR* 41 (1968), 1–18.

[75] See references in n. 2 above. The first article of deposition accuses Richard of extorting
money from his people in order to satisfy his favourites, Given-Wilson, *Chronicles of the
revolution*, 172–3; the fifteenth stated that the king ought to have lived honestly off the
revenues and profits of the realm without burdening his people. But Richard raised so many
grants and taxes on his subjects that he oppressed them greatly with poverty, ibid. 177; the
twenty-sixth accuses the king of having appropriated lands, goods, and incomes from his
subjects, not because they were legally forfeit, but because it pleased the king to feel that they
were at his disposal, ibid. 180.

[76] The twenty-first article states that Richard extracted pardons from all those who had
been implicated with the Appellants in 1397 in return for money, ibid. 179.

[77] See Usk, *Chronicon*, 174 and 190; *Westminster Chronicle*, 207 and 243; Walsingham,

the earl of Arundel, probably caused the murder of the duke of Gloucester, and banished the earl of Warwick. More fateful was his appropriation of Henry Bolingbroke's Lancastrian inheritance in 1398 after he had banished the earl of Hereford along with Thomas Mowbray.[78] That the nobility should be called 'half-goddes' is intriguing: the phrase insinuates the barons into a scheme of sacral iconography which Richard was concerned to have all to himself.[79]

It seems to me that this passage articulates what Ricardian iconography attempts to edge out of representation.[80] While the earlier descriptions of the entry of Cupid and Alceste may be seen to reproduce key features of Richard's regal image, here kingship is framed within a more institutionalized context. In G. 368–9, there may well be a reference to the king's coronation oath, but in contrast to the use of coronation symbolism in the Diptych as an occasion for regal display, here, the reminder of sworn obligation is prised free from a ceremonial context.[81] Rather than reproducing regalian parade, Alceste's words remind the king of his obligations to the nobility; the nobility who find no place in the regal self-aggrandisement of the Diptych or of the Westminster portrait. The passage challenges the way that Ricardian image-making strove to create subjects held in thralled allegiance to a divinely appointed monarch. We are reminded here of the *business* of kingship: taxes, petitions, and just handling of the law.[82] Divine sanction and symbolically patterned pageant give way to pragmatics and contractual

Historia Anglicana, ii. 140, 148, and 224, and Johannis de Trokelowe et Henrici de Blaneforde, *Chronica et Annales*, ed. H. T. Riley (London, 1886), 209.

[78] For these events, see Saul, *Richard II*, 366–404.

[79] Lindley observes the king's 'propensity to envisage himself in the context of a heavenly court rather than his earthly one', 'Absolutism and regal image', 64.

[80] Monnas notes that the Livery Rolls 'give an unruffled account of the regular provision of magnificent garments for the king and his court, which sits oddly at variance with the turbulent political events of his reign', 'Fit for a king', 177.

[81] At Richard's coronation the traditional order of events was altered so that the king took his oath before, not after the acclamation by the people; Saul, 'The kingship of Richard II', 40. After the Merciless Parliament of 1388, during a solemn mass in Westminster Abbey, Richard renewed his coronation oath while the lords renewed their oaths of homage, Saul, *Richard II*, 195. The text of the articles of deposition was prefaced with Richard's coronation oath, as if to emphasize his having broken it, Given-Wilson, *Chronicles of the revolution*, 172.

[82] J. A. Tuck observes that 'the importance of petitions in medieval government can hardly be over-emphasised', 'Richard II's system of patronage', in F. R. H. DuBoulay and Caroline Barron, eds., *The reign of Richard II: essays in honour of May McKisack* (London, 1971), 1–20, p. 4. Article 23 in the *Record and Process* accuses Richard of not having listened to the advice of lords and justices at councils, Given-Wilson, *Chronicles of the revolution*, 179.

obligations. While the earlier descriptions of Cupid and Alceste reproduce details of Ricardian image-making, Alceste articulates what that representation sought so strenuously to suture. As I argued earlier, to maintain power, Richard required the institutionalized support of counsel, parliament, and baronial cooperation, all of which is sutured in the elaboration of his regal image. Alceste exposes what the image-making covers up.

More widely, *The Prologue to the Legend of Good Women* can be seen to expose the process of suture, to reveal how suture attempts to construct and maintain a monosemic political representation which permits no opposition. Alceste's speech follows Cupid's challenge to the narrator for daring to enter his royal presence and his formal accusation that the writer is guilty of heresy:

And thow my foo, and al my folk werreyest,	Thow art my mortal fo and me werreyest,
And of myn olde servauntes thow mysseyest,	And of myne olde servauntes thow mysseyest,
And hynderest hem with thy translacioun,	And hynderest hem with thy translacyoun,
And lettest folk from hire devocioun	And lettest folk to han devocyoun
To serve me, and holdest it folye	To serven me, and holdest it folye
To serve Love. Thou maist yt nat denye,	To truste on me. Thow mayst it nat denye,
For in pleyn text, withouten nede of glose,	For in pleyn text, it nedeth nat to glose,
Thou hast translated the Romaunce of the Rose,	Thow hast translated the Romauns of the Rose,
That is an heresye ayeins my lawe,	That is an heresye ageyns my lawe,
And makest wise folk fro me withdrawe.	And makest wise folk fro me withdrawe.
(F. 322–31)	(G. 248–57)

The passage inheres in a number of topical controversies. The charge that the narrator has slandered Cupid's old servants chimes with the impeachment of some of Richard's most prominent supporters in the Merciless Parliament of 1388, an impeachment which led to the execution, amongst others, of Richard's old tutor Simon Burley.[83] It is also striking, given Richard's insistence on allegiance and obeisance, that the narrator is accused of preventing his people from acts of devotion towards him.[84] Of most particular relevance to my argument, however, is that Cupid accuses the narrator of heresy because he has translated the

---

[83] Saul gives an account of these events, *Richard II*, 176–95. Burley was executed despite the intercession both of Anne and Richard on bended knees.

[84] Michael Hanrahan in 'Seduction and betrayal: treason in the *Prologue* to *The Legend of Good Women*', *Chaucer Review*, 30 (1996), 229–40, argues that the language of treason in the *Prologue* is a response to the struggle for the control of 'treason' as a concept in the 1380s. Fiona Somerset traces the Ricardian expansion of the concept of treason and the efforts of

Romance of the Rose. Why this text? One answer would be because it was a work that had attracted controversy over its interpretation. The words 'pleyn text' and 'glose' feature in both versions of the passage, and draw attention to the debate over whether *The Roman* was to be read literally or allegorically.[85] The possibility of a text offering different meanings is exactly what Ricardian self-representation, with its insistence and accretion, attempted to prevent. While the proliferation of image-making strove to assert a single meaning only—the sacral majesty of Richard II—Cupid displays extreme nervousness about the dissemination of a text whose meaning was publically contested.

Cupid's charge that the narrator has committed heresy is suggestive of Richard's own attempts to suppress unorthodoxy. In 1382 the Chancellor was empowered to issue commissions to the Sheriffs to arrest unorthodox preachers and detain them until their appearance before a church court, and in 1388, further commissions were issued for the seizure of Wycliffite writings for examination by the Council.[86] Walsingham narrates a story in which Richard forced Sir Richard Stury, one of the knights in his service, to abjure the heresy, warning him that if he ever went back on his word, he would have him executed.[87]

In his rebuff to the narrator, Cupid links heresy with translation. Biblical translation was not officially declared heretical until the publi-

Henry IV to annul previous convictions for treason, *Clerical discourse and lay audience in late medieval England* (Cambridge, 1998), 140–53.

[85] Cf. *Book of the Duchess*: 'And alle the walles with colours fyne | Were peynted, bothe text and glose, | Of al the Romaunce of the Rose' (332–4). Ruth Ames notes that it is customary to date the quarrel over the *Romaunt* to 1399, when Christine de Pisan's *Epistre au Dieu d'Amours* appeared, but that the reference in the *Prologue* to the *Legend of Good Women* suggests that the debate had begun earlier. '. . . there is reason to think that the argument that boiled over in the early 1400s had been simmering for some years', 'The feminist connections of Chaucer's *Legend of Good Women*', in Julian N. Wasserman and Robert J. Blanch, eds., *Chaucer in the eighties* (Syracuse, NY, 1986), 57–74, pp.59–60. Ames traces the literary connections between England and France in the last decades of the fourteenth century. See also John V. Fleming, 'The moral reputation of the *Roman de la Rose* before 1400', *Romance Philology*, 18 (1965), 430–5. The materials relating to the explosion of the quarrel are edited by Eric Hicks, *Le débat sur le Roman de la Rose* (Paris, 1977).

[86] Barron, 'Introduction', in Gordon *et al.*, *The regal image*, 28, drawing on *Rot. Parl*, iii. 124–5 and *CPR* 1385–9, 430. See also H. G. Richardson, 'Heresy and the lay power under Richard II', *EHR* 51 (1936), 1–26.

[87] Johannis de Trokelowe et Henrici de Blaneford, *Chronica et Annales*, 183. See also discussion in Richard G. Davies, 'Richard II and the church', in Goodman and Gillespie, *The art of kingship*, 83–106, pp. 91–4.

cation of Arundel's *Constitutions* in 1409,[88] but connections between translating and heterodoxy had certainly been made before this.[89] Knighton makes the comment that the Lollard laity thought English to be of more value than Latin.[90] In *Confessio*, Gower rhymes 'Lollardie' with 'heresie' and states that it is better to dig and build ditches than to know all that the Bible says:

> . . . causeth forto bringe
> This newe Secte of Lollardie,
> And also many an heresie
> Among the clerkes in hemselve.
> It were betre dike and delve
> And stonde upon the ryhte feith,
> Than knowe al that the bible seith
> And erre as somme clerkes do.
>
> (Prol. 348–55)

As Anne Hudson has noted, the *Opus Arduum*, written between Christmas 1389 and Easter 1390, refers to the persecution of those 'qui scripta ewangelica in Anglicis penes se detinent et legunt . . . qui ut lolardi deffamantur'.[91]

That Cupid should charge the narrator with heresy is directly relevant to Chaucer's treatment of the politics of representation. Heresy defines what dominant culture will not permit within its terms. What is deemed

[88] The seventh of these forbids the translation of any text of sacred Scripture into English, and the ownership of any translation of the Bible made in the time of Wyclif or later without the express permission of the diocesan, and this permission was only to be given after the translation had been inspected, Wilkins, *Concilia Magnae Britanniae*, iii. 317.

[89] The resonances in these lines to the controversy over Wycliffite translation have been discussed by Sheila Delany, *The naked text*, 120–3.

[90] Cited in Hudson, *The premature reformation*, 190, from Knighton, *Chronicon*, ii. 155: 'Lollardis qui mutaverunt Evangelium Christi in Evangelium aeternum, id est, vulgarem linguam et communem maternam, et sic aeternam, quia laicis reputatur melior et dignior quam lingua Latina.'

[91] Anne Hudson, 'Lollardy: The English heresy?', in *Lollards and their books* (Hambledon, 1985), 141–63, p. 157, quoting from Brno University Library MS Mk 28 fo.161[v]. Hudson traces the treatment of the issue of scriptures in the vernacular in the 1380s and 1390s, pp. 152–63, concluding that it is not 'unreasonable to claim lollardy as the heresy of the vernacular', p. 163. See in the same volume, 'The debate on Bible translation, Oxford, 1401', 67–84. Cf. Margaret Aston, 'Wyclif and the vernacular', *Studies in Church History*, Subsidia 5 (1987), 281–330. Somerset notes, *Clerical discourse*, 11, that from the early 1380s onwards, it became controversial for orthodox as well as heretical writers to use English. Strohm explores how the burning of heretics existed in the textual imagination in the late fourteenth century before the passing of *De Haeretico Comburendo*, *England's empty throne*, 36–40.

to be oppositional to the maintenance of dominant culture is cast out, adjudged unorthodox.[92] By accusing the narrator of heresy, Cupid is figured as a king who will not tolerate a form of representation different from what he demands to be the norm. His hostility towards translation and his legislation which forbids it may be seen to stem from the fact that to translate a text is to expose it for appropriation by those who may find meanings in it oppositional to those endorsed by dominant culture. Anne Hudson has noted that the argument that the English Scriptures lead to heresy was extended into the secular field by the contention that they also led to rebellion: 'the preaching of Wyclif and his followers was seen in retrospect by Walsingham and the compiler of the *Fasciculi Zizaniorum* as instrumental in the Peasants' Revolt.'[93]

Leaving aside the particular terrain of Bible translation, it is, in many ways, unsurprising that Cupid should show such a hostile attitude to the very process of translation. The overt sense of 'translate' here is to turn one text into the language of another. But, translation does not make something new that is identical to the source text, a problem that the writer of the Wycliffite *Tractatus de Regibus* tried to explain away by arguing that: 'Sythen witte stondis not in langage but in groundynge of treuthe, for tho same witte is in Laten that is in Grew or Ebrew, and trouthe schuld be openly knowen to alle manere of folke . . .'.[94] That the writer should seek to defend translation by saying that knowledge rests, not in material language but in truth, articulates the counter-argument: the objection to translation on the grounds that a text translated from one language to another is not materially the same work. One thing is changed into another.[95] In *The Clerk's Tale*, the word 'translate' is used of Griselda's rise from peasantry to courtliness:

---

[92] Strohm has argued that 'the Lollard was from the beginning less a real threat to orthodox control than orthodoxy's rhetorical plaything', ibid. 34.

[93] Hudson, 'Lollardy', 158.

[94] Quoted from ibid. 141. An excerpt from the work, including this passage, is printed in *Selections from English Wycliffite writings*, p. 25.

[95] Percival discusses the significance of 'translation' in this passage, *Chaucer's legendary good women*, 136–40, and notes that: 'in the ludic context of the *Legend* the conception of translation as a sanctioned transgressive rather than passive activity allows Chaucer to identify with the traitors in the stories he is about to tell', p. 139. For the argument that there was no differentiation between close and free translation in the Middle Ages, see Rita Copeland, 'The fortunes of "non verbum pro verbo": or why Jerome is not a Ciceronian', in Roger Ellis, ed., *The medieval translator: the theory and practice of translation in the middle ages* (Cambridge, 1989), 15–35.

> Unnethe the peple hir knew for hire fairnesse
> Whan she *translated* was in swich richnesse.   (IV. 384–5)

As the variant readings 'transmuwed' and 'transformed' attest,[96] 'translated' in these lines means to change the form of one thing into that of another. Cupid's hostility to translation is to the process itself because translation represents a challenge to the construction of the same. Cupid's refusal to countenance the differentiality produced by translation is parallel to the Ricardian insistence on absolute monosemy in the construction of the regal image.

Cupid's attempt to police differential representation is seen also in the commission and penance he enjoins on the narrator:

Syn that thou art so gretly in hire dette,	Syn that thow wost that calandier is she
And wost so wel that kalender ys shee	Of goodnesse, for she taughte of fyn lovynge,
To any woman that wol lover bee.	And namely of wifhod the lyvynge,
For she taught al the craft of fyn lovynge,	And alle the boundes that she oughte kepe.
And namely of wyfhod the lyvynge,	Thy litel wit was thilke tyme aslepe.
And al the boundes that she oghte kepe.	But now I charge the upon thy lyf
Thy litel wit was thilke tyme aslepe.	That in thy legende thow make of this wyf
But now I charge the upon thy lyf	Whan thow hast othere smale mad byfore.
That in thy legende thou make of thys wyf	
Whan thou hast other smale ymaad before.	(G. 533–40)
(F. 541–50)	

James Simpson has argued that Cupid may be seen as a cupidinous reader, one who imposes his will on the type of material he reads and forces it to yield up interpretations which accord with his brutalized male desire. Cupid wants one story, that of Alceste, and he wants it explicit, and in G, he goes on to command the narrator to write such narratives since she hyperbolically contains all wifely virtue.[97] The king tries to enforce one kind of representation, and a monosemic one at that. Cupid wants the narrator to create a portrait of Alceste which would function as the determinant of a fixed set of meanings around the representation of women. She is to be the 'kalender' (F. 542; G. 533). Cupid's attempt to exert total control is an attempt at suture in the field of literary sexual politics that reproduces a number of the suturing practices in the construction of Ricardian iconography. The king tries to anchor himself as a nodal point to privilege his version of womanhood within a larger discursive field. He tries to predetermine in

---

[96] See *Riverside Chaucer*, 1127.

[97] James Simpson, 'Ethics and interpretation: reading wills in Chaucer's *Legend of Good Women, SAC* 20 (1998), 73–100, p. 92.

advance the representation of women within the field of literary sexual politics in a way that is analogous to how Ricardian iconography attempted to fix Richard's sacral majesty as the centre point in the larger discursive field of representing kingship.

But this intransigent attempt to control representation is as doomed as Richard's was. The tales which follow the Prologue, for so long thought to be boring,[98] need not be seen to be cravenly flat or mono-semic. They can be read to articulate a variety of representations of women that are oppositional to, or different from, Cupid's controlling brief. Fyler has commented that Cupid's command to tell simply the gist of each life 'leads to a wonderfully comic exercise in censorship and distorted emphasis'.[99] The attempt to fix representation is exposed for being precisely that: a fix. Besides, given that the narrator begins the Prologue by raising the whole issue of hermeneutics in the first place, if he were to cooperate in the reproduction of the same, it would be solely because his intellectual insight was censored by tyrannical rule:

A thousand tymes have I herd men telle	A thousand sythes have I herd men telle
That ther ys joy in hevene and peyne in helle,	That ther is joye in hevene and peyne in helle
And I acorde wel that it ys so;	And I acorde wel that it be so;
But, natheles, yet wot I wel also	But natheles, this wot I wel also
That ther nis noon dwellyng in this contree	That there ne is non that dwelleth in this contre

[98]   The critical tradition which argued that Chaucer got bored with these repetitive stories is represented by W. W. Skeat in *The complete works of Geoffrey Chaucer* (Oxford, 1900), vol. iii, p. xxii. Cf. Robert Burlin, *Chaucerian fiction* (Princeton, 1977), who calls the *Legend* a 'colossal blunder', p. 34. R. W. Frank, however, defends Chaucer against the charge that he got bored with the poem, *Chaucer and the Legend of Good Women* (Cambridge, Mass., 1972), 189–210.

[99]   John Fyler, *Chaucer and Ovid* (New Haven, 1979), 99; Simpson argues that: 'the *Legend* is more the *representation* of straitjacketed art, where the strictures of the straitjacket pull violently', 'Ethics and interpretation', 95. Ames comments it might more aptly be named 'the legend of bad men', 'The feminist connections', 67. Delany argues that the movement of the poem is that of a double subversion of the narrator's commission, 'Rewriting woman good: gender and the anxiety of influence in two late medieval texts', in *Medieval literary politics: shapes of ideology* (Manchester, 1990), 80. Cf. Percival, *Chaucer's legendary good women*, 4; Frank, *Chaucer and the Legend*, 35–6; Kiser, *Telling classical tales*, 97–154; and Priscilla Martin: 'far from presenting a "naked text" in which the facts speak for themselves, Chaucer has produced a story which reads one way if you know the sources and another if you don't', *Chaucer's women* (London, 1996) 2nd edn., 205. Rowe discusses how Chaucer's treatment of the legends dramatizes the irrationality of the programme imposed on the narrator in the *Prologue* as a means of exploring the creative difficulties of writing poetry, *Through nature to eternity*, 47–79.

That eyther hath in hevene or helle ybe,	That eyther hath in helle or hevene ybe,
Ne may of hit noon other weyes witen	Ne may of it non other weyes witen
But as he hath herd seyd or founde it writen;	But as he hath herd seyd or founde it writen;
For by asay ther may no man it preve.	For by assay there may no man it preve
But God forbede but men shulde leve	But Goddes forbode but men shulde leve
Wel more thing then men han seen with ye!	Wel more thyng than men han seyn with ye!
(F. 1–11)	(G. 1–11)

These lines confidently (even provocatively) assert the truth of books over experience, but the poem as a whole clearly sets up a debate between textuality and experientiality. Helen Phillipps writes that the poem:

constantly returns to the issue of how and whether texts can faithfully present their subject: literary tradition provides us with the spectacle of misogynist texts which misrepresent women's real experience of fidelity and feminist texts that vindicate them; questions of intentionality and interpretation make the content and meaning of texts problematic . . . Chaucer talks provocatively of creating a 'Nakede tixt' but, as the *Legend* shows, there is no such thing as a text that directly represents reality, that is, the experience of people in the past; there is no unmediated text freed from issues of intentionality and interpretation.[100]

In its concern with hermeneutics, *The Legend* explores the relationship between the 'real' and its representation. And with the 'real' exposed as representation, the claim for monosemic purchase in any discursive field is revealed as a strategy to gain power and control. Once the strategy is revealed, and the edge of representation disclosed, the means of resisting suture is available. To practise suture means to interpellate subjects into the suturing process.[101] Ricardian iconography attempted to suture the king's subjects (in both senses of the word) into the spectacle of regal display, where the only subject position available to them was one of allegiance and obeisance. Cupid attempts to suture the narrator in a similar way, to take up and reproduce a subject position within the field of literary sexual politics which he has predetermined. But we might

---

[100] *Chaucer's dream poetry*, ed. Phillipps, 286. David Wallace comments that the description of the cycle of seasons (F.125–39): 'is penned by a poet-artificer, a craftsman deploying rhetorical figures while pretending to aspire to the ideal of fashioning a "naked text in English"' (G. 86), *Chaucerian polity: absolutist lineages and associational forms in England and Italy* (Stanford, Calif., 1997), 352; Cf. Burlin, *Chaucerian fiction*, 36.

[101] 'Suture designates the production of the subject on the basis of its chain of discourse', Laclau and Mouffe, *Hegemony and socialist strategy*, 88.

read the narrator in *The Prologue* as a figure for the resistance to suture. With his knowledge that the real is representation, he refuses the reproduction of the same that Cupid enjoins upon him. In the tales which follow, he does not reinscribe Alceste as the 'kalender', or the nodal point, in the representation of women. He offers up representations that do not fall squarely within the king's edict. He refuses to be sutured; refuses to take one particular kind of representation for real. In effect, the narrator scripts himself into the position of a dissident subject.[102]

Critics who have written on Richard's regal image often conclude their accounts with some variation on the following: either that Richard mistook the illusion of the stage for the world; or focused on symbol rather than substance; or took refuge in image rather than gritty reality.[103] I do not think these oppositions are tenable. Laclau and Mouffe explain: 'there are not *two* planes—one of essences and the other of appearances, since there is no possibility of fixing an *ultimate* literal sense for which the symbolic would be a second, and a derived plane of signification.'[104] As Chaucer's *Prologue to the Legend of Good Women* shows us so well, representation is all, both image and reality, and both symbol and substance. Representation is a battle in which claimants to power contest ownership of the will to truth, the desire to possess discourse.[105] I have tried to argue that the contours of this conflict are articulated in Chaucer's *Prologue to the Legend of Good Women*. For all the literary play of Chaucer's text, however, this was a battle, which in Richard's case, was played out with deadly consequences.

[102] In *De quadripartita regis specie* presented to Richard in 1391/2, the writer states that nothing is more likely to force a king to impose penalties on his subjects than an act of disobedience, *Four English political tracts of the later middle ages*, ed. J.-P. Genet (Camden Society, 4th Series 18, London, 1977), 35–6. Lee Patterson argues that the poem registers Chaucer's desire to escape from subjection to a court, and to aristocratic values generally, that are felt as increasingly tyrannical, *Chaucer and the subject of history*, 237.

[103] e.g. Barron, 'Richard II and London', in Goodman and Gillespie, *The art of kingship*, 129–54; Saul, *Richard II*, 467; id. 'The kingship of Richard II', in *The art of kingship*, 55; id., 'Richard II's ideas of kingship', in Gordon *et al.*, *The regal image*, 31; Scheifele, 'Richard II and the visual arts', 261 and 271.

[104] Laclau and Mouffe, *Hegemony and socialist strategy*, 98.

[105] Laclau and Mouffe: 'Representation is the terrain of a game whose result is not predetermined from the beginning', ibid. 119.

CHAPTER FIVE

'From pig to man and man to pig':[1] The 1381 Uprisings in Chaucer's *The Nun's Priest's Tale*

REPRESENTATION WAS A dangerous social practice not only for Richard II but also for those involved in the uprisings in 1381, whether they were engaged in insurrection, or attempting to curb the disturbances. Only one of Chaucer's works mentions the civil disturbances in 1381. The reference is embedded in the account of the chase at the end of *The Nun's Priest's Tale*, where the cacophony of the peasants pursuing the cockerel-snatching fox is said to exceed the shouting of Jack Straw and his fellows as they set about killing the Flemish merchants.[2] Critical opinion is divided on the precise import of this passage, but it is frequently noted that the chase reproduces key features of the representation of the 1381 rebels found in other contemporary accounts: the noise, unruliness, mayhem, and the mingling of human and animal behaviour, which characterize the treatment of the uprising in the chronicles and John Gower's *Vox Clamantis*.[3] I want to argue, however,

---

[1] The quotation is from the last line of George Orwell's *Animal Farm*.

[2] John M. Ganim, 'Chaucer and the noise of the people', *Exemplaria*, 2 (1990), 71–88, suggests that there might be an allusion to Jack Strawe in *Troilus and Criseyde*, IV. 184–5: 'The noyse of peple up stirte thanne at ones, | As breme as blase of strawe iset on-fire'. J. Stephen Russell sees allusions to the revolt in *The House of Fame*, ll. 935–49, 'Is London burning? A Chaucerian allusion to the rising of 1381', *Chaucer Review*, 30 (1995), 107–9.

[3] Ian Bishop, '*The Nun's Priest's Tale* and the Liberal Arts', *RES* 30 (1979), 257–67, suggests that Chaucer parodies Gower's account of the revolt; and Steven Justice argues that Chaucer is writing for a coterie audience, with satirical criticism of Gower, *Writing and rebellion: England in 1381* (Berkeley, 1994), 211–18. Other critics who draw parallels between the characteristics of Chaucer's fox chase and contemporary accounts of the revolt include: David Aers, '"Vox populi" and the literature of 1381', in *CHLME* 440–51; Lillian M. Bisson, *Chaucer and the late medieval world* (London, 1998), 157–8; Richard W. Fehrenbacher, '"A yeerd enclosed al aboute": literature and history in *The Nun's Priest's Tale*', *Chaucer Review*, 29 (1994), 134–48; Ganim, 'Chaucer and the noise of the people'; R. James Goldstein, 'Chaucer, Freud, and the political economy of wit: tendentious jokes in *The Nun's Priest's*

that the resemblances between the reference to 1381 in *The Nun's Priest's Tale* and accounts in other contemporary works are superficial. Chaucer's rhetorical constructions in the *Tale* and his handling of narrative distance and voice produce a very different socioliterary representation of the events of 1381 from those found in the works of his contemporaries.

It is well known that the contemporary accounts of the uprisings in 1381 depict the insurgents in the most unflattering terms. Those who took part in the revolt are frequently characterized by the chroniclers as 'peasants' and 'rustics'; hence the popular (mis)-conception of the events of 1381 as 'The Peasants' Revolt'. Gower presents the rebels exclusively as peasants: 'rustici'.[4] Walsingham refers to the rebels as 'rustici' or 'bondes' and, with reference to the rebels at the Tower of London, as 'the most abject of peasants'.[5] Historians who have examined legal documents relating to the series of uprisings have shown how this rhetorical fervour is misleading. Far from being exclusively peasants and bondmen, the social composition of the rebels comprised significant numbers of artisans and tradesmen, as well as a smattering of lesser gentry and clerics in minor orders.[6]

The designation of the rebels as peasants and/or bondmen is characteristic of the way that commentators on the uprising strove to put as much social distance as possible between themselves and those who took part in the revolt. Accounts in the chronicles and poetic records, excluding Chaucer, are written from an utterly authoritative perspective, and seek to present the rebels in the worst possible light, and as far removed from any kind of civilized discourse as possible.[7]

Tale', in Jean Jost, ed., *Chaucer's humour* (New York, 1994), 145–62, pp. 154–7; Ralph Hanna III, 'Pilate's voices/Shirley's case', in *Pursuing history: Middle English manuscripts and their texts* (Stanford, Calif., 1996), 267–79, pp. 273–5; Derek Pearsall, 'Interpretative models for the Peasants' Revolt', in Patrick J. Gallacher and Helen Damico, eds., *Hermeneutics and medieval culture* (New York, 1989), 63–71; Larry Scanlon, 'The Authority of fable: allegory and irony in *The Nun's Priest's Tale*', *Exemplaria*, 1 (1989), 43–68; and Peter W. Travis, 'Chaucer's trivial fox chase and the Peasants' Revolt of 1381', *Journal of Medieval and Renaissance Studies*, 18 (1988), 195–220.

[4] See ll. 172; 175; 513; 558, English translation in *The major Latin works*, ed. Stockton, 49–90.

[5] Walsingham, *Historia Anglicana*, i. 454; 459 and 477.

[6] The social composition of the rebels is examined by Rodney Hilton, *Bondmen made free: medieval peasants and the English rising of 1381* (London, 1973), 176–85.

[7] Studies which analyse the authoritative representation of the rebels, and the insurgents' attempt to create a counter discourse include: Susan Crane, 'The writing lesson of 1381', in

In Gower's *Vox Clamantis* the narrative perspective is authoritative in the extreme.[8] The title of the poem 'the voice of one crying' invokes the figure of St John the Baptist, and the prophetic voice that cries in the wilderness. Gower capitalizes on the fact that he shares the same name as the Baptist, entrusted with proclaiming the Messiah, and also points out that he shares the same name as St John the divine who wrote the Book of Revelation.[9] In yoking the authority of his own writing with these two biblical authorities, John Gower makes great claims for the truth of his own writing. As a result, his pronouncement on the events of 1381 and his interpretation of them are invested with prophetic validity.[10]

Gower's account of the rebels' approach to London is characteristic of his description of the rebels :

> Mille lupi mixtique lupis vrsi gradientes
> A siluis statuunt vrbis adire domos:
> Non erat in terris monstrosum quicquid abortum,
> Seu genus, vnde furor ledere posset humum,
> Quin venit et creuit, spersus velut imber ab austro
>
> .   .   .   .   .   .
>
> Tunc in aperta loca que monstra prius latuerunt
> Accedunt, paribus suntque recepta suis:
> Belua vasta, ferox, siluis que palustribus exit,
> Qui tantum rabie non furit, immo fame
>
> .   .   .   .   .   .

Barbara Hanawalt, ed., *Chaucer's England: literature in historical context* (Minneapolis, 1992), 201–21; Richard Firth Green, 'John Ball's letters: literary history and historical literature', in Hanawalt, ed., *Chaucer's England*, 176–200; Justice, *Writing and rebellion*; Paul Strohm, *Hochon's arrow: the social imagination of fourteenth-century texts* (Princeton, 1992), 33–56; and A. J. Prescott, 'Writing about rebellion: Using the Records of the Peasants' Revolt of 1381', *History Workshop Journal*, 45 (1998), 1–27.

[8] Gower had finished *Vox* by 1381, but he went back and added a new first book to the poem in which he directly talks about the events of 1381, see *The Latin works*, ed. Macaulay, iv. pp. xxxi–xxxii; and John H. Fisher, *John Gower: moral philosopher and friend of Chaucer* (New York, 1964), 101–4.

[9] See the end of the Prologue: 'Insula quem Pathmos suscepit in Apocalipsi, | Cuius ego nomen gesto, gubernet opus' ('May the one whom the Isle of Patmos received in the Apocalypse, and whose name I bear, guide this work' (58–60)).

[10] At the beginning of Chapter 2, Gower further aligns himself with the prophetic validity of the Book of Revelation with the line: 'Iam fuerat raptus spiritus ipse meus' ('My spirit itself was indeed stolen away' (166)). Justice discusses Gower's claims to prophetic status, *Writing and rebellion*, 209–10. On Gower's interpretation of the 1381 uprising, see Andrew Galloway, 'Gower in his most learned role and the Peasants' Revolt of 1381', *Medievalia*, 16 (1993), 329–47.

Agresti furia iurat siluestris, vt vno
Legibus excussis iura furore ruent:
Tantus adest numerus seruorum perdicionis,
Cingere quod murus vix valet vllus eos.
Cum furor vrget opus, remanet moderacio nulla,
Set magis in vetitum quodlibet ipse ruit:
Sponte sua properant, nichil est prohibere volentes.

A thousand wolves and bears approaching with the wolves determined to go out of the woods to the homes of the city. There was no monstrous thing or species on earth whose fury could hurt the land but that it came forth and multiplied . . . Then the monsters which previously had lurked in hiding went out into the open and were received by their companions. The fierce and mighty beast, which used to rage not so much from fury as from hunger, came out of the woods and marshes . . . They swore with savage rage in the woods that they would trample on justice in a mad frenzy by overthrowing all laws. So great was the number of these slaves of perdition that scarcely any wall could contain them. Since madness prompted the goings on, all restraint was gone, and the madness plunged into any—and everything forbidden.

(*Vox*, I. 883–901)

Gower writes the rebels out of civilized discourse; they are monsters: beasts who inhabit woods and marshlands rather than the civility of the city. Portrayed as demonic animals, the mob cannot be contained by any human structure. Walls built by human beings fail to hold irrationality and anger. A promiscuous chaos tramples on human justice. Gower's description of the attack on London presents the fall of civilization itself. Details of this characterization are frequent in the chroniclers' accounts. Knighton also calls the rebels wolves,[11] the Monk of Westminster terms them 'rabid dogs' running wild through the countryside,[12] and Thomas Walsingham associates them with the inhabitants of hell:

a most horrible shouting broke out, not like the clamour normally produced by men, but of a sort which enormously exceeded all human noise and which could only be compared to the wailings of the inhabitants of hell. Such shouts used to be heard whenever the rebels beheaded anyone or destroyed houses, for as long as God permitted their iniquity to be unpunished.

Words could not be heard among their horrible shrieks but rather their

---

[11] Quoted in Dobson, *The Peasants' Revolt of 1381*, from *Chronicon Henrici Knighton*, ii. 132–8.

[12] Quoted in Dobson, *The Peasants' Revolt*, 199, from Higden, *Polychronicon*, IX. 1–6.

throats sounded with the bleating of sheep, or, to be more accurate, with the devilish voices of peacocks.[13]

This comparison of the language of the rebels to animal noise or tumultuous uproar is a common motif. The frequency of this trope is an example of the way that the chroniclers created textual social difference between themselves and the rebels. Gower writes a long passage comparing the shouts of the insurgents to many different kinds of animals, from asses to wasps (*Vox*, I. 799–830), and the macaronic poem *Tax has Tenet Us Alle* describes how 'laddus loude thay loȝe' when they slew the archbishop. Here noise is a sign of sacrilege.[14] The writer of *The Anonimalle Chronicle* extends this trope even further. In his account, the rebels are said to have dragged Sudbury away from the chapel in the Tower, even as he is reciting the words of the liturgy. The chronicler tells us that 'when he was at the words "Omnes sancti orate pro nobis"', the commons entered and dragged him off and executed him. The clerical Latin of the murdered archbishop stands in sharp contrast to the 'hideous cries and horrible tumult' of the rebels.[15] The narration of the incident captures in miniature the gap which the chroniclers strove to create between their own civilized discourse and the barbarous cacophony of the insurgents.[16] While, as Prescott has shown in examining accounts of the riots in Britain in 1981, the depiction of dissenters as noisy animals is not confined to the late fourteenth century,[17] it is important that the 1381 accounts are written in Latin (or in the case of Froissart, in French). The brutality of the insurgents is marked off as textually different from the civilized discourse of the chroniclers, with its claim to erudition and order.[18] The use of this textual strategy puts as much social difference as possible between the writers and the rebels.

Given the challenge to normative social hierarchy posed by the risings in 1381, such a strategy is hardly surprising. There are many references in the accounts to how the rebels strove to usurp their social

[13] Quoted in Dobson, *The Peasants' Revolt*, 173, from Walsingham, *Historia Anglicana*, i. 456–67.

[14] *Political poems and songs*, ed. Wright, i. 224–6.

[15] Quoted in Dobson, *The Peasants' Revolt*, 161–2.

[16] John Bowers explores this in relation to Walsingham's narration of the execution of John Ball, seeing Walsingham's Latin framing of Ball's English letter, 'full of obscurities' as a condemned text, '*Piers Plowman* and the police: notes toward a history of the Wycliffite Langland', *YLS* 6 (1992), 1–50.

[17] Prescott, 'Writing about rebellion', 1–3.

[18] The emergence of English as a discourse of power and authority in the late fourteenth century is examined by Fisher, 'A language policy'.

positions and break down the boundaries of social order. This is Walsingham on the beginnings of the unrest:

For the rustics, whom we call 'nativi' or 'bondsmen', together with other country-dwellers living in Essex sought to better themselves by force and hoped to subject all things to their own stupidity. Crowds of them assembled and began to clamour for liberty, planning to become the equals of their lords and no longer to be bound by servitude to any master.[19]

And these are his remarks on the behaviour of the rebels in London:

For who would ever have believed that such rustics, and most inferior ones at that, would dare (not in crowds but individually) to enter the chamber of the king and of his mother with their filthy sticks; and, undeterred by any of the soldiers, to stroke and lay their uncouth and sordid hands on the beards of several most noble knights. Moreover, they conversed familiarly with the soldiers asking them to be faithful to the ribalds and friendly in the future . . . The rebels, who had formerly belonged to the most lowly condition of serf, went in and out like lords; and swineherds set themselves above soldiers although not knights, but rustics.[20]

The relish with which Walsingham narrates this vignette suggests his outrage at the violation of social decorum and natural hierarchy which the 1381 revolt represented. The rebels are dirt whose filthy sticks are a squalid imitation of knightly sword.[21] Here, Walsingham aligns himself with a strong tradition in the representation of peasants which associates them with dirt of all kinds, including excrement.[22] Gower also presents a number of vignettes of social reversal, including a passage in which the rebels arm themselves not with chivalric weaponry, but with stakes, poles, and a rusty sickle: 'est ibi vanga loco gladii' ('the mattock took the place of the sword' (*Vox*, I. 843–70, l. 859). Accounts of such reversals are not confined to the chroniclers. Prescott cites the indictment of one Geoffrey Lister, the Norfolk rebel leader, who assumed judicial powers and appointed some members of the gentry to serve him in a mock royal court.[23] Description of such behaviour shows how the actions of the rebels were seen to be caught up in the kind of festival revelry in

[19] Quoted in Dobson, *The Peasants' Revolt*, 132.

[20] Quoted from ibid. 171–2.

[21] As Mary Douglas explains, defilement or dirt is 'matter out of place . . . It implies two conditions: a set of ordered relations and a contravention of that order . . . dirt is that which must not be included if a pattern is to be maintained', *Purity and danger: an analysis of the concepts of pollution and taboo* (London, 1966), 35 and 40.

[22] See Paul Freedman, *Images of the medieval peasant* (Stanford, Calif., 1999), 143–53.

[23] Prescott, 'Writing about rebellion', 17.

which social distinctions were reversed or parodied. In his narration
of events at Bury St Edmunds, Walsingham recounts how the rebels
executed John Cavendish, Chief Justice of the kingdom, and John de
Cambridge, prior of the abbey, and set their heads on the top of
two lances as if they were talking and kissing. Walsingham terms the
'absurdly improper action' a 'jest'.[24]

The reportage of these outrageous violations of social decorum can
be seen to spring from anxiety about the frequent demands from the
rebels for all lordship to be abolished, save that of the king, and for all
goods to be held in common. This is Froissart's version of the appeal:

These unhappy people . . . began to stir, because they said they were kept in
great servage, and in the beginning of the world, they said, there were no
bondmen, wherefore they maintained that none ought to be bond, without he
did treason to his lord, as Lucifer did to God; but they said they could have
no such battle for they were neither angels nor spirits, but men formed to the
similitude of their lords, saying why should they then be kept so under like
beasts; the which they said they would no longer suffer, for they would be all
one, and if they laboured or did anything for their lords, they would have
wages therefor as well as other.[25]

The principle of equality was expounded very forcibly in a sermon
given by the rebel leader John Ball, a priest in minor orders. Walsingham
states that Ball preached this sermon at Blackheath on the text of a
proverb: 'Whan Adam dalf and Eve span | Wo was thanne a gentil-
man?'[26] This couplet is found in Latin and in several vernacular
languages, although it appears to have become a proverbial statement
only in the later Middle Ages.[27] Ball's use of the proverb asserts the
fundamental equality of all people, the illicit nature of servitude, and the
hollowness of claims for innate nobility. Froissart gives a stirring account
of Ball's sermon:

[24] Quoted in Dobson, *The Peasants' Revolt*, 245. Studies of the place of revelry in the 1381
uprisings include: Margaret Aston, 'Corpus Christi and corpus regni: heresy and the Peasants'
Revolt', *Past and Present*, 143 (1994), 3–47; T. Pettit, '"Here comes I, Jack Straw": English
folk drama and social revolt', *Folklore*, 95 (1984), 3–20; and Paul Strohm, '"Lad with revel to
Newegate": Chaucerian narrative and historical meta-narrative', in Robert R. Edwards, ed.,
Art and context in late medieval narrative (Cambridge, 1994), 163–76.

[25] Quoted in Dobson, *The Peasants' Revolt*, 370.

[26] Walsingham, *Historia Anglicana*, ii. 32; cf. *Chronicon Angliae*, 321. On the implications
and contexts of Ball's sermon, see Justice, *Writing and rebellion*, 14–23, 102–19, 233–7.

[27] See Albert B. Friedman, '"Whan Adam delved" . . . contexts of an historic proverb' in
Larry D. Benson, ed., *The learned and the lewed: studies in Chaucer and medieval literature*
(Cambridge, Mass., 1974), pp. 213–30.

We be all come from one father and one mother, Adam and Eve: whereby can they say or shew that they be greater lords than we be, saving by that they cause us to win and labour for that they dispend? They are clothed in velvet and camlet furred with grise, and we be vestured with poor cloth: they have their wines, spices and good bread, and we have the drawing out of the chaff and drink water: they dwell in fair houses, and we have the pain and travail, rain and wind in the fields; and by that that cometh of our labours they keep and maintain their estates.[28]

In some ways, it is remarkable that the chroniclers preserved such revolutionary sentiments, but it is important that the medium of Latin and/or French would be accessible to an audience comprised chiefly of those who had most to fear from the rebels' actions: the nobility, clerics, and anyone associated with the imposition of the hated poll tax. As Walsingham comments, it was dangerous at this time to be caught with an ink-pot at your elbow.[29] Moreover, the chroniclers present the rebels' concern to ensure that all goods were in common simply as acts of plunder, looting, and destruction. *The Anonimalle Chronicle* reports that when the rebels arrived at the manor house in Essex of the Treasurer, Sir Robert Hales, they ate his fine victuals, 'drank three casks of good wine and threw the building to the ground'.[30] The fine wines in the London cellar belonging to the bishop of Chester suffered the same fate.[31] Walsingham narrates how the rebels sacked the Savoy Palace of John of Gaunt after having 'tasted various wines and expensive drinks at will'. Once inside the palace they tore cloths and silk hangings, crushed rings and precious jewels to fine mortar, and used one of the duke's precious garments for shooting practice. Failing to damage it sufficiently, they then tore it to pieces with axes and swords.[32] This kind of reportage frames the rebels' demand for equality, an end to servitude, and for all goods to be held in common, simply as another kind of mindless, animal-like violence. The seizure of food, wine, and fine clothes is presented not as political protest but senseless destruction by coarse hooligans. Knighton, for example, describes the rebels as being so drunk that, sated with pillaging and executions, they lay sleeping in the streets 'like slaughtered pigs'.[33] While the educated prose of the

---

[28] Quoted in Dobson, *The Peasants' Revolt*, 371.
[29] Quoted in ibid. 364.
[30] Quoted in ibid. 125.
[31] Quoted from *The Anonimalle Chronicle*, Dobson, *The Peasants' Revolt*, 157.
[32] Quoted from ibid. 169–70.
[33] Quoted from ibid. 185.

chronicles may preserve the demands made by the insurgents, the narrative stance is relentlessly dismissive, refusing, either through narrative distance, or through choice of imagery, to give any political credence to the rebels' agenda. Dissident power is dispersed through discourses of filth, uncouthness, bestiality, madness, senseless destruction, grotesquerie, and noise.

A crucial difference between these accounts and the reference to the rising in *The Nun's Priest's Tale* is that Chaucer writes, not in Latin, or in French, but in the vernacular. Simply in terms of choice of language, Chaucer does not obtain the same kind of narrative distance from the rebels as that in the other accounts. To be sure, the *Nun's Priest's Tale* is not actually a narrative account of events of 1381, but nevertheless it is a tale which can be seen to be deeply enmeshed in the issues raised by the revolt, and from a narrative perspective which is radically different from those writing in Latin and French. The difference is not simply one of writing in English: the diction and rhetoric of social description proceeds from a narrative position which is very far removed from the disparagement and distance of other contemporary accounts.

This is apparent right from the start of the tale, in the description of the poor, aged, peasant woman and her meagre life:

> A povre wydwe, somdeel stape in age,
> Was whilom dwellyng in a narwe cotage,
> Biside a grove, stondynge in a dale.
> This wydwe, of which I telle yow my tale,
> Syn thilke day that she was last a wyf
> In pacience ladde a ful symple lyf,
> For litel was hir catel and hir rente;
> By housbondrie, of swich as God hire sente,
> She foond hirself, and eek hir doghtren two.
> Thre large sowes hadde she, and namo,
> Three keen and eek a sheep that highte Malle.
> Ful sooty was hire bour and eek hir halle,
> In which she eet ful many a sklendre meel.
> Of poynaunt sauce hir neded never a deel.
> No deyntee morsel passed thurgh hir throte;
> Hir diete was accordant to hir cote.
> Repleccioun ne made hire nevere sik;
> Attempree diete was al hir phisik,
> And exercise, and hertes suffisaunce.
> The goute lette hire nothyng for to daunce,
> N'apoplexie shente nat hir heed;

No wyn ne drank she, neither whit ne reed;
Hir bord was served moost with whit and blak
Milk and broun breed in which she foond no lak,
Seynd bacoun, and somtyme an ey or tweye,
For she was, as it were, a maner deye.

(VII. 2821–46)

The widow has a tiny cottage, a very small income, and disposable goods, and supports herself in reduced circumstances. She does not appear to be a bondwoman and, indeed, has her own dairy business. The description may be seen to extol the virtues of Christian patience and humility, and contentment with a simple life.[34] Fehrenbacher has argued that the highly rhetorical style of this passage is employed 'in an attempt to efface both the social inequities the tale threatens to bring to light as well as the "pastoral" voice capable of articulating these concerns'.[35] I would argue that, far from effacing social concerns, the textuality of this passage is insistently social. We are told that the widow has a 'bour' and 'halle', diction which is relevant to spaces in an aristocratic house or castle but completely inappropriate to describe a two-roomed cottage.[36] The description is grounded in social difference: it tells us what the widow's cottage is not like.[37] The same technique is used in describing the widow's diet. We are told that she never needed much in the way of spicy sauces, no dainty morsel passed her lips, she did not suffer from over-eating, gout did not prevent her from dancing, and she did not drink red wine. We are told more about what she does not eat than what she does: milk and brown bread, singed bacon, and the odd egg or two.

The effect of these negations is very similar to the portrait of the Parson in *The General Prologue*, where the technique of telling us what the priest did not do, e.g.: 'he ne lefte nat' (492) describes the faults of negligent priests even while an individual example of pastoral responsibility emerges. In the *Nun's Priest's Tale*, the description of the diet and living conditions of a member of the third estate is simultaneously an

---

[34] See Bisson, *Chaucer and the late medieval world*, 159–60.

[35] Fehrenbacher, '"A yeerd enclosed al aboute"', 139.

[36] Stephen Knight observes that the irony is clear enough but a 'number of editors have missed the important point that it is a one room cottage—bower and hall are one', *Ryming craftily: meaning in Chaucer's poetry* (Sydney and London, 1973), 213.

[37] In the French *Roman de Renart* the fenced yard where the hens live belongs to a rich landowner, not a poor widow, Helen Cooper, *Oxford guides to Chaucer: The Canterbury Tales* (Oxford, 1996), 2nd edn., 342.

account of those of the first estate—the nobility. What Gower and the chroniclers were very anxious to keep textually separate: the labourers and the nobility, are here rhetorically enmeshed. While the chroniclers recorded the rebels' attacks on aristocratic houses, and their predilection for sampling fine food and wine, as social and spatial transgression, the rhetoric of Chaucer's passage, inter-envelops the space and diet of labourers and the nobility.[38]

This absence of social diegesis is characteristic of the tale in its entirety. Rhetorical construction is socially freighted in a manner which erodes hierarchy and distance. Chauntecleer, the cockerel, is the widow's property—her 'catel' and one of her precious means of sustenance. He is presented through the courtly rhetorical scheme of 'descriptio'—where a person is described from top to toe,[39] or in Chauntecleer's case, from his comb to his toenails:

> His coomb was redder than the fyn coral,
> And batailled as it were a castel wal;
> His byle was blak, and as the jeet it shoon;
> Lyk asure were his legges and his toon;
> His nayles whitter than the lylye flour,
> And lyk the burned gold was his colour.
> This gentil cok hadde in his governaunce
> Sevene hennes for to doon al his plesaunce
> Whiche were his sustres and his paramours.
>
> (VII. 2859–67)

A barnyard animal belonging to a peasant is here described in terms of aristocratic property, wealth, and values. While the widow's cottage is surrounded with a dry ditch and sticks, Chauntecleer's comb is crenellated like a castle wall. Ostensibly defensive structures, crenellations were, in reality, signs of aristocratic wealth. In contrast to other texts written in the aftermath of 1381, there is no textual distance created here between peasant property and aristocratic building. Chauntecleer's

---

[38] In *Mirour de L'Omme*, Gower contrasts the obedient rustics of former times, content with a diet of coarse bread, milk, and cheese, with the greedy and disloyal rabble of his own times, 26425–81. Compare the demands of the labourers in *Piers Plowman* for a diet more refined than bean-baked bread, B. VI. 302–11, where the impropriety of the claims for a better diet is registered through the use of French diction: 'chaud' and 'plus chaud' (310).

[39] The rules are set down in Geoffrey Vinsauf's *Poetria Nova* in Faral, *Les arts poétiques*, 589–99. The device features in *The Knight's Tale* with the description of Emily, I. 1035–55, and in *The Miller's Tale*, which answers the disembodied portrait of Emily with an uncovering of Alison's sensuality. Here, Chaucer bends the rules by starting, not at the head, but at Alison's loins, I. 3233–70.

colours are compared to precious metals: coral, jet, azure, and burnished gold, suggestive both of heraldic emblazoning, and of the costly materials used by the aristocracy to create fine works of art. The comparison of his toenails to the lily flower associates Chauntecleer with a symbol used to denote the virginity of the Virgin Mary.[40] It was also used of courtly women, for example, Emily in *The Knight's Tale* (I. 1036). The lexis of the passage blends French courtly diction with native English vocabulary. Chauntecleer is 'gentil', has 'paramours' in his 'governaunce' for the satisfaction of his 'plesaunce'. A chicken which procreates in the dust is invested with the courtly language of refined love, even as the presence of the comic English words 'hennes' and 'sustres' reminds us that the subjects of the description are animals. As in the opening description of the widow's cottage, the registers of courtliness and peasant sustenance are inseparable.

There is also social blurring in the allegorical resonances of the tale. In literary critical history, *The Nun's Priest's Tale* was a frequent site of battle between allegorical and humanist critics.[41] Critics steeped in patristic literature teased out all kinds of 'fruyt' from the 'chaff' of this tale, from seeing it as an allegory of a priest (Chauntecleer) being deceived by a friar (the fox),[42] to readings in which Chauntecleer is a complex 'imitatio Christi' whose encounter with the fox evokes both the crucifixion of Christ and his temptation in the wilderness.[43] One allegorical reading in particular has relevance for the context of 1381: the view that the tale is a tragicomic allegory of the Fall of Man. First advocated by Speirs, and subsequently adopted by Huppé, and Levy and Adams, these readings interpret Chauntecleer and Pertelote as Adam and Eve, the beam on which they perch as the Tree of Knowledge, and the chaos of the farmyard chase at the end of the tale as the sublunary chaos unleashed by the Fall of Man.[44] The extent to which allusions such as these produce a totalizing allegorical reading of the tale is open to debate, but it is hard to ignore the fact that these allusions are present and that integral to the

---

[40] For example in the Annunciation scene in the Bowet Window, York Minster Choir; see Clifford Davidson, *Drama and art* (Kalamazoo, Mich., 1977), 42–3, plate V.

[41] The debate has been well chronicled and discussed by S. H. Rigby, *Chaucer in context: society, allegory and gender* (Manchester, 1996), 78–99.

[42] C. Dahlberg, 'Chaucer's cock and fox', *JEGP* 53 (1954), 277–90.

[43] R. Neuse, *Chaucer's Dante: allegory and epic theater in the Canterbury Tales* (Berkeley, 1991), 93–4; p. 97.

[44] John Speirs, *Chaucer the maker* (London, 1951), 185–93; B. F. Huppé, *A reading of the Canterbury Tales* (New York, 1967), 174–84; B. S. Levy and G. R. Adams, 'Chauntecleer's paradise lost and regained', *Medieval Studies*, 29 (1967), 178–92.

rhetorical constructions of the tale Chauntecleer is a type of Adam and his wife a type of Eve. As I have argued earlier, however, these chickens are items of peasant property who are also figured as members of the aristocracy. In socio-textual terms, then, both the labouring and the noble estates are represented by the figures of Adam and Eve. This aligns the textuality of the tale with the social levelling of the proverb used as the text of John Ball's sermon. While the textual strategies of Gower and the chroniclers strove to reassert hierarchical control over the third estate, the rhetoric of *The Nun's Priest's Tale* can be seen to reproduce the social equality demanded by John Ball.

   It is important to keep these rhetorical constructions in mind when reading the end of the tale and the passage which contains the reference to the 1381 uprising:

> This sely wydwe, and eek hir doghtres two
> Herden thise hennes crie and maken wo,
> And out at dores stirten they anon,
> And syen the fox toward the grove gon,
> And bar upon his bak the cok away;
> And cryden, 'Out! Harrow and weylaway!
> Ha, ha! The fox! and after hym they ran,
> And eek with staves many another man.
> Ran Colle *oure* dogge, and Talbot and Gerland,
> And Malkyn, with a dystaf in hir hand;
> Ran cow and calf, and eek the verray hogges,
> So fered for the berkyng of the dogges
> And shoutyng of the men and wommen eeke,
> They ronne so hem thoughte hir herte breeke.
> They yolleden as feendes doon in helle;
> The dokes cryden as men wolde hem quelle;
> The gees for feere flowen over the trees;
> Out of the hyve cam the swarm of bees.
> So hydous was the noyse, a, benedicitee!
> Certes, he Jakke Straw and his meynee
> Ne made nevere shoutes half so shrille
> Whan that they wolden any Flemyng kille,
> As thilke day was maad upon the fox.
> Of bras they broghten bemes, and of box,
> Of horn, of boon, in whiche they blewe and powped.
> And therwithal they shriked and they howped;
> It semed as that hevene sholde falle.

(VII. 3375–401)

At first sight this passage looks similar to the portraits of bestial chaos discussed earlier: the animals break out of the spaces where they ought to be contained: the geese fly over the trees, the bees swarm out of the hive. These images are intensified by a rhetorical instability between the animal and the human: the dogs have human names, the pigs are frightened both by the dogs and men and women, and the ducks cry out as though they fear that the humans are going to kill them.[45] There is also barbaric, demonic noise: similes compare all this yelling to that of devils in hell, quacking ducks and the 'parping, shrieking, blowing and hooping' of those in pursuit of the fox. The cacophony of the chase, which seems as if it will bring down the very heavens, exceeds that of the 1381 rebels. While this all seems very similar to how the chroniclers and Gower strove to write the rebels of 1381 out of civilized discourse, by associating them with madness, devils, inhuman noise, and anarchy, the similarities are all on the surface.[46] The acts of rhetoric committed by Chaucer have a very different socio-textual resonance.

Social confusion is created in this passage because of earlier rhetorical constructions. Chauntecleer has been rhetorically set up both as an animal, and as a member of the nobility. Furthermore, the cockerel has been snatched by a fox who has been likened to a flattering courtier. This is the narrator's address to the audience after the fox has success-fully flattered the cockerel into singing with his eyes shut, and hence made himself into easy prey for the fox's breakfast:

> This Chauntecleer his wynges gan to bete,
> As man that koude his traysoun nat espie,

[45] The confounding of the human and the animal is said by Monica E. McAlpine to merge the fictional and historical worlds of the tale, 'The triumph of fiction in "The Nun's Priest's Tale"' in Edwards, *Art and content*, 79–92, , p. 90; Travis notes that the names 'Talbot' and 'Gerland' are ambiguous: are they canine or human? And how the merging of humans and animals yokes together the two worlds of literary and historical narration by the curious bond of sound, 'Chaucer's trivial fox chase', 211 and 217.

[46] Fehrenbacher argues that with the conflation of animal sound and human language, the attempt made by the tale to repress history breaks down. The repressed returns, and when it does it is monstrous; an animalistic, incoherent mob of murderers, a familiar way of repre-senting the voice of peasants, '"A yeerd enclosed al aboute"', 144–5. Ganim argues that the chase scene conflates two great cataclysms of the late fourteenth-century English society: the revolt and the plague, but by placing them in an ironic context, their horror is rendered comic. Chantecleer is both courtly and a parody of courtliness. Cf. the comments by Aers, *CHMEL*, Bisson, *Chaucer and the late medieval world*, and Hanna, 'Pilate's voice/Shirley's case', which all draw similarities between the sound of the fox chase and contemporary representations of the peasant.

So was he ravysshed with his flaterie.
Allas! ye lordes, many a fals flatour
Is in youre courtes and many a losengeour,
That plesen yow wel moore, by my feith,
Than he that soothfastnesse unto yow seith.
Redeth Ecclesiaste of flaterye;
Beth war, ye lordes, of hir trecherye.

(VII. 3322–30)

Daun Russell the fox is framed as a sycophantic courtier: a type familiar from advice to princes literature of the time, and a type that has already featured earlier in *The Canterbury Tales*.[47] The address to 'ye lordes' (3325) frames the audience as aristocratic, but, in contrast to the pleasure that such an audience might have gained from reading accounts of 1381 in other contemporary works, it might have felt much more uncomfortable with *The Nun's Priest's Tale*: that is, if it paid close attention to its rhetorical constructions.

On one level, because both the cockerel and the fox have been fashioned as courtly subjects, the chase at the end of the tale describes a peasant mob and animals going in pursuit of members of the aristocracy.[48] The images of mayhem and disorder signal the anarchy of

[47] e.g. Placebo in *The Merchant's Tale*, IV. 1478–518. Prudence warns her husband of the dangers of flatterers in *The Tale of Melibee*, VII. 1171–94, where there is also a reference to Ecclesiastes ('Salomon seith that', 1177). Gower inveighs against flatterers in all three of his major works: *Mirour*, 26545–7; *Confessio*, VII. 2165–694; and *Vox*, VI. 545–80, where the revised version attaches more blame to Richard's inability to repress flattery. Compare also ll. 645–52, 681–2, and 759–60. Other closely contemporary criticisms of flattery include: *On the Times* in *Political poems and songs*, ed. Wright, i. 270–8; *Historical poems*, ed. Robbins, p. 49/29–32; *De quadripartita regis specie*, *Four English political tracts*, ed. J.-P. Genet, 92. The contemporary chroniclers frequently criticize Richard for failing to provide himself with honest and trustworthy counsellors, see *Eulogium*, iii. 382; *Westminster Chronicle*, 69; *Historia Vitae R. II*, p. 86: Knighton, *Chronicon*, ii. 219. The sixteenth and twenty-third articles of deposition against Richard in the September 1399 Parliament accuse Richard of being unwilling to follow wise counsel, see Given-Wilson, *Chronicles of the revolution*, 177–8 and 23. *Richard the Redeless* is unsparing in its criticism of the king's willingness to listen to flatterers and false counsellors, e.g. I. 136–201; II. 116–139; III. 110–19; 198.

[48] Scanlon argues that Chauntecleer is the voice of royal male authority in the barnyard; the status quo from which the narrative begins and to which it returns, 'The authority of fable', 56. He notes that 'making the fox a flatterer casts Chauntecleer in the role of a prince or great lord, about to be trapped in the discursive exchange of his own court', p. 61. Of the conclusion, he writes that when Chauntecleer invites the fox to address the anarchic mob as churls and invite them to turn back, he is asking the fox to perform the same gesture as Richard II in his treatment of the mob at Mile End, namely, to restore order through the power of his voice. But as a result of flattery, the authority of that voice has been dissipated,

that social upheaval reminiscent of the slaughterous actions of the 1381 rebels.[49] Simultaneously, however, keeping in mind the description of the widow at the start of the tale, this is simply the account of a poor woman, with no access to aristocratic dainties, taking desperate measures to recapture a vital means of food production which has been snatched from her by a sweet-talking courtier. The wildness of the chase is an index of the desperation of the widow and the household, for, as a result of the intrusion of the courtly fox, their means of survival is under threat. The vast gulf between the nobility and the rebels, so strenuously maintained in the chroniclers and Gower, is not present here. The correspondences between the labourers and the nobility are fluid. Chauntecleer is both a member of the aristocracy and the means of livelihood for a poor widow. The chase is both an unruly event and a legitimate act to restore rightful ownership. The discursive terrain resonates with contemporary accounts of how the rebels claimed equality with their social superiors, imitated their practices, demanded that all goods be in common, and commandeered aristocratic possessions, but while in these contemporary accounts, such actions are narrated with derision and dismissal, in *The Nun's Priest's Tale*, rhetorical ambivalence erodes the textual distance between estates. The hullabaloo which is likened to Jack Straw's gang killing Flemish merchants describes an upheaval in which the social status of characters and actions is mobile.

Volatility of social status is also constructed by other textual devices used in the tale; namely, generic expectation and voice. In terms of generic affiliations, *The Nun's Priest's Tale* is most readily apprehensible as a beast fable. This genre is one which could lend itself to the kind of didactic writing that Gower employs in his *Vox Clamantis*. Chaucer's use of the beast fable, by contrast, produces excessive, and conflicting, patterns of signification which resist authoritative condemnation of the 1381 rebels. Scheps has argued that the blurring of distinctions between humans and animals in the tale reaches the point where the whole idea of fable as a genre is ridiculed. Of the chase sequence he writes:

Especially significant is the way in which the Nun's Priest . . . makes no attempt to distinguish between human and animal responses here because there is no distinction to be made . . . just as the distinction between human and

pp. 63–4. This is an attractive reading, but I differ in interpretation in placing more emphasis on the mobility of rhetorical construction than the textual force of flattery in the tale.

[49] The reference to the distaff carried by a woman might be seen to echo Gower's account of the ignoble weapons carried by the rebels. In *Vox*, it is carried by a man, I. 851.

animal behaviour has been deliberately blurred throughout the tale, so too is the traditional distinction between 'fabula' and 'moralitas' . . . in opposition to the perilously easy identification of men and beasts which the beast fable ordinarily requires us to make, the Nun's Priest demonstrates a profound understanding of the grave inadequacy of such an identification, and thus he refuses to make it complete. By involving his animal characters in learned disputation, he anthropomorphizes them; but by making their arguments irrelevant to the central action of the fable, he in effect returns them to the level of beasts.[50]

Robert Jordan observes how the slippage in the levels of illusion—where a man is a protagonist in a tale told by a chicken, who in turn is the protagonist in a tale told by a man—produces 'illusionary ambiguity and instability'.[51] Jill Mann has argued that such an interpretation of the tale is not simply a modern projection of modern values and attitudes onto a medieval text. Pointing to the existence of earlier mock-heroic beast epics such as *The Romance of Reynard* and Nigel Longchamps's *Speculum Stultorum*, she notes how there was a tradition of beast narrative which exposed the hollowness of moral, intellectual, and aesthetic abstractions. In *The Nun's Priest's Tale*, the irony and satire of amoral beast epic undercuts the potential of beast fable for serious teaching. The tale is the ultimate epitome of Chaucer's continuously human suggestion of the relativity of things.[52]

In contrast to the strategies used by Latin or French writers to distance the actions of the rebels from authoritarian civilized discourse, *The Nun's Priest's Tale* is conspicuous in its lack of narrative authority and containment. While the Latin and French works exert strict narrative control over licence and excess, the *Nun's Priest's Tale* revels in plenty and confusion. One instance of this, as we have seen, is the comic refusal to segregate the animal and the human, and the courtly and the labouring. Another instance is how the tale's encyclopedic embracement of diverse discourses disperses linear didacticism. Helen Cooper has observed how the tale can be seen as 'an encapsulation of everything

[50] Walter Scheps, 'Chaucer's anti-fable: "reduction ad absurdum"', in *The Nun's Priest's Tale*', *LSE* 4 (1970), 1–10, pp. 4–7.

[51] Jordan, *Chaucer's poetics*, 147. Cf. Helen Cooper, *The structure of 'The Canterbury Tales'* (London, 1983), 'relativity is therefore built into the genre in all kinds of ways, not least in the balance between the animal world and the humans they almost, but never quite, represent. Morality is, after all, inapplicable to animals; the fox can no more be blamed for eating poultry than the cock for polygamy', p. 188.

[52] Jill Mann, 'The *Speculum Stultorum* and the *Nun's Priest's Tale*', *Chaucer Review*, 9 (1975), 262–82.

that *The Canterbury Tales* is'.[53] Beast fable coexists with beast epic, alongside dream vision, sermon exempla, philosophical debate, tragedy, comedy, biblical allegory, rhetorical apostrophe, and scientific exposition. Jordan comments:

Its command of forms is indeed encyclopedic, and because it is composed of so many modes of discourse, it is a tale whose center is hard to locate, shifting as it does among different rhetorical domains . . . no doubt one of the meanings, or 'moralites' of the tale is the futility of seeking fixed meanings, even in authoritative texts.[54]

It is striking that the most clear reference to 1381 in Chaucer's works should come in the Canterbury Tale most celebrated for its play of textuality. Whilst courting the fixity of meaning and clear-cut moral that a fable could encode, the tale resists closure of interpretation at every turn. An instance of this is the equivocal nature of victory at the end of the tale. Both the fox and the cock are beguiled, but both escape punishment and their ultimate destinies remain un-narrated. As Doron Narkiss explains:

there is something unusual about a fable that ends so symmetrically, without the clear-cut victory of one party over the other. The 'double-unit' fable may appear as merely a multiplication of fable, but is actually a negation of fable's traditional persuasive function. Fable persuades by making a point about power, and a neat reversal, such as here, in which power is shared, and each character has a chance to crow over his rival, questions the validity of the moral . . . Chaucer's use of the fable highlights interchangeability, a propensity for doubling, repetition and substitutions. It is this ambiguating propensity that opens the fable to interpretation, and casts doubt on the finality of fable as a revealer of ultimate truths.[55]

To include a reference to 1381 in a tale in which power is shared between actants whose social status is not clear-cut is a far cry from the absolute denunciations of the Latin and French writers. Further, as a number of critics have noted, while 'moralites' and 'sententiae' are scattered profusely throughout the tale, no *final* moral is offered.[56]

[53] Cooper, *Structure*, 180.

[54] Jordan, *Chaucer's poetics*, 138.

[55] Doron Narkiss, '"The fox, the cock and the priest": Chaucer's escape from fable', *Chaucer Review*, 32 (1997), 46–63, pp. 53 and 60.

[56] Scheps notes the surprising number of morals and sententiae throughout the tale, observing that they are atypical in number for a beast fable, and also contradictory rather than complementary, 'Chaucer's anti-fable', 4–5.

Notoriously, at the end of his tale, the Nun's Priest invites his audience to extract the 'moralite':

> Taketh the moralite, goode men
> For Seint Paul seith that al that writen is,
> To oure doctrine it is ywrite, ywis;
> Taketh the fruyt, and lat the chaf be stille.

(VII. 3440–43)

With this final playful comment, the tale gestures towards didactic closure only to confuse even further the relationship between story and morality, fruit and chaff. The textual pyrotechnics of the tale have occluded any distinction between these relationships. Scheps argues that any distinction between 'fruyt' and 'chaff' is 'virtually impossible',[57] while Boitani argues that it is impossible to move to a level of allegory in the tale; the priest 'makes us turn away from non-literal exegesis while inviting us to pursue it'.[58] For Cooper, 'meaning is subverted by the insistent fictionality of the text . . . all such ethical claims are enfolded within other layers that stress storytelling and fictionality'.[59]

Crucial in this fictional layering is the play of different voices in the tale. The pilgrim teller of the tale is a member of the second estate. But in contrast to the monk Thomas Walsingham, he provides no authoritative containment and denunciation of the events of 1381. The Nun's Priest is a notoriously evasive and shadowy figure. In contrast to John Gower's assertive identification with prophetic biblical voice in *Vox Clamantis*, the Nun's Priest is not named, and he receives no description in *The General Prologue*. The point of origin for the tale remains opaque, and as a result we are left with an unanchored play of voices.[60] The emphasis on speech is itself important. In contrast to the efforts in other accounts of 1381 to assert textual distance between the civility of their written Latin and French and the bestial orality of the rebels, there is an

---

[57] 'Chaucer's anti-fable', 5.

[58] Piero Boitani, '"My tale is of a cock"—or the problem of literal interpretation', in Richard G. Newhauser and J. A. Alford, eds., *Literature and religion in the later middle ages: philological studies in honor of Siegfried Wenzel* (New York, 1995), 25–42, p. 41.

[59] Cooper, *Oxford guides*, 348. Cf. Cooper, *Structure*, 187, where she notes that the real trouble with the priest's final formulation 'is that it shows Chaucer so brilliantly as the poet of the chaff: it is the surface that matters, not the trite little moral fruits that can be extracted from it'.

[60] Jordan notes that the tale is told by 'a farrago of voices that Chaucer found suitable, if not necessary, for the multiplicity of subjects, situations, and perspectives that constitute this multifarious work', *Chaucer's poetics*, 136.

insistence on multiple voices in *The Nun's Priest's Tale* and frequently a collapse of the hierarchical distinction between written authority and orality. A cockerel quotes Saints' lives (3120–1), the Bible in Latin (3163–4); a hen quotes Cato (2940–1) and a fox boasts of how well read he is in 'Daun Burnel the Asse' (3312) in addition to referring to Boethius's treatise *De Musica* (3294). To add to the confusion, it is frequently unclear who exactly is speaking. At one point in the tale, there are at least, as Helen Cooper has pointed out, seven levels of narration: Chaucer; Chaucer the pilgrim; the Nun's Priest; Chauntecleer; the 'auctor' Chauntecleer has read who tells of men's dreams; the men whose dreams are recounted; the dreamer within the second tale who narrates a prophetic dream to his companion not to sail; and the anonymous man within this prophetic dream:

> And seyde him thus: 'If thou tomorwe wende,
> Thow shalt be dreynt; *my tale is at an ende*'
>
> (VII. 3079–82)[61]

No resolution is supplied to this debate on the efficacy of dreams. In relation to Chauntecleer's dream and his subsequent abduction by the fox, the teller provides no clear link between cause and effect. Is his dream coincidental with his snatching by the fox, or is it a foretelling of it? This casual, open-ended treatment of dream vision could hardly contrast more starkly with the prophetic urgency and ardour of Gower, nor the absence of controlling narrative frame more strongly with the authoritarian narrative stance of the chroniclers.

This absence of authoritarian control is perhaps seen most strikingly at the moment in the tale where Chauntecleer (or is it?) tries to evade responsibility for the comment that woman was responsible for the Fall:

> Wommennes conseils been ful ofte colde;
> Wommannes conseil broghte us first to wo
> And made Adam fro Paradys to go.
>
> (VII. 3256–68)

Narrative authority is thrown to the winds by the teller's lily-livered comment:

> Thise been the cokkes wordes, and nat myne;
> I kan noon harm of no womman divyne   (3265–6)

The socio-textual distance, so characteristic of other treatments of 1381,

---

[61] Cooper, *Structure*, 6 (italics hers).

is here completely collapsed. Ostensibly, the teller is a priest, but far from exerting textual authority and providing a governing interpretation he passes the buck to a chicken.[62] But even this much is not clear-cut. The lines beg the question: who is speaking here? Is it Chaucer the narrator, the pilgrim, a priest, or a barnyard cockerel rhetorically fleshed out in the trappings of the aristocracy? In contrast to the way that the Latin and French writers marked out vernacular voice as bestial noise, here, in terms of voice, all three estates could be said to be speaking at once.

And here, I want to return to the long passage on the fox chase. In terms of my interpretation of the tale, perhaps the most crucial word is a pronoun—'oure' in l. 3383. *The Riverside Chaucer* notes that it is an example of the 'domestic plural' (p. 941). What interests me is that it is a first-person plural, and with the use of this pronoun, all narrative distance from the events of 1381 is lost; the voice of the teller merges with that of the participants within the tale. One might read the Nun's Priest at this point as an example of one of the number of minor clergy who joined in the risings. More important, in my view, than identifying the Nun's Priest exclusively as a minor clerical rebel is to note that an ostensibly clerical voice joins in with the uproar of social upheaval, and that the successive de-centrings of vocal authority in the tale erode any kind of socio-textual distance from events.

Paul Strohm has argued that the actions of the 1381 rebels may be seen as genuinely transgressive for the following reasons: disrespect for hierarchy and status; encouragement of reversal, and erasure of the line between spectatorship and participation.[63] All these are features of carnival and all of these are features of the textual revelry of *The Nun's Priest's Tale*. Especially important with regard to the relationship of the tale to the works of Chaucer's contemporaries is the last: the erasure of the line between spectatorship and participation. This is an erasure performed spectacularly by the pronoun 'oure' in l. 3383, where in contrast to the authoritarian ocular framing of the events of 1381 in the writings of Chaucer's contemporaries, here, there is no difference between the voice of description and the voice of rebellion.

The formal characteristics of *The Nun's Priest's Tale*: its rhetoric, allegory, use of sententiae, narrative voice, and encyclopaedic play of discourses are charged with social resonance. The tale is not just *about*

---

[62] Boitani observes that in these lines a priest leaves exegesis to a cockerel, and thus loses authority over all interpretation, 'My tale is of a cock', 33.

[63] Strohm, *Hochon's arrow*, 56.

the uprisings in 1381; it participates in the contest for representation which was such a key feature of the revolts. The tale is both a dazzling foray into the arts of fiction-making *and* an example of the social struggle for empowerment. Chaucer's social practice in this tale, presumably one which John of Gaunt skipped, is as radical as his exploration of social semantics in *The Manciple's Tale*.

CHAPTER SIX

'Blessed are the horny hands of toil': Wycliffite Representations of the Third Estate[1]

ACCORDING TO Adam Usk, Wyclif's followers 'most wickedly did sow the seed of murder, snares, strife, variance, and discords, which last unto this day, and which, I fear, will last even to the undoing of the kingdom'.[2] Usk was not alone in associating Wycliffites with civil dissent and unrest. Walsingham stated that the failure of the late Archbishop Sudbury to suppress the heresy of Wyclif and his followers was the primary cause of the revolt in 1381.[3] Both Walsingham and Knighton frame John Ball as a follower of Wyclif, the latter terming him 'Wycliffe's John the Baptist'.[4] While modern criticism is generally sceptical of the notion that Wyclif and/or his followers were the *cause* of the uprisings in 1381, it is hard to ignore the considerable body of contemporary opinion which apparently believed that there was a very strong connection between Lollardy and insurrection.[5] When one turns to what the Wycliffites actually wrote themselves, however, rather than what was written about them, it is clear that Lollard texts are unanimous and univocal in their declaration of obedience to secular authority. The king must be obeyed, even if he be a tyrant, and members of civic

---

[1] Quotation from James Russell Lowell, *A glance behind the curtain*, I. 201.

[2] Usk, *Chronicon*, 3–4.

[3] T. Walsingham, *Chronicon Angliae*, ed. E. M. Thompson (London, Rolls Series, 1874), 310–11.

[4] Ibid. 320–1; Knighton, *Chronicon*, ii. 151.

[5] For discussion of the connection, see Margaret Aston, 'Lollardy and sedition', repr. in *Lollards and reformers* (Hambledon, 1984), 1–47; Anne Hudson, '*Piers Plowman* and the Peasants' revolt: a problem revisited', *YLS* 8 (1994), 85–106; and Justice, *Writing and rebellion*, 67–101. Hudson notes that the furthest that Wyclif went in condemning the commons in *De blasphemia* was to say that 'they acted rather outside the law', '*Piers Plowman*', 97; while Justice argues that Wyclif's programme of disendowment put into circulation a vocabulary that could be put to insurgent use, even if Wyclif himself stressed secular obedience to the king, *Writing and rebellion*, 89–101.

society must be ordered according to the normative tripartite division into lords, clergy, and labourers.[6] How is such a polarity of view possible? If the stated opinions of the Lollards on civil society were so declaredly orthodox, and even quietist, how could contemporary commentators associate them with a series of uprisings for which the third estate—the peasants, or 'rustics', as the commentators term them—were held to be chiefly responsible?[7] This chapter is, in part, an attempt to answer that question.[8]

Apart from the tract titled by Matthew *Of Servants and Lords*, there is no sustained discussion of the third estate in Wycliffite prose texts.[9] From collation of localized comments in other tracts about the place and function of the third estate, however, a coherent and consistent Wycliffite view of this social group does emerge, especially in the discussion of labourers. While they strenuously maintain the place of labourers within overt support for a three-estate structure of civil society, Wycliffite texts are much less vitriolic in their views of the commons and far less condemnatory of labourers than is the norm. As I shall argue, much of the reason for this stems from how the commons are viewed within Wycliffite ecclesiology. For all the declared support for a traditional three-estate structure, Wycliffite representations of the third estate can be seen to have a radical potential and to harbour dissident energy. Wycliffite texts can be seen to rewrite the contemporary, normative language of social description in the ways that they refigure social relationships between the commons and the lords, but, even more profoundly, in how they refashion social relationships between the commons and the material Church.[10] The most radical attention to the position of labourers is seen in the distinctive Wycliffite treatment of the figure of the ploughman. The fullest representation of this figure occurs in *Pierce the Ploughman's Crede*, a depiction which is entirely consonant with localized discussion in the prose texts, but which is distinctively different from the treatment in *Piers Plowman*.

---

[6] See Hudson, *The premature reformation*, 362 and 366–7; and *English Wycliffite sermons*, ed. Pamela Gradon and Anne Hudson (Oxford 1996), iv. 152–60.

[7] See discussion in Chapter 5 above.

[8] The discussion is also continuous with my exploration of the language of social description in Chapters 1–3 and the politics of representation examined in Chapters 4 and 5.

[9] *The English works of John Wyclif hitherto unprinted*, ed. F. D. Matthew (EETS OS 74 1880, 2nd rev. edn., 1902), 226–43; hereafter referred to in the notes as Matthew. This tract appears to attempt to distance Wycliffite thought from the riots of 1381 and is discussed further below.

[10] Cf. discussion of the language of social description in Chapter 1.

Overwhelmingly, Wycliffite prose texts represent the third estate through the figure of the peasant labourer.[11] The artisan class is scarcely visible and the peasants depicted are the rural poor rather than labourers with their own plot of land.[12] That Lollard tracts should focus their treatment of the third estate on the rural poor peasant is itself significant. As Paul Freedman has recently shown, there is a tension in medieval images of the peasant. There are two intertwined traditions: on the one hand, the peasant was held to be a figure of utter contempt and ridicule, and on the other, seen to be much closer to God than members of the other two estates because of his poverty and simple way of life. As Freedman illustrates, both these discourses are held in tension and reinforce one another.[13] One reason for this duality is the existence of contradictory legacies on the value of labour. One tradition held that all labour was the result of sin, and toil was Adam's punishment for the Fall. The other tradition argued that it was not toil *as such* that was a consequence of the Fall, but the difficulty and hardship of labour that was enjoined on Adam for his transgression. It was argued that God laboured over his Creation, and even before the Fall, Adam worked happily to maintain the garden in Paradise. Wall-paintings survive which showed Adam being taught to labour by an angel before his disobedience.[14] This dual legacy is often found interrelated in medieval commentaries on the value of labour. For example, Jacques de Vitry, taking as his text Zachariah 13: 5 ('homo agricola ego sum'—'I am a husbandman'), asserts that Holy Scripture praises agriculture and manual labour, but as a penance enjoined by God after the Fall. If labourers work gladly to fulfil this penance they will be praised by God, and many poor tillers do so. If, however, they are like brute animals, concerned only to eat and drink, then they will lose grace in this life and all their labour will be for nothing.[15] The sermon combines elements both of the tradition of contempt for peasants and their bestial habits, and the tradition which valued the exemplary 'simplicitas' of peasants,

[11] There is some localized attention to merchants and lawyers which I discuss below.

[12] For the distinction between peasants with no land or less than a full holding, and those who could support themselves from their tenements, see R. H. Hilton, 'Reasons for inequality among medieval peasants', in *Class conflict and the crisis of feudalism: essays in medieval social history* (London, 1985), 139–51; and Werner Rösener, *Peasants in the middle ages*, trans. Alexander Stützer (Cambridge, 1992), 191–207.   [13] Freedman, *Images*, 31–3.

[14] Ibid. 28–9.

[15] Quoted ibid. 33 from Jacques de Vitry, 'Sermo ad agricolas et vinitores et alios operarios', in J.-Th. Welter, *L'exemplum dans la littérature religieuse et didactique du Moyen Age* (Paris, 1927), 458.

and appreciated their toil for the sustenance of society. Both of these traditions employ distinctive tropes which appear time and again in medieval texts.

In the Middle Ages, the 'contempt' branch of peasant discourse was the more voluminous. Chiefly depicted as unpleasant and boorish, coarse and dull-witted, they are also seen as subhuman, even devilish, and a menace to the rest of society. Peasants were seen to be quint-essentially stupid, especially ignorant in matters of theology,[16] and as the antithesis of all that is civilized. This latter takes a variety of forms. Fre-quently, peasants are compared to animals. Commentators on the events of 1381, as I have discussed above, tapped this rich seam of contempt with relish,[17] but it is also seen in other contexts. The Luttrell Psalter, for example, contains *bas de page* illustrations of peasants working away at rustic occupations alongside semi-human, grotesque baboons.[18]

Allied to the tradition of framing the peasant as non-civilized and animalistic is his frequent association with base bodily functions and filth. As a keeper of animals and fertilizer of fields, the peasant was ripe for comparison to manure and other forms of animal waste. A late fourteenth-century Lombard poem which traces the origin of the 'vilein' class, argues that the first such was born from the flatulence of an ass.[19] The association of the third estate with bodily functions of all kinds, from farting, belching, and pissing, to unbridled 'swyving' is memorably portrayed in the final three tales of the first fragment of *The Canterbury Tales*. Alongside the insistently bodily portrayal of the peasant class—a group, which, if their detractors were to be credited, had no control over their sphincter muscles—was their representation as dirt, or pollution.[20] In recounting the entry of a group of rebels into the

---

[16] For instance the tale told by John of Bromyard in which a peasant was asked to identi-fy the three persons of the Trinity. He coped reasonably with God the Father and God the Son: he knew them well enough 'for he tended their sheep', but came rather unstuck on the Holy Spirit: 'I know not that third fellow; there is none of that name in our village.' Cited in G. G. Coulton, *The medieval village* (Cambridge, 1925), 265–6.

[17] See Chapter 5 above.

[18] See Michael Camille, 'Labouring for the lord: the ploughman and the social order in the Luttrell Psalter', *Art History*, 10 (1987), 423–54. Freedman collects continental depictions of peasants as animals, denizens of the forest, ill-formed, mis-shapen, black, and ugly, *Images*, 140–3.

[19] Cited ibid. 147 from Paul Meyer, 'Dit sur les vilains par matazone de Calignano', *Romania*, 12 (1883), 14–28.

[20] Cf. Mary Douglas's analysis of the anthropological significance of dirt in the previous chapter, *Purity and danger*.

queen's bedchamber in 1381, Walsingham states that the swineherds carried 'filthy sticks' in imitation of the knightly sword and laid their 'uncouth and sordid hands on the beards of several most noble knights'.[21] Here, the tradition of peasants as dirt is wedded to the familiar view of peasants as socially insubordinate and anxious to ape the behaviour of their social superiors. Gower, in Book IX of *Vox Clamantis*, associates the toil of peasants with the punishment of Adam, but states that scarcely any husbandman wishes to do such work, rather he wickedly loafs around everywhere. He describes the peasant as sluggish and grasping, desiring the leisures of great men: 'born of a poor man's stock and a poor man himself, he demands things for his belly like a lord' (*Vox*, IX. 561–70; 572; 582ff., and 648).

A further trait of the presentation of peasants as agents of social disturbance and upheaval, not content with their place, is their depiction as liars and thieves, their theological ignorance and stupidity contrasted with their cunning in outwitting their social superiors.[22] Chroniclers of the 1381 uprising frequently depict the actions of the rebels in terms of senseless plundering and looting,[23] even though, as in the destruction of John of Gaunt's Savoy palace, the insurgents are said to have thrown rich gold and jewels into the Thames and to have punished any of their fellows who tried to keep such things for themselves.[24]

Perhaps the most telling condemnation of the peasant seen in the discourse of contempt is their portrayal as separate from humanity. They are devilish[25] or 'foreign', or an outcast. Pictorial representations showed peasants as dark, swarthy, and with non-European physiognomy.[26] Some representations depict figures who are separate from civilization, not just culturally, but biologically; their bodies are deformed, either through anatomical disproportion, or through having horns on their

[21] Quoted from Dobson, *The Peasants' Revolt*, 172. For further examples of peasants as dirt see Freedman, *Images*, 143–54.

[22] For examples from the continental fabliau tradition, see ibid. 206. This tradition is important in the framing of the miller in *The Reeve's Tale*, who, however, fails to outwit his social superiors, the clerks, as with a characteristically fabliau denial of patriarchal authority, Maleyne, the miller's daughter, enables the clerks to turn the tables on her father. Cf. the miller in *The General Prologue* who knew how to charge thrice the proper toll for his corn, I. 562.

[23] See *The Anonimalle Chronicle*, quoted in Dobson, *The Peasants' Revolt*, 125 and 157, and Walsingham, *Historia Anglicana*, i. 456–7, quoted in Dobson, *The Peasants' Revolt*, 169–70.

[24] See ibid. i. 457; Knighton, *Chronicon*, ii. 134–5; and *The Anonimalle Chronicle*, 141–2.

[25] As by Gower and Walsingham, for example; see previous chapter.

[26] See Freedman, *Images*, 139.

heads.[27] The figure of Cain was seen to be the archetypal first peasant because he was a tiller of the soil in contrast to his brother Abel, the archetypal shepherd, who was a keeper of sheep. Cain served as a figure for a number of outcast races from giants to the Plinian races, and, by extension, peasants became co-opted into this discourse of racial otherness.[28]

This discourse of contempt and subjugation, however, is not the whole story. The peasant could not be cast as 'other' unequivocally because his work was necessary to sustain Christian society. Peasants were also seen as spiritually superior to their social betters. Freedman argues that their spiritual benefit derived from three things, none of which produced any special reward here on earth: labour that feeds the world, poverty rather than comfortable simplicity, and oppression.[29] Christian teaching extolled the virtue of hard labour as penance, and a tradition of pious rural rectitude ran in tandem with the tradition of the peasant as treacherous, alien scum. Honorius quotes Psalm 127 : 'Blessed are those who eat the labour of their hands' in a passage which states that the majority of 'agricolae' will be saved, because they live simply and feed the people of God by their sweat.[30] One of the additions made by Chaucer to his source in *The Clerk's Tale* is a verse which describes the idyllic situation of Griselda's small village: the poor live off their own labour, by which the earth yields its abundance.[31] St Jerome, in a letter that was to become a 'locus classicus' on this topic, also contrasted the holy rusticity of peasants with sinful eloquence: 'melius est . . . rusticitatem sanctam habere quam eloquentiam peccatricem'.[32]

Sermons and topical poems were also important in fostering the

---

[27] Freedman (ibid. 90–1) notes the example in an early fourteenth-century Roman law manuscript (Tübingen, Universitätsbibliothek Ms Mc 295, fo.153ʳ) in which runaway serfs with horns on their heads are led in bonds before a judge.

[28] Freedman, *Images*, 92 (fig. 7), notes the example of St John's College, Cambridge, MS K.26 fo. 6ᵛ, which shows Cain with horns, kinky hair, and carrying a scythe. Cf. Michael Camille, *Mirror in parchment: the Luttrell Psalter and the making of medieval England* (London, 1998), 190–1. Lee Patterson discusses the significance of the tradition of associating peasants with Ham, Cain's son, with reference to *The Miller's Tale*, *Chaucer and the subject of history*, 264–70. I discuss the figure of Cain more fully below.

[29] See Freedman, *Images*, 218.

[30] Honorius Augustodunensis, *Elucidarium* 2.61, 'Ex magna parte salvantur, quia simpliciter vivunt et populum Dei suo sudore pascant', *L'Eluciadarium et les lucidaires*, ed. Yves Lefèvre (Rome, 1954), 429. Cited in Freedman, *Images*, 216.

[31] *The Clerk's Tale*, IV. 199–203.

[32] Jerome, *Epistola*, 52, ch. 9, quoted in Freedman, *Images*, 378.

tradition of the necessary, virtuous peasant. Political writing, as I discussed with reference to *Pearl*, often made recourse to the image of the body politic to figure a realm operating in mutual harmony and for common profit.[33] The labourers are usually represented as the feet, not in a derogatory fashion, but as enabling the whole body to stand. For instance, *Digby* poem 15 likens men's legs to craftsmen who work with their hands, because they bear up the whole body as a tree bears up the branches. The feet are the ploughmen, all true tillers of the land, and all that dig the earth, and on them, all the world stands. The toes are likened to the poor, virtuous peasant:

> The toes of þe mennys feet,
> þo y likne to trewe hyne
> þat traualyle boþe in drye and weet,
> In þurst, in hungere, and in pyne,
> In het, in cold, in snow and slet,
> Many hiȝe none, er þey dyne,
> And wiþ good mete selde met;
> But after howsel þey drynke no wyn[34]

Without toes, the poet continues, a man cannot stand or rise; master and servant depend on one another. The writer of the fifteenth-century poem *The Crowned King* reminds Henry V of this fact: it is the 'swope', 'swepe', and 'swynke' of the 'pouere peple' that provides the king with his food, and it is their labour which enables the king to have glittering gold, fine clothes decorated with precious gems, doughty castles, and fortified towns. And yet, says the poet, the most precious plant is that which the poor dig out of the earth with their plough. The allegiance and love of the labourers is much more valuable to the king than his 'mukke'—his wealth; and the king should heed their petitions.[35]

In sum, then, the tradition of peasant representation is fissured. The peasant is both the virtuous, spiritually blessed bedrock of Christian society, *and*, more frequently, the seditious 'other'; a greedy, filthy, lying, ignorant, and deformed body. What is most striking in Wycliffite texts is how this dual legacy of peasant representation is split. Overwhelmingly, the third estate, as represented by the rural poor labourer,

---

[33] See discussion in Chapter 3.

[34] *Digby* poem 15 in Kail, *Twenty six political and other poems*, ll. 65–72. Cf. Thomas Brinton's sermon preached in London in 1373 which describes the feet of the body politic as the farmers and labourers who support the whole body firmly, *The sermons of Thomas Brinton*, ed. Devlin, p. xxiii, and pt. III, Sermon 28.

[35] *The Crowned King*, 61–72, in *The Piers Plowman tradition*, ed. Barr.

is invested with the characteristics of the ameliorative strain of peasant discourse. The virulent tradition of peasant contempt is not obliterated, however. It is highly visible, but instead of being used of the peasant labourer, its features are used to describe friars, monks, and prelates. In Wycliffite texts, it is members of the second estate who are demonized, accompanied by an idealization of the place and worth of those belonging to the third.

At the root of the favourable view of peasant labourers in Wycliffite texts is that they live in praiseworthy poverty. Their discussion of this topic is entirely consonant with Wyclif's own views, expounded most fully in *De Civili Dominio*, II., chapters 7–10. Wyclif believed that the apostolic poverty of the early Church should form the true model for later Christian behaviour. While not condemning riches as such, he asserts that the evangelical poor should renounce all civil possession; the endowment of the Church was intended, not for the enrichment of the clergy, but for the care of the poor in the world. To avoid revolt, a king should dispense goods wisely, rule prudently, and avoid collusion in the appropriation of goods into the dead hand of the Church. The temporalities of the Church would be better dispensed if they were in the hands of the laymen.[36]

Discussion of this issue by his followers runs along similar lines. Wycliffite texts show a passionate concern with poverty.[37] Christ is the holy exemplar of praiseworthy indigence. *The Rosarium Theologie* states that he was 'moste pore, als wele as vnto mekenes of spirite as vnto renoncyng of ciuile lordeschepe',[38] a view extended in a sermon for Christmas Day which interprets Christ's humble birth, and the angelic visitation to the shepherds, to show that Christ was not born into this world 'to regne on mennus bi worldely excellence and temperal power, but in pore estaat and semple to lede his lyif, and so to regne þorouȝ grace vertuously in mennes soules'.[39] Lollard texts are not alone in using

---

[36] Discussion drawn from Anne Hudson, '"Poor preachers, poor men; views of poverty in Wyclif and his followers', in *Häresie und vorzeitige reformation im spätmittelalter: herausgegeben von Frantižek Šmahel undet Elisabeth Müller-Luckner* (Munich, 1998), 41–53, 47–49. I am grateful to Professor Hudson for an offprint of this article. Wyclif's views on poverty are also discussed by Justice, *Writing and rebellion*, 75–101; and Margaret Aston, 'Caim's castles: poverty, politics and disendowment', in *Faith and fire: popular and unpopular religion*, (London, 1993), 95–131.

[37] As noted in *English Wycliffite sermons*, iv. 159.

[38] Christina von Nolcken, ed., *The Middle English translation of the Rosarium Theologie* (Heidelberg, 1979), p. 94/11–13.

[39] *Lollard sermons*, ed. Cigman, p. 61/316–19.

Christ's humble birth as an example of praiseworthy rural poverty; Griselda's father in *The Clerk's Tale* is the poorest of the poor folk in the village, but, as the narrator states, 'But hye God somtyme senden kan | His grace into a litel oxes stalle'.[40] What is distinctive about Wycliffite texts, however, is the use of this image as an argument against the temporal endowment of the Church. The fourteenth point of *The Twenty-Five Articles* explicitly contrasts the apostolic poverty of Christ and his disciples with the 'possessioun' enjoyed by the contemporary Church: 'Jesus Crist hade not by worldly lordschipe whereupon he schuld bowe his heved.' The first apostles could not become disciples of Christ until they had renounced their nets and boats, and even their family. On what basis, then, can contemporary priests claim the status of apostles, and yet be greater worldly lords than earls, dukes, kings' uncles, and princes?[41]

An integral part of the praise of virtuous poverty in contrast to temporal possession is the Wycliffite stress on the necessity of the labourer. Far from being outside civil society, alien and deformed, his toil is essential to the health of the realm, and in contrast to associating labourers with filth and dirt because they work on the land, the Lollard sermon for Septuagesima Sunday, based on the parable of the vineyard, exalts the 'grobbyng aboute þe erþe' of 'þe comyne peple', their 'erynge, and dungynge, and sowynge, and harwynge'. The commons are the root of the three types of workers in the spiritual vineyard. With their 'trwe labour', they 'bere vp and susteyne þe oþere tweie parties of þe chirche, þat is: kny3tes and clerkis'.[42] In *Lanterne of Li3t*, Christ's true Church is described as the elect. The 'praedestinati' are represented by each of the three estates, but the 'symple labureris' are mentioned first. They 'parten her trewe traueile; þerfore þei representen þe good

---

[40] *The Clerk's Tale*, IV. 206–7.

[41] *Select English works of John Wyclif*, ed. Thomas Arnold (Oxford, 1869–71), 3 vols., iii. 475; hereafter referred to as Arnold; cf. similar views in ibid. 415 and Matthew, 425.

[42] *Lollard sermons*, ed. Cigman, p. 86/206–14; cf. Arnold, iii. 207. Christ's church is also figured according to the normative tripartite division in *Jack Upland*, and here, the office of the commons is to 'truli laboure for þe sustinaunce of hem silf, & for prestis and for lordis doynge wel her office', *Jack Upland, Friar Daw's Reply and Upland's Rejoinder*, ed. P. L. Heyworth (Oxford, 1968), p. 54/16–17. In *Super cantica sacra* labouring the earth is seen, not as a sign of filth, but as a spiritual necessity, Arnold, iii. 30–1. Thomas Wimbledon also uses the parable of the vineyard to model the three estates of society, stating that it is the duty of the labourers to 'trauayle bodily and wiþ here sore swet geten out of þe erþe bodily liflode for hem and for oþer parties', *Wimbledon's Sermon: Redde rationem villicationis tue: a Middle English sermon of the fourteenth century*, ed. I. K. Knight (Pittsburgh, 1967), p. 63/44–6.

loue of þe Hooli Goost'.[43] With a reconfiguration of the tradition of peasant contempt, here, poor simple labourers are seen as the first group of God's elect because they share out the fruits of their honest labour.

This privileging of the work of the third estate is a common strain in Wycliffite texts. Allegiance is declared to the normative, tripartite division of society into lords, clerics, and labourers,[44] but closer inspection reveals a distinctive treatment of this topos. *Jack Upland* draws an analogy between the three estates and the persons of the Trinity. Upland states that the three estates were created by God, with the lords to represent the Father, priests to represent the Son, 'and þe comouns to presente þe good lastinge wille of þe Holi Goost'.[45] Transgression against this tripartite ordering of civil society or the Church is hotly condemned. An expansion to a sermon written for the first Sunday in Lent criticizes the sin of pride and upward mobility in all three estates, but the poor are seen to be less blameworthy than the lords and clergy.[46] Indeed, the conclusion offers a remedy against social strife by enjoining the hearer to bestow generous alms on the truly poor. This will be pleasing to God, 'help of alle seyntis, and þe endles blisse of heuene'. The saints, who can help to bring the congregation to the 'blisse of heuene' are said to have been 'pore men'.[47] While the sermon is anxious to support the three-estate structure and criticize any estate that usurps its allotted role, the poor are seen to be potentially less blameworthy, and closer to the promise of eternal life, than the other two estates.

Often, in criticisms of the third estate, it is lawyers and merchants who are singled out rather than the poor labourer, as in William Taylor's sermon, where merchants are condemned for enhancing their

[43] *The Lanterne of Li3t*, ed. Lilian M. Swinburn (EETS OS 151 1917), p. 33/11–13.

[44] See *English Wycliffite sermons*, iv. 15. The tract *Tractatus de Regibus* states briefly and simply that society is comprised of these three estates, *Four English political tracts*, ed. J.-P.Genet, 6 and 14.

[45] *Jack Upland*, p. 54/4–10. *The clergy may not hold property* likewise compares each of the three estates to the respective figures of the Trinity. This formulation figures God's Church. The commons correspond to the true love or good will which the Holy Spirit owes to þe father and to the Son. Consequently, the commons 'owiþ true loue & obedyente wille to þe statis of lordis & prestis', Matthew, 363.

[46] *Lollard sermons*, ed. Cigman, p. 137/207–11. This sermon contains a rare example of more economically tuned criticism of the labourers than is common in Wycliffite texts. They are wretched knaves who plough and cart, who, nonetheless, desire costly apparel, and whereas they used to serve for ten or twelve shillings in a year, now demand twenty or thirty, plus a livery to boot, pp. 137–9.

[47] Ibid. 147–8.

wealth and worldly station 'bi vnleeful meenes'.[48] *Of Servants and Lords* criticizes the guile of merchants and lawyers alongside the deceitfulness of servants: the latter 'traueilen faste' in the presence of their master but in his absence are idle, and mess about unproductively, claiming that they are unable to work harder and more honestly than they do. Gower might have written this, but not, perhaps the sentence that comes after: '& ȝit generaly in clerkis regneþ most gile, for þei disceyuen men bi here veyn preieris & pardons & indulgencis'.[49] While there is nothing exclusively Wycliffite in this particular criticism, the tract as a whole is much more lenient towards the vices of the first and third estates than it is to the second. Of all the estates, it is the clerics who are the most vicious.

The exculpation of the third estate from the grievous sins committed by the second pervades *Þe Ten Comaundementis.* Their faults are attributed to the neglect of the clergy. Surprisingly, there is no criticism of peasant idleness.[50] Instead: 'pore men of þo comyne, for hor bisye travel, synnen lesse in envye and in oþer synnes þen done men above hom þat traveilen not þus'.[51] Priests are seen as far more idle than labourers, a sin which is much more damnable in them as they have the higher office. And while labourers sin in lechery because they go together 'as bestis', priests are not only lecherous themselves, but, more seriously, abuse the system of absolution, as a result of which labourers are deprived of the possibility of atoning for their sin.[52] *Þe Ten Comaundementis* is characteristic of Wycliffite texts in its overt support for a normative three-estate structure, while privileging the plight of the poor labourer who is seen to be the victim of the corruption and abuses of members of the Church.[53]

[48] *The sermon of William Taylor* in *Two Wycliffite texts*, ed. Anne Hudson (EETS OS 301 1993), ll. 439–42; cf. Matthew, 185–6, where merchants are criticized for maintaining the great houses of the friars; and pp. 182 and 234 (on lawyers), and pp. 237–8 (on both).

[49] Matthew, 238. Cf. *The order of priesthood*, where priests are said to be 'more worldly & vicious þan þe comune peple, þat bi hem þe peple takiþ ensaumple & boldnesse in synne', Matthew, 167, and *Of prelates*, where prelates are blamed for the wickedness of the lords, clerics, and commons, and said to lead them to hell for breaking of God's commandments, Matthew, 88.

[50] Cf. *Jack Upland*, ll. 40–2, where it is Antichrist who urges the commons to leave their true labour and become idle. The traditional criticism of labourers is diverted into a criticism of the father of the false church. [51] Arnold, iii. 133.

[52] Ibid. 166.

[53] Cf. *Lollard sermons*, ed. Cigman, p. 240/1145 where clerics are said to prevent literacy in the third estate, and actively to lead labourers astray, Matthew, 94, and to oppress the commons by magnifying their sermons above the law of God, *Lanterne*, p. 120/10–11.

In texts such as *De Blasphemia Contra Fratres*, support for the labourer against the vices of the clergy is given a radical twist. The 'foundement' of the church is said to be 'comyners and laboreres'. However, more 'ordiris and sectis' have been 'clotirde on hom'. This is seen to be contrary to God's ordinance because these new sects do not labour for the profit of the Church and are instead 'raveyners' who rob the people. Since the new orders have come in, the Church has been 'payred in everiche membre'.[54] Friars, monks, and false prelates are seen in Wycliffite texts to be superfluous to the three-estate structure, to be outside society in ways reminiscent of how the discourse of contempt figured the labourer as 'other' and the antithesis of civilization. In contrast to the necessary work of the labourers who are the foundation of the Church, new orders are an idle superfluity. In a sermon on the parable of the vineyard for Septuagesima Sunday, the labourers delve around the roots in case evil herbs grow and 'bastard braunchis wiþowten byleue'. These branches must be cut away because they represent the superfluity in the Church, the prelates whom God has not ordained and who contravene His ordering of the estates.[55] Wycliffite texts maintain that the three estates should be sufficient without the new orders which are not grounded.[56] In a rewriting of the language of social description, friars, monks, canons, and emperors' clerks are seen as an additional estate which is outside God's ordained structure of the Church.[57]

This superfluous estate is seen to compromise obedience to secular and civil rule.[58] The writer of *Of Servants and Lords* urges all people to be content with their allotted role, and counsels obedience to earthly lords with fear, quaking, and trembling. Yet, he says, the devil moves some men to say that Christian men need not be servants to heathen lords—nor to Christian—because they are brethren in blood and Christ redeemed Christian men on the cross with his blood.[59] Far from being

---

[54] Arnold, iii. 418.

[55] *English Wycliffite sermons*, ed. Anne Hudson, i. 380–81/53–68; cf. p. 512/75–85 where the three estates established according to God's law are contrasted to the new sects; and Arnold, iii. 239 where the friars are again called bastard branches, crept in by the devil. By contrast, Wimbledon likens the branches of the vineyard to sins which priests must cut away with the sword of their tongue, *Wimbledon's Sermon*, p. 63/39–41.

[56] Matthew, 364.

[57] Arnold, iii. 184.

[58] On Wyclif's theory of dominion and discussion by its followers, see Hudson, *Premature reformation*, 46, 362, and 366–7.

[59] Matthew, 227–43.

in cahoots with seditious rebels, as Walsingham, Usk, and Knighton accused, this follower of Wyclif deplores the civil disobedience which stems from misplaced belief in commonality of all things. It is also important that the formulation of this statement removes the blame from members of the third estate, and attributes such notions of equality to the 'fend', the father of the Church of Antichrist.

While Wycliffite texts portray the commons performing their duty meekly and truly,[60] worldly priests and feigned religious trumpet their 'newe feyned obedience founden of synful men', which was never taught or commanded by Christ.[61] In this splitting of the dual legacy of peasant discourse, the poor labourer is shown to be a model of civil obedience while the friars strive against secular and civil authority. Jack Upland states that the various sects brought in by Antichrist are not obedient to bishops, liegemen, or kings because they neither till nor sow, weed, or reap. They are without place.[62] In contrast to the labourer, they perform no necessary work and cannot be accommodated within the structure of human society. It is not peasants who make the land lawless, but the friars.[63] In a reregistering of 1381 anti-peasant discourse, *Þe Grete Sentence of Curs Expouned* states: 'alle þe newe lawis þat clerkis han maad ben sutilly conjectid by ypocrisie, to brynge doun power and regalie of lordis and kyngis þat God ordeynede, and to make hem self lordis, and alle at here dom.'[64]

Instead of perceiving the commons to be a threat to social order, they are seen to be the victims of the lawlessness of the sects and prelates who have no place. Through building, the sects destroy the pasture that ought to be in common to produce food;[65] they live in rich houses while the labourers are condemned to poverty,[66] and the privileges of the sects rob the poor.[67] In contrast to the pomp and luxury of these new orders, workmen are forced to beg even if their work beasts are distressed, and their wife and children hungry and naked;[68] poor men labour, but new sects waste their goods, both through wicked pomp

[60] Matthew, 276.
[61] Ibid. 279–80; cf. ibid. 38, where prelates are asked to cease slandering 'pore men' by saying that they will not obey their lords.
[62] *Jack Upland*, p. 57/69–78.
[63] Arnold, iii. 384.
[64] Ibid. 298.
[65] *English Wycliffite sermons*, i. 266/53–5.
[66] *SEWW* 85/72; Matthew, 186.
[67] Ibid. 97, 118, 128–9.
[68] Matthew, 214.

and self-indulgence, and drinking at taverns.[69] The bread of poor men is turned into masonry: sects have fine buildings and the poor, hollow bodies and shrunken flesh.[70] Friars are seen to deceive the lords and commons through their false teaching, such as holidays for saints, and articles of belief which deny poor men's rights.[71] The poor labourer is exonerated while traits of traditional anti-peasant discourse: lying, greed, luxury, ignorance, and sloth, are transferred to the new orders and prelates.

Further, it is the superfluous estate rather than the peasantry who are keen to usurp social rank. They behave like kings and lords, merchants and reeves, and prefer to ape secular lordship rather than engage in poor, honest labour.[72] The commons bear the burden of this social climbing, being oppressed by the taxes necessary to support this superfluous estate.[73] Friars, monks, and prelates are seen both to flout their clerical estate and to rob the commonwealth by stealing temporalities that ought to belong to secular lords. *Þe Grete Sentence of Curs* accuses worldly prelates of slander for claiming that they live as Christ and his disciples did in apostolic poverty. This is seen to camouflage 'here owene raveyne, bi whiche þei stelen fro lordis and comyns here temperal lordischip and goodis . . . ȝif it be resonable þat a man schal be hangid for stelyng of fourtene pens, moche more schulden þes blasphemeris of God, þat stelen so many lordischipis and temperal goodis from comynte of seculeris, and wasten hem in synne'.[74] The writer argues that prelates would rather 'rere baner aȝenst þe kyng and his lordis and comyns, þan temperal lordischipis schulden turne to þe kyng and lordis, and þei on spiritualte, as God ordeyned'.[75] In contrast to the humble obedience of the poor labourer, Wycliffite texts figure the estate without order as treacherous thieves, and agents of civil dissent.

The insistence of prelates to gather tithes is also seen as a sign of their usurpation of social rank and their oppression of the poor. Nicholas

[69] Ibid. 149; Arnold, iii. 474; Matthew, 152.

[70] *Lanterne*, p. 38/3–14; Von Nolcken, *Rosarium*, p. 70/24–31.

[71] Arnold, iii. 233; 490; 455.

[72] Matthew, 139; *Lollard sermons*, ed. Cigman, 137; Matthew, 366; 172; 265 and 376.

[73] e.g. ibid. 22; 233; 279.

[74] Arnold, iii. 292.

[75] Ibid. 276. In repeating the charge, the writer refers to 'oure' king, lords, and commons, to invoke a discourse of solidarity against the prelates, p. 276. In *Wynnere and Wastoure*, to raise a banner ('rere baner') against the king is seen to be a sign of treason which deserves death, ll. 131–3.

Hereford, in his Ascension Day sermon, argued that if the king were to remove the possessions and riches of these orders as he should, then he would not have to tax the poor commons.[76] Writers on this subject are at pains to make a difference between the withdrawing of tithes from worldly prelates, and the withholding of rents from secular lords: 'summe men þat ben out of charite sclaundren pore prestis wiþ þis errour, þat seruantis or tenauntis may lawefully wiþholde rentis & seruyce fro here lordis whanne lordis ben opynly wickid in here lyuynge'.[77] The agents of civil disobedience are seen to be members, not of the third estate, but the second. The idealized view of the rural poor labourer that emerges in Wycliffite texts serves as a foil against which to contrast the superfluity and corruption of the material Church. The commons, through their honest toil and true obligation to secular authority, are seen to be more worthy and meritorious than the grasping superfluity and luxury of the material Church.

In reversing the orthodox relationship between the third and second estates, Wycliffite texts maintain that the 'lewed', or labourers, are better priests than the temporal clergy of the new orders. The discourse of bestial animal imagery is frequently mobilized in this reconfiguration: the superfluous estate are characterized as wolves of hell,[78] bears,[79] dogs,[80] hounds returning to their vomit,[81] vipers,[82] and, swine.[83] They are given over to drunkenness and gluttony; bodily excesses of all kinds,[84] and associated with muck, dirt, and stink.[85] The trope of the bizarre appearance of the peasant is reregistered to frame comments on the irregular clothing of the new orders,[86] and the description of dissident peasants as a rebellious multitude, threatening the order of civilization, appears as the multitude of new orders without number which cause strife and dissension within the realm.[87]

---

[76] See the edition by Simon N. Forde, 'Nicholas Hereford's Ascension Day sermon 1382', *Medieval Studies*, 51 (1989), 205–41; and discussion in Hudson, '"Poor preachers, poor men"', 50–1.   [77] Matthew, *Of servants and lords*, 229.

[78] e.g. *English Wycliffite sermons*, i. 439/37; Matthew, 149 and 151.

[79] e.g. *English Wycliffite sermons*, i. 439/38.

[80] e.g. Matthew, 104, 110, 319; Arnold, iii. 440.

[81] e.g. Matthew, 253.

[82] e.g. ibid. 161; *Lanterne*, p. 111/12.

[83] e.g. Matthew, 156, 165–6, 243.

[84] e.g. ibid. 152, 165–6, 182, 267–8.

[85] e.g. ibid. 134, 182,

[86] e.g. *Jack Upland*, pp. 59–60/130–43.

[87] e.g. Matthew, 162, 212, 236, 222.

And, while traditionally it was the peasant who was ridiculed for his ignorance, in Wycliffite texts this accolade goes to the superfluity of clergy. Ignorant of the Bible, prelates blabber all day like magpies and jays from costly books of 'mannus ordynaunce'.[88] They are more worldly and vicious than the common people, and people laugh them to scorn for their ignorant leading of services and their reading of the gospel and epistle, and yet: 'ignoraunce of good lif & goddis hestis is werse þan ignoraunce of latyn or of ony oþer langage'.[89] The superfluous estate is seen to be ignorant not only of clerical knowledge, but more importantly, also of the simple good works, and true faith of honest Christians. Members of the third estate are, in this respect, better priests than the temporal clergy. Lollards claimed 'þat þer schulde be bot oo degre aloone of prestehod in þe chirche of God, and euery good man is a prest and haþ power to preche þe word of God'.[90] *Lanterne of Liзt* notes that Christ's disciples were not graduate men in schools, but 'symple ydiotis' inspired in heavenly teaching by the grace of the Holy Spirit.[91]

With the espousal of such beliefs, the second estate becomes, not simply superfluous, but disappears altogether. The sacerdotal duties of the temporal priesthood are better performed by the third estate; absolution, for example, according to the writer of *Of Confesssion* might be performed better by good 'lewed men' than wicked priests.[92] While worldly prelates despoil the poor, simple priests help them and bestow alms,[93] and true, honest priests advise the commons how to preserve charity and reason.[94] Together with the denial of transubstantiation in the sacrament of the Eucharist, and the belief that auricular confession is unnecessary since contrition alone is necessary to wipe out sin, sacerdotal authority is eliminated and the dividing line between clerical and lay removed.[95] The Wycliffite investment in the honest simplicity of the poor third estate redraws the map of social relations. Overt support for the normative tripartite estate structure is predicated on the existence of

[88] Ibid. 194.

[89] Ibid. 167.

[90] *SEWW* 19/16–18. The quotation is from the accusations made against the Lollards by the bishops.

[91] *Lanterne*, p. 5/16–19.

[92] Matthew, 333.

[93] Arnold, iii. 293.

[94] Arnold, iii. 359.

[95] For further discussion on these points and views of Wyclif and his adherents, see Hudson, *Premature reformation*, 325–7.

a fourth, superfluous estate, represented by the new orders and false prelates. Even more radical is the logical extension of the argument for the temporal disendowment of the clergy, the redefinition of the Church as the predestined congregation of the Church in heaven,[96] and the belief in the priesthood of all believers. All these produce a model of civic society predicated on a two-estate structure: the lords and the commons.

Such is the Wycliffite investment in the 'sanctitas' of the 'lewed' that writers adopt the role and voice of members of the third estate as a narrative position from which to preach their views. *The Twelve Conclusions of the Lollards* affixed to the doors of Westminster Hall during the parliament of 1395, demanding the reformation of the Church, are presented by 'we pore men, tresoreris of Cryst and his apostlis'.[97] Lollard preachers appropriated for themselves the epithets 'true', 'pore', and 'simple' as terms of approbation in opposition to the temporal possessions of the Church. In contrast to the deceit, corruption, and false preaching of the material Church the words of the humble Lollard preacher are true.[98] Friars persecute those who speak the truth,[99] while the author of *The Twenty Five Articles*, states that 'pore men' answer accusations made against them honestly, and: 'þat if þei erren in ony poynt of þeire onswerynge, þei submytten hem to be correctid openly to þo kynge and his chivalrye and þo clergye and comyns, ʒe, by deþe, if hit be justly demed lawefulle'.[100] The voice of the poor and the honest is subject to temporal correction and castigation

---

[96] See *SEWW* 116/21–6: 'but, howeuere we speken in diuerse names or licknessis of þis holi chirche, þei techen nouʒt ellis but oo name, þat is to seie, "Þe congregacioun, or gedering-togidir of feiþful soulis þat lastingli kepen feiþ and troupe, in word and in dede, to God and to man, and reisen her lijf in siker hope of mercy and grace and blisse at her ende, and ouercoueren, or hillen, þis bilding in perfite charite þat schal not faile in wele ne in woo"'.

[97] *SEWW* 24/1. In his written defence of the charges against him Walter Brut terms himself an 'agricola'—a husbandman—despite his academic education, see *Registrum Johannis Trefnant*, ed. W. W. Capes (Canterbury and York Society 1916), 257–8.

[98] See Gloria Cigman, '"Luceat lux vestra": the Lollard preacher as truth and light', *RES* NS 40 (1989), 479–96. See also *SEWW* 146, n. 50, and the Lollard use of the term 'true men' or 'true cristen men' to refer to themselves. Hudson notes that Wyclif often refers to himself as 'quidam fidelis' which accords with the claim that Wyclif and his followers were alone in the true line of descent from Christ and the primitive Church. See also, Hudson, 'A Lollard Sect Vocabulary', in *Lollards and their books*, 165–80.

[99] e.g. Arnold, iii. 231.

[100] Ibid. 457. Cf. Matthew, 225, where the lords and commons are called upon to correct the clergy.

in a way that the members of the superfluous estate, through their contravention of obedience to secular authority, refuse. As Justice observes of the 1395 bill, in claiming to issue from the hands of 'pore men' Wycliffite texts speak as if they embody 'the collective voice of England's poor'.[101] This is diametrically opposed to Gower's narrative strategy in *Vox Clamantis*. So alarmed is Gower by the challenge to civil order posed by the greedy, exploitative members of the third estate, that in Book V he mobilizes 'the people's voice' against them, a voice which, in the words of David Aers, calls for the law to launch against them an 'unspecified but terrorizing pre-emptive strike'.[102]

For Gower, the figure of the ploughman is the source of the 'evil disposition widespread among the common people'.[103] This remark is representative of a sub-strain of anti-peasant discourse which figures those who work at the plough as the very worst representatives of the peasant class. Just as peasant discourse as a whole is fractured into an ameliorative and a pejorative strain, however, so too is the tradition of the representation of the ploughman.[104] There is biblical warrant for the plough itself as a sign of fruitful labour, and by extension, a metaphor for good preaching,[105] and a sermon attributed to Berthold speaks of Christ willingly ploughing the field of Christianity himself, with the wood and iron of the plough symbolizing the wood and iron of the Cross.[106] Before the late fourteenth century, possibly the most well-known favourable depiction of a ploughman, rather than a symbolic plough, was in the poem *De Duello Militis et Aratoris*, which, as Edward Wheatley has shown, was part of the *Liber Catonianus*, a standard compilation of school-texts used in the Middle Ages.[107]

Until the appearance of the figures of the ploughman in Chaucer's

---

[101] Steven Justice, 'Lollardy', in *CHMEL* 662–89, pp. 672–3.

[102] David Aers, '"Vox populi" and the literature of 1381', in *CHMEL* 440.

[103] Gower, *Vox*, V. 574.

[104] See Freedman, *Images*, 223–35.

[105] See Proverbs 12: 11 and 20: 4; Isaiah 28: 24 and 1 Corinthians 9: 10. For ploughing and preaching see Stephen A. Barney, 'The plowshare of the tongue: the progress of a symbol from the Bible to *Piers Plowman*', *Medieval Studies*, 35 (1973), 261–93. This metaphor was used in Gregory's *Moralia*, and was thus widely disseminated through the Middle Ages; see Freedman, *Images*, 34.

[106] Berthold von Regensburg, *Vollständige ausgabe seiner predigten*, I: 14, quoted in Freedman, *Images*, 380, n. 77. Freedman also notes the existence of a Byzantine Hymn in which Mary is described as the 'nourisher of the loving ploughman', p. 224.

[107] Edward Wheatley, 'A selfless ploughman and the Christ/Piers conjunction in Langland's *Piers Plowman*', *Notes and Queries*, 40 (238) (1993), 135–42.

General Prologue and *Piers Plowman*, however, the tradition of representing the plougher rather than the plough was overwhelmingly negative.[108] The progenitor of the husbandman was seen to be Cain, the
first to till the land, while the spiritual ancestor of shepherds, and by
extension, priests, was Abel. Tillers were thus associated with disobedience, murder, fratricide, and outcasts. Further, it was shepherds, not
ploughmen, who were the first to receive word of the birth of Christ.[109]
Artistic representations of Cain as ploughman are wholly pejorative: for
instance, the portrait in the Holkham Bible which shows him ploughing furiously, but pointlessly.[110]

   Wycliffite texts continue the tradition of the negative representation
of Cain, but instead of representing the peasant labourer, he represents
the superfluous fourth estate. In counterpoint, shepherds, represented
by Abel, are the *true* priests. A sermon for the birth of Christ says that
angels led the shepherds to the nativity because they lived a simple and
holy life: 'for God louede Abel betture þan Caym þat was his broþur.
And þe furste was an herde, and þe toþur a tylinge man; and tylynge
men han more of craft þan han herdus in þer dedis.'[111] This is as
unflattering a view of tilling men as exists in Wycliffite texts. Here,
while Abel is associated with an honest, simple life, the symbolic force
of Cain receives no mention. Elsewhere, the progeny of Cain are the
damned, while Abel's children are persecuted true priests.[112] *The Clergy
May Not Hold Property* states that Abel, the true shepherd is dead, and
Cain, as possession, usurps the care of souls.[113] The true Church is Abel's

---

[108] See Elizabeth D. Kirk, 'Langland's plowman and the recreation of fourteenth-century
religious metaphor', *YLS* 2 (1988), 1–21. The case of Chaucer and Langland is discussed
below. In Iolo Goch's *Cwydd y Llafurwr* the figure of the ploughman is praised as both a
literal and figurative lynchpin of a stable, ordered society, see Morgan Thomas Davies,
'Plowmen, patrons and poets: Iolo Goch's *Cwydd y Llafurwr* and some matters of Wales in the
fourteenth century', *Medievalia et Humanistica*, 24 (1997), 51–74. Davies argues that the figure
of the ploughman also validates Iolo's profession as a minstrel. Andrew Breeze has argued that
Piers Plowman was an influence on Iolo Goch's poem, 'A Welsh addition to the *Piers Plowman*
group?', *Notes and Queries*, 238, NS 40 (1993), 142–51. Camille, *Mirror in parchment*, 188, notes
the depiction of a foolish ploughman trying to work an illogical assemblage, a nonsense
plough, which does not touch the soil, in the margins of the East Anglian Gorleston Psalter.
[109] See Freedman, *Images*, 34.
[110] See Edmund Reiss, 'The symbolic plow and plowman and the Wakefield *Mactacio
Abel*', *Studies in Iconography*, 5 (1979), 3–30, p. 11. See also Kirk, 'Langland's plowman', 3.
[111] *English Wycliffite sermons*, vol. ii. 209–10/88–100. In other sermons, there is the standard
equation between Christ and the shepherd, *English Wycliffite sermons*, i. 439/18–19.
[112] *English Wycliffite sermons*, ii. 106/6–15; cf. *Lollard sermons*, ed. Cigman, p.30/699–703.
[113] Matthew, 374.

while the fiend's Church belongs to Cain.[114] Wycliffite writers were not slow to catch onto the acrostic potential of the Middle English spelling of Cain as 'Caim' and to spell out the initial letters of the four orders of friars from his name.[115] The friars are linked with Cain in a variety of texts, and their friaries referred to as Cain's castles. The writer of *De Officio Pastorali* states that true priests should not belong to a false order, but live in poverty as Christ did: 'not in hye castels of caym & lustful fode as boris in sty'.[116]

The corollary of the Wycliffite alignment of friars and false prelates with Cain is that the figure of the ploughman is freed from all negative characteristics. Instead, Christ himself is seen as an earth-tiller;[117] there is praise for the labour that the apostles performed with their hands, in contrast to criticism of hypocrites who disdain such travail.[118] When contrasting the true Christian life of the third estate to the vicious living of the prelacy, the distinction between the merit of shepherd and ploughman is collapsed. They, and their prayers, are seen to be equally meritorious in the sight of God if they live well and love God well.[119] Most crucially, the good ploughman is oppositional to the evil prelate or friar:[120]

Cristen men shulden wel wite þat good lif of a plouman is as myche wrþ to þe soule as preyer of þis frere, al ȝif it profite sumwhat.[121]

A symple pater noster of a plouȝman þat his in charite is betre þan a þousand

---

[114] *Lanterne*, p.133/14–15.

[115] Wyclif had used the acrostic in *Trialogus*, ed. G. Lechler (Oxford, 1869), iv. 33, p. 362. Apart from Fitzralph, who used the acrostic in one of his London sermons in 1357, see Penn R. Szittya, *The antifraternal tradition in medieval England* (Princeton, 1986), 129, there appear to be no instances of the use of this acrostic outside medieval texts; see further, Barr, *Signes and sothe*, 126–7. Szittya (pp. 229–30) comments that the friars are linked with Cain because he is the archetype of all those who wander without place or number within a divine order, governed by the principles laid down in Wisdom 2: 21. Friars are also invested with the characteristics of Cain even when he is not named, for instance, as the cursed of God, Matthew, 91, and as aliens, like Jews, murderers, and other enemies to the realm such as Frenchmen, Arnold, iii. 492–3; 516.

[116] Matthew, 425; cf. p. 12. *Jack Upland*, p. 58/86; and for discussion, Aston, 'Caim's castles'.

[117] Christ is depicted elsewhere as a tiller, drawing on John 15: 1 and 20: 15, and Christ is shown with a spade in a fifteenth-century alabaster; see Freedman, *Images*, 224–5, fig. 11.

[118] Matthew, 236.

[119] Matthew, 173 and 321.

[120] *Upland's Rejoinder* accuses friars of stealing ploughmen from the true life, p. 109/261–2.

[121] *English Wycliffite sermons*, ed. Anne Hudson (Oxford, 1990), iii. 313/20–1.

massis of coueitouse prelatis & veyn religious ful of coueitise & pride & fals flaterynge & norischynge of synne.[122]

In Wycliffite texts, the figure of the ploughman is an exemplar of poverty, simplicity, honesty, and *necessary* social labour in contrast to the idle cunning and superfluity of ungrounded members of the second estate. These latter, like Cain, are treacherous villains, and like Cain, are outcasts both from earthly civil society, and from heaven.

Of course, it cannot be claimed that the revalorization of the negative image of the ploughman is exclusively Wycliffite. There remain the instances of Chaucer's ploughman in the *Prologue*, and the figure of Piers in *Piers Plowman*.[123] Yet, when these are compared to what is the fullest exposition of the ploughman in Wycliffite texts, namely Peres in *Pierce the Ploughman's Crede*, the distinctiveness of the Lollard appropriation of the ploughman figure is apparent. While the undoubtedly Wycliffite *Plowman's Tale* was fathered onto the Ploughman from *The General Prologue*, Chaucer's figure is exemplary, but lacking in the distinctively Wycliffite conception of the figure.[124] To be sure, he lives in peace and perfect charity, loves God and his neighbour best, is an honest labourer,[125] and works for the poor without payment, none of which would be out of place in a Wycliffite text (though a Lollard reader might have frowned on his prompt payment of tithes).[126] That he is cast

[122] Matthew, 274.

[123] The ideal of kingship in *Richard the Redeles* is said to be to labour on the law 'as lewde men on plowes' (III. 267).

[124] For reasons of space (and of date) I have excluded *The Plowman's Tale* from this study. While the frame of the tale juxtaposes the virtuous toil of the ploughman against the vices of the clergy, and has the ploughman consoling the griffin at the conclusion, it is likely that this is a sixteenth-century addition to fourteenth-century material; see Andrew Wawn, 'The genesis of *The Plowman's Tale*', YES 2 (1972), 21–40; id., 'Chaucer, *The Plowman's Tale* and reformation propaganda: the testimonies of Thomas Godfray and *I Playne Piers*', *Bulletin of the John Rylands Library*, 56 (1973), 174–92; and Anne Hudson, 'The legacy of *Piers Plowman*' in *A companion to* Piers Plowman, ed. John A. Alford (Berkeley, 1988), 251–66, p. 257. Some original lines do preserve the typical Wycliffite opposition between the virtuous ploughman and Antichrist's Church, however: 'What knoweth a tyllour at the plowe | The Popes name and what he hate? | Hys Crede suffyseth to hym ynowe' (453–5), and 1041–4, of the monks: 'had they ben out of religioun, | They must have honged at the plowe, | Threshynge and dykynge fro towne to towne, | With sory mete, and not halfe ynowe', quoted from *Six ecclesiastical satires*, ed. James Dean (Kalamazoo, Mich., 1991).

[125] Jill Mann, *Medieval estates satire*, notes that this, and the other positive qualities of the ploughman might be seen as an inversion of the usual derogatory remarks about peasants, pp. 69–71.

[126] See Anne Hudson, *Premature reformation*, 342–5, for the range of Wycliffite views on the

as the brother of the virtuous Parson is suggestive of the Wycliffite link between the sanctity of ploughmen and poor priests,[127] but there is a crucial dimension lacking: this ploughman is not explicitly contrasted with figures from the superfluous fourth estate.[128] Further, in Chaucer's portrait, as Christina von Nolcken observes of the difference between *Piers Plowman* and Wycliffite texts, 'the perspective is bounded by the temporal, whereas the Wycliffites seek to superimpose the archetypal on the temporal'.[129] And what else is the Wycliffite splitting of the plough-man tradition, in order to impe Cain onto the friars, but one such superimposition?

The treatment of ploughmen in *Piers Plowman* is much more com-plex.[130] In addition to his appropriation by the 1381 rebels,[131] the figure of Piers was also the inspiration for the unequivocally Lollard *Pierce the Ploughman's Crede*.[132] It is not hard to see how a reader with Wycliffite sympathies might warm to the presentation of ploughmen in *Piers*.[133] In

granting of tithes. At the moderate end of the spectrum, Lollard writers were content with the granting of tithes even if they criticized draconian methods of obtaining them irrespec-tive of the circumstances of the payer. More radical was the view that the individual was due to pay his tithes so long as the recipient had earned them, and the most extreme that, in keep-ing with apostolic poverty, priests should not be paid tithes at all.

[127] Hudson, *Premature reformation*, 391, notes the closeness of the portrait of the Parson to Wyclif's ideal of apostolic priesthood, and further that there is, significantly, no mention of the Parson's celebration of the Mass or to his role as a confessor. Mann observes that the link between the Parson and Ploughman illustrates the close union inspired by two ideals of Christian virtue, *Medieval estates satire*, 68. Through the series of negatives in his portrait, the Parson is implicitly contrasted to corrupt contemporary priests, see ibid. 55–67.

[128] Mann notes his absence of suffering in contrast to ploughmen in *Piers Plowman*, *Medieval estates satire*, 72–3; a contrast which is applicable also to the depiction of ploughmen in Wycliffite texts.

[129] Christina von Nolcken, '*Piers Plowman*, the Wycliffites and *Pierce the Ploughman's Crede*', *YLS* 2 (1988), 71–102, p. 88.

[130] Mann suggests that Chaucer's Ploughman was influenced by *Piers*, *Medieval estates satire*, 68–73, and Helen Cooper examines the relationship between the two prologues in 'Langland's and Chaucer's Prologues', *YLS* 1 (1987), 71–81.

[131] For discussion of the rebels' letters which refer to *Piers Plowman*, see Hudson (*Premature reformation* and '*Piers Plowman* and the Peasants' Revolt'); Richard Firth Green, 'John Ball's letters'; Justice, *Writing and rebellion*, and Bowers, '*Piers Plowman* and the police'.

[132] *Pierce the Ploughman's Crede*, in *The Piers Plowman tradition*, ed. Barr. There is clear support for Wyclif (528–30) and Walter Brut (657–70).

[133] For the relationship between *Piers* and Wycliffite beliefs see Pamela Gradon, '*Piers Plowman* and the ideology of dissent', *PBA* 66 (1980), 179–205; Hudson, *Premature reforma-tion*, 398–408; David Lawton, 'Lollardy and the *Piers Plowman* tradition', *MLR* 76 (1981), 780–93. Lawton concludes that Lollards had Langlandian sympathies, p. 793; Justice, *Writing*

the *Prologue* ploughmen are 'ordeyned' for the profit of the whole community and fulfil their obligations, garnering what wasters, those who
'putten hem to pride' will consume.[134] While this does not reproduce
exactly the dynamic in Wycliffite texts whereby the ploughman is seen
to be necessary and the fourth estate superfluous, a Lollard reader might
'concretize' it to yield up this very sense.[135] Piers is Truth's 'pilgrym atte
plow for pouere mennes sake' (B. VI. 102),[136] and displays admirable
social husbandry in his organization of the ploughing of the half acre,
which, in its substitution for the pilgrimage, might have pleased the
sensibilities of a Lollard reader.[137] Although a labourer, Piers also appears
as a priestly figure; he opposes the priest in the tearing of the pardon
scene in the B text (B. VI. 105–48),[138] explains the significance of the
tree of Charity to Will (B. XVI. 21 ff.),[139] and is at the apex of the
apostolic ploughing at the conclusion of the poem (B. XIX. 214–337).
Most particularly, while it is Piers who establishes the Barn of Unity, it
is the friars, part of Antichrist's army, who cause its destruction by selling penance (B. XX. 53–64; 313–71). Conscience sets off at the end of
the poem seeking to *haue* Piers the Plowman in a quest that has been
seen as moving outside the institutional Church.[140]

and rebellion; von Nolcken, '*Piers Plowman*'; and Barr, *Signes and sothe*, 122–5. On ploughmen,
see Malcolm Godden, 'Plowmen and hermits in Langland's *Piers Plowman, RES* NS 35 (1984),
129–63.

[134] *Piers Plowman*, B. Prol. 119–20 and 20–2. See discussion of these lines by Cooper,
'Langland's and Chaucer's Prologues', 78–9.

[135] 'Concretization' is the term used by Wolfgang Iser to describe the way that the reader
realizes the schematic aspects of a text by filling in the gaps of indeterminacy it inevitably
contains, *The act of reading: a theory of aesthetic response* (Baltimore, 1978), 171–9. Szittya notes
that Piers is the true labourer, while the friars are the false beggars who do not work, *The
antifraternal tradition*, 284.

[136] The line is the same in A, but in C, altered to 'to pore and ryche' (VIII. 111).

[137] Lollard texts are generally, though not universally, hostile to physical acts of pilgrimage, see Hudson *Premature reformation*, 307–9.

[138] The quarrel is substantially abbreviated in C and the tearing of the pardon cut. Aers,
'"Vox populi"', notes how readers could have found in *Piers* congenial materials for dissent,
with Piers Plowman as the opposer of official priests, and finally the absent leader of what has
finally become a thoroughly corrupt Catholic Church, pp. 438–9.

[139] In the C text, Liberium Arbitrium replaces Piers, Passus XVIII.

[140] Kirk notes how Conscience seeks to 'haue', not to 'know' Piers Plowman—'to have
him means infinitely more than becoming a labourer', 'Langland's plowman', 19. On
leaving behind the institutional church, see David Aers, *Chaucer, Langland and the creative
imagination* (London, 1980), 61. See also Simpson, *Piers Plowman: an introduction to the B text*,
234–43.

Nothing in *Piers Plowman*, however, is straightforward. Criticism of the contemporary Church shares many issues with Wycliffite polemic, including the prophetic disendowment of the religious and their return to the pristine apostolic state (B. X. 316–329; cf. B. XV. 563: 'Takeþ hire landes, ye lordes, and let hem lyue by dymes; | If possession be poison, and inparfite hem make'), but when it comes to the friars in Passus XX, Conscience, in a rather enigmatic line, wishes that they had a 'fyndyng' rather than oppose him and flatter out of need (B. XX. 384–5). Clearly, the friars are figured as corrupt in the poem (and useless as guides to Will in Passus VIII), but there is no suggestion of the typical Wycliffite complaint that they are 'ungrounded'.[141] Nor are the friars associated with Cain. Wit's long disquisition on the progeny of Cain in B. Passus IX. 119–60 reproduces all the negative characteristics with which he was invested, but to characterize illegitimacy, not to vilify unnecessary mendicants.[142]

As in Wycliffite texts, there is passionate concern with the poor, most movingly in two additions to the C text (IX. 70–158; XIII. 1–96),[143] while the A text finishes with the lines:

> Þanne pore peple as plouȝmen, and pastours of bestis,
> Souteris and seweris—suche lewide iottis
> Percen wiþ a *Paternoster* þe paleis of heuene
> Wiþoute penaunce at here partyng, into þe heiȝe blisse.

> (A. XI. 310–13)

The similarity to the elevation of the 'paternoster' of a ploughman over the masses of a priest in *How Satan and His Priests*[144] is striking. And while in the B and C texts, the dramatic force of these lines is attenuated since they do not form a conclusion, the revisions bring the sentiment closer in line to Wycliffite representations of the third estate. There is a progressive elimination of the artisan class. 'Souteres' remain in B (X. 461) but 'pouere commune laborers' are added (460). C runs:

---

[141] Szittya notes that they are the only religious group whose institution poses a danger to the church, *The antifraternal tradition*, 284.

[142] The characteristics listed are exactly those that are grafted onto Cain in Wycliffite texts but there is no explicit association with the friars in *Piers*. Clergy prophesies that before the king comes to reform the clergy, Cain shall awake, but 'Dowel shal dyngen hym adoun and destruye his myȝte' (B. X. 329– not in C). There is no explicit association between Cain and superfluous orders.

[143] See Derek Pearsall, '"Lunatyk lollares" in *Piers Plowman*', in Piero Boitani and Anna Torti, eds., *Religion in the poetry and drama of the late middle ages in England* (Cambridge, 1990), 163–78.   [144] Matthew, 274.

Ne none sonnere ysaued ne saddere in bileue
Then ploughmen and pastours and pore comune peple.
Lewed lele laboreres and land-tulyng peple
Persen with a *Paternoster* paradys oþer heuene
And passen purgatorie penaunceles for here parfit bileue.

(XI. 296–300)

Shepherds are still present, but the presence of tillers is amplified at the expense of the artisan class, which produces a profile of the third estate very much in keeping with Wycliffite representation. 'Parfit bileue' ('pure' in B. X. 464) is also added in both texts, which suggests that the faith of husbandmen is truer than that of the clever clerics with all their book learning.

Once again, however, as with the oppositional depiction of fraternal corruption and Piers's apostolic ploughing, the crucial dimension lacking is that the clergy are unnecessary. The relationship between the clergy and labourers is comparative ('sonner'; 'saddere'). In Wycliffite texts, the comparative is deployed to assert that husbandmen are necessary to society while the material Church is harmful and otiose.[145] There is a further important difference between the Wycliffite representation of the ploughman and that in *Piers*. In keeping with von Nolcken's distinction between archetypal and temporal representation, the figure of Piers, for all his typological transformations, is still recognizably an actual fourteenth-century ploughman.[146] For all the concern with the poor, and the amelioration of the ploughman figure, Langland does not idealize the third estate. As Christopher Dyer has shown, Piers is not a tenant labourer; he owns both his plough and his plot of land. He is a small landowner, and in Passus VI, he is shown to be pitted against the poorest of the rural poor. Piers's confrontation with the wastrel labourers foregrounds contemporary economic concerns and reproduces the kinds of tensions experienced in actual local villages.[147] Individual lines and passages of *Piers Plowman* can be adduced to show

[145] Hilton, *Class conflict*, 250, notes briefly that Wycliffite poems contrast the idle clergy, especially the friars, with the ploughman at work.

[146] Kirk explores this in detail ('Langland's plowman'). On the figural interpretation of Piers, see Elizabeth Salter, *Piers Plowman: an introduction* (Oxford, 1969), 83–105.

[147] Christopher C. Dyer, '*Piers Plowman* and plowmen: a historical perspective', *YLS* 8 (1995), 155–76. On Langland's treatment of labour issues, see Anne Middleton, 'Acts of vagrancy: the C Version "autobiography" and the Statute of 1388', in Steven Justice and Kathryn Kerby-Fulton, eds., *Written work: Langland, labor and authorship* (Philadelphia, 1997), 208–317.

compatibility with Wycliffite ideas, but taken as a whole, the poem does not reproduce the particular delineation of the third estate common in Wycliffite texts. Lacking is the sustained idealization of the rural poor as a foil against which to argue for the superfluity of monks, friars, and prelates.

Nor, despite the contemporary elevation of the authority of the figure of Piers over the author of the poem, does Piers emerge as the spokesman for the whole poem.[148] In *Pierce the Ploughman's Crede*, by contrast, the ultimate speaker of truth in the poem *is* the ploughman, whose voice at the conclusion merges with that of the narrator and the poet in his insistence on the truth of what he has told.

> . . . all that euer I haue seyd soth it me semeth
> And all that euer I haue writen is soth, as I trowe,
> And for amending of thise men is most that I write.　(836–8)

Entirely consonant with representations of the third estate in Wycliffite texts as 'pore' men and 'simple', endowed with a corrective voice fit to speak as reformers for the whole of civic society, this ploughman/narrator/poet is bearer of the truth against the calumny of 'thise men' the friars. The satiric strategy of the whole poem is based on the contrast between the virtuous ploughman and the corrupt friars.[149] The singularity of the friars: 'neyther in order ne out' (45), and their contravention of secular and ecclesiastical regulation is ingeniously exposed by having a representative of each of the four orders expose the illegitimacy of the others. All that Peres does when he condemns them is to confirm their very own words. While at ll. 511–14 and ll. 75–6, Peres draws back from a full-blooded condemnation of the existence of the friars per se by praising the founding ideals of St Francis, in ll. 482–7, he says that fraternal orders were instituted by the devil.[150] Satan sent them into the Church to destroy it:

---

[148] See Anne Middleton, 'William Langland's "kynde name": authorial signature and social identity in late fourteenth-century England', in Lee Patterson, ed., *Literary practice and social change in Britain, 1380–1530* (Berkeley, 1990), 15–82; and Barr, *Signes and sothe*, 5–7.

[149] David Lampe, 'The satiric strategy of *Peres the Ploughman's Crede*', in B. S. Levy and P. S. Szarmach, eds., *The alliterative tradition in the fourteenth century* (Kent, Oh., 1981), 69–80.

[150] This is in line with Wyclif's initial admiration of the friars because of their apostolic founding ideals. After the friars' denunciation of his views on the Eucharist, he turned against them, and between 1382 and 1384, denounced them in pamphlets and sermons; see A. Kenny, *Wyclif* (Oxford, 1985), 93–4; and A. Gwynn, *The English Austin friars in the time of Wyclif* (Oxford, 1940), 211–79.

> Of the kynrede of Caym he caste the freres,
> And founded hem on Farysens feyned for gode.   (486–7)[151]

As in other Wycliffite texts, the friars are the progeny of Cain, and additional to the Church; they are 'put in' by the devil (505–6). They are invested with all the traits of anti-peasant discourse which Wycliffites transfer to the friars: covetous ignorance (336–7; 357; 497; 591–2; 820); physical grotesqueness (244; 459); bodiliness (44–51; 55; 73; 92; 221–25; 339–40; 594); animals (225; 357; 375; 644; 648; 663); dirt (226; 644; 752); lying (359; 379); stealing (68–70); usurpation of social rank (204–5; 499); bizarre clothing (550–4; 608), and sloth (726). They also oppress the poor (216–18; 721–9).

Peres, with his honest toil, is a perfect example of labouring charity, offering to 'lene' the narrator 'lijflode' as soon as he meets him (445). Probably the most graphic example of the reregistration of peasant muck to symbolize the harsh virtue of true husbandry is the description of Peres wading ankle-deep through the fen, toes poking out of his tattered shoes, as he drives the plough. His four heifers are so painfully thin that you could count their ribs (symbolic presumably of the scarcity of preaching based on the four gospels). The painful poverty of his wife and children is further laid on with a trowel (421–42). In contrast to Piers, this ploughman is an idealized representative of the poorest rural labourer: 'Peres . . . the pore man, the plowe-man' (473). There is no suggestion that he owns the land he tills, nor even that the land is good; it seems to consist of sticky mire and ice.[152] The figure is socially deracinated: as in Wycliffite prose texts, there is no attempt to frame the peasant labourer within contemporary economic conditions.[153] The ploughman is a non-institutionalized true preacher who is able, and willing, to teach the 'lewed' narrator his creed, an act which the friars, too much concerned with conning money from him and slandering each other, were distressingly unable to perform. Peres is a true priest in contrast to the idle superfluity of the mendicant orders:

> Thei vsen russet also somme of this freres,
> That bitokneth trauaile and trewthe opon erthe.
> Bote loke whou this lorels labouren the erthe,

---

[151] Cf. the comparison of a friary to a 'heyghe helle-hous of Kaymes kynde' (559).

[152] Though, as Camille points out, ploughing was an activity which chiefly took place in winter, *Mirror in parchment*, 183.

[153] The exception is the criticism of the labourers demand for higher wages and livery, see n. 46 above.

But freten the frute that the folk full lellich biswynketh.
With trauail of trewe men thei tymbren her houses,

.   .   .   .

And ryght as dranes doth nought but drynketh vp the huny,
Whan been withe her bysynesse han brought it to hepe,
Right so, fareth freres with folke opon erthe;
They freten vp the furste-froyt and falsliche lybbeth.   (719–29)

The collectively responsible, true labour of the husbandman is contrasted with the false greed of the friars.[154] That which should belong to the ploughman (2 Timothy 2: 6: 'The husbandman that laboureth must be first partaker of the fruits') is gobbled up by the fraternal orders to nourish vain building and parasitic gluttony. Figuring the friars as drones places them outside the hard-working community of bees, and thus, outside civil society.[155] This passage encapsulates in miniature the textual dynamic of Lollard representations of the third estate. *Crede* is a straightforward verse depiction of the relationship between the second and third estates seen in Wycliffite prose texts.[156] While greatly amplified from the local vignettes in the prose, the presentation of the ploughman is much closer in spirit to these texts, than it is to *Piers Plowman*, however much the figure of Peres was inspired by Langland's poem.

Were Usk, Walsingham, and Knighton correct, then, in attributing civil sedition to Wyclif and his followers? The answer must be both yes and no. Wyclif condemned the murder of Archbishop Sudbury,[157] and there is no call in Wycliffite texts for all goods to be in common, or for any subversion of secular authority. And yet, the logical outcome of Wycliffite representations of the third estate is to rewrite the language of social description and to redraw the map of civil society in a fashion which resonates with the claims of the rebels. To uphold the sanctity of the third estate while arguing for the superfluity of the second, or

---

[154] Camille observes that the plough was an absolute essential in the life and prosperity of all levels of society, *Mirror in parchment*, 180.

[155] This, as Lawton has observed, 'Lollardy', 791, is very similar to the exemplum of the community of bees in *Mum and the Sothsegger*, 966–1090. I discuss this analogy in the next chapter.

[156] There is a long passage (744–69) which condemns the upward mobility of artisans and beggars, which has been seen as a vicious satire of labourers with economic aspirations; Kathryn Kerby-Fulton, '*Piers Plowman*', in *CHMEL* 513–38, p. 537. I think that the invective is directed primarily at how the fraternal orders subvert secular hierarchy by making the sons of shoemakers and beggars members of their orders, from which they can go on to be made bishops, and force the nobility to kneel to them (748–56).

[157] *De blasphemia*, 190/20; see further, Hudson, 'Poor preachers, poor men', 44–6.

indeed its eradication, brings Wycliffite polemic close to the insurgents' refiguring of the political community encapsulated in their apparent watchword: 'wyth Kynge Richarde and the trew communes'.[158] The sentiments are not identical, to be sure: Wycliffite texts do not call for the abolition of the lords, but the rebels' watchword does, necessarily, require the disappearance of the clerical estate.

In celebrating the virtuous worth of the poor labourer, Wycliffite texts can also be seen to voice support for exactly the social group who were blamed for revolt (even if the demographic composition of the rebels was rather different). And in promoting the 'commune vois' of the 'pore' and 'simple' as necessary and astringent correction of the corruptions in the civic community, Wycliffite texts nourish the potential of vernacular literacy as an agent of sedition.[159] The distinctiveness of this representation is foregrounded when compared with a text such as *The Pore Caitiff*. While this is a work which (dubiously) has been seen to have Wycliffite affiliations, its treatment of the third estate is very different from the characteristic depiction in Lollard texts.[160] MS Bodley 938, which preserves the fourteen chapters of the *Caitif*, interleaved with some Wycliffite additions, brings out the contrast very tellingly.[161] There is stalwart support for the plight of the poor. To eat the bread of poor men is considered to be an act of manslaughter, for anyone to misappropriate their property is to kill the child in the sight of the father, and anyone who withdraws sustenance from a poor man deprives him of his very blood (fos. 135^{a-b}). Significantly, however, there is no accusation against the second estate for such oppression. And while Wycliffite texts praise acts of charity towards the poor, in the section

---

[158] The watchword is reported in *The Anonimalle Chronicle*, ed. V. H. Galbraith (Manchester, 1970), 139: 'Et les ditz comunes avoient entre eux une wache worde en Engleys, "With whom haldes yow?" et le respouns fuist, "Wyth kynge Richarde and wyth the trew communes"'.

[159] Cf. Margaret Aston, 'Lollardy and sedition', in *Lollards and reformers*, 215.

[160] See Sr. M. Teresa Brady, '*The Pore Caitif*: an introductory study', *Traditio*, 10 (1954), 529–48, esp. 543–8.

[161] Brady (ibid.) discusses these insertions on p. 533; cf. Hudson, *The premature reformation*, 425, and n. 154, where printed versions of some of these additions are noted. See also, Brady, 'Lollard interpolations and omissions in manuscripts of *The Pore Caitif*', in Michael G. Sargent, ed., *Cella in seculum: religious and secular life and devotion in late medieval England* (Cambridge, 1989), 183–203. MS Bodley 938 is not one of the manuscripts discussed. This manuscript is said to contain six such tracts interleaved between two parts of the *Caitiff*, between fos. 50^a and fo. 117^b. There is also Wycliffite material prior to fo. 50^a, most notably in 'The Pater Noster', fo. 24^a, which calls for the Gospel to be declared in English, and states that it is Antichrist who prevents this help to the 'lewed'. Cf. Arnold, iii. 98.

The Loue of Jesu, the writer states that even if you 'ȝiue alle þingis þat
ȝe han to pore men, but if ȝe schulen loue þis name iesu, ȝe traueile
in ydel for whi oonli siche schulen be gladdid of iesu' (fo. 185ᵇ). This is
a hierarchy of devotional obligation not likely to have issued from a
Lollard quill. Further, while the interests of the poor are championed,
there is no attendant idealization of the labourer. Glossing the third
precept of the ten commandments, for example, the writer states that it
is better to plough on the sabbath than to attend dances and taverns,
which is how labourers would spend their time, selling their souls to the
devil, if not engaged in work. They are also warned against performing
their labour by deceit or trickery (fo. 141ᵃ). Most crucially, at no point
is the labourer, or ploughman, held up as essential and uncorrupted to
form a contrast with the superfluity of friars or prelates. *The Pore Caitif*
is demonstrably orthodox in its representation of the third estate.

But to free, as Wycliffite texts do, the husbandman from the curse of
Cain, and ban the 'fourth estate' instead, is to call for a total realignment
of what is considered 'inside' and 'outside' both the civic community,
and the Church triumphant. Well might writers belonging to the
second estate be offended and alarmed by their Wycliffite adoption into
the family of Cain. After all, who would wish to be part of a family from
hell? Even the self-assured Cain in *The Wakefield Pageant* hardly has a
free choice in the matter:

> Now fayre well, felows all, for I must nedys weynd,
> And to the dwill be thrall, warld withoutten end:
> Ordand ther is my stall, with Sathanas the feynd.[162]

---

[162] *Mactacio Abel*, 463–5, *The Wakefield pageants in the Townley Cycle*, ed. A. C. Cawley
(Manchester, 1958).

CHAPTER SEVEN

Coded Birds and Bees:
Unscrambling *Mum and the Sothsegger*
and *The Boke of Cupide*

> The formation and understanding of messages (encoding and decoding) is made possible by codes—a set of rules or an interpretative device known to both transmitter and receiver, which assigns a certain meaning or content to a certain sign. We recognize the signifier, long blonde hair for example, as a sign of femininity when we interpret it through the code of femininity as the signifier as a certain signified, woman . . . Codes are forms of social knowledge which are derived from social practices and beliefs although they are not laid down in any statute. Codes organize our understanding of the world in terms of 'dominant meaning patterns', patterns which vary from culture to culture and from time to time . . .[1]

To be sure, between late medieval poetry and twentieth-century advertising, there lies 'a great gap of time' and a diversity of cultural practices. For all that, the concept of code as Dyer formulates it is helpful, I think, in providing a linguistic framework within which to identify, not only the ideological work performed by selling commodities, but the socioliterary practice of *The Boke of Cupide* and *Mum and the Sothsegger*. The verbal signs of these texts are embedded in, and produced by, particular forms of social knowledge. To decode their meaning, it is necessary to gauge how their selection of linguistic items and textual devices is informed by shared sets of assumptions which were current when they were composed.

Both *The Boke of Cupide* and *Mum and the Sothsegger* were written at a time in which the emergence of Lollardy produced new forms of religious writing with distinctive tropes, vocabulary, and cohesions.[2] The

[1] Gillian Dyer, *Advertising as communication* (London and New York, 1982), 131–5.

[2] Though, as I discuss in more detail below, *Cupide* was written before the institutional censorship of Lollardy, while *Mum* was composed after the imposition of statutes to curb the spread of heresy.

distinctiveness of Wycliffite expression was recognized by the contemporary Knighton,[3] and, as both Hudson and von Nolcken have shown, 'sect vocabulary' and an appeal to common constructions are very important features of Lollard texts.[4] To view Wycliffite texts as coded, however, is not to argue that they were written in a kind of secret language that only their supporters could understand. Nor do I intend to suggest that these texts court a game of hide and seek in playing the kinds of literary games with coded symbols that Gower, for example, sported with so adroitly.[5] Rather, I want to argue that authors and audiences of texts written during the emergence and suppression of Lollardy shared assumptions about the cultural significance of certain linguistic signs in accordance with their advocacy of, or simply familiarity with, the particular form of social knowledge constituted by Wycliffism.

Writers who might not necessarily advocate Lollard views could, in their deployment of available linguistic resources, produce texts which were seen to articulate Wycliffite sentiments if read by someone familiar with the cultural value of key terms in the religious debate.[6] Similarly, writers who wished to express Lollard ideas without writing overt polemic, especially after measures had been passed to suppress the heresy,[7] could deploy a common currency of linguistic features which were recognizable to fellow advocates, thus allowing them access to the particular Wycliffite inflection of the discussion.[8] For orthodox readers, however, even though they might recognize suspicious features, it was hard to prove conclusively that such a text was heretical because nothing explicitly unorthodox was articulated. Heretical sense was pro-

---

[3] *Chronicon*, ii. 186–7.

[4] See Hudson, 'A Lollard sect vocabulary', in ead., *Lollards and their books* (Hambledon, 1985), 165–80; and Christina von Nolcken, '"A certain sameness" and our response to it in English Wycliffite texts' in Richard Newhauser and J. A. Alford, eds., *Literature and religion in the later middle ages: philological studies in honour of Siegfried Wenzel* (Binghamton, NY, 1995), 191–208. Von Nolcken interprets the common diction as proceeding from the Wycliffite concern to present themselves as writing both as, and from, a group, noting that there is far more evidence that Wycliffites studied and heard texts in groups than that they did these things as individuals, p. 200.   [5] See Chapter 5 above.

[6] A classic example is *Dives and Pauper*, which Bishop Alnwick thought contained multiple errors and heresies and was adduced in evidence against the Bury St Edmunds chaplain Thomas Bert, while the staunchly orthodox Abbot Whetehamstede commissioned a copy of the work for the library of St Albans; see discussion in Hudson, *Premature reformation*, 417–21.

[7] Especially *De Haeretico Comburendo* 1401, see *Rot. Parl*, iii. 467; *Stat. Realm*, ii. 125–8, and Arundel's Constitutions of 1409; see D. Wilkins, ed., *Concilia Magnae Britanniae et Hibernae* (4 vols., London, 1737), iii. 314–19.

[8] Cf. the comments by Anne Hudson, *Premature reformation*, 153.

duced by the decoding of the reader. I want to suggest that *The Boke of Cupide* is a product of the first of these scenarios and *Mum* a product of the second. The distinction between the two, and the character of the social knowledge which informs them, is a matter of date.

One of the most familiar ways to mine the social knowledge encoded in texts is to examine how they might reproduce the known ideological views of their authors.[9] *The Boke of Cupide* would seem to present an easier case here than *Mum*, though the situation is rather complicated. While there is no annotation in the sole surviving manuscript of *Mum* which gives us any clue about its author,[10] one of the five manuscripts which preserves *Cupide* concludes with the words 'Explicit Clanvowe'.[11] Assuming this to be correct, the question remains, which Clanvowe—father or son? Scattergood assigns the poem to Sir John Clanvowe, who died in 1391,[12] while other scholars prefer his son Thomas, thus making the poem a product of the fifteenth century.[13] As I hope my discussion below will demonstrate, it seems to me more likely that John, rather than Thomas, composed the poem. This is not because I want to line up with either Walsingham or McFarlane and claim Clanvowe as a 'Lollard knight';[14] rather, because the religious environment of Richard II's court, and Clanvowe's circle of friends within it, provide exactly the conditions to produce works which can be seen to be informed by Lollard issues whether or not the author was a personal advocate of

---

[9] To engage in this is to mobilize what Foucault terms 'the author function'. One of the functions of mobilizing the concept of the author is to put brakes on the endless proliferation of meaning, or as Foucault puts it: 'The author allows a limitation of the cancerous and dangerous proliferation of significations within a world where one is thrifty not only with one's resources and riches, but also with one's discourses and their significations. The author is the principle of thrift in the proliferation of meaning', M. Foucault, 'What is an author?', quoted from David Lodge, ed., *Modern literary criticism and theory* (London, 1988), 196–210, p. 209.

[10] The surviving witness, MS British Library Add. 41666, is defective. The opening of the poem is missing; it ends abruptly at l. 1751 and many of the margins are torn.

[11] In CUL MS Ff.1.6 (The Findern Manuscript), fo. 28ʳ.

[12] See *The works of Sir John Clanvowe*, ed. V. J. Scattergood (Cambridge, 1975), 23–5.

[13] See Skeat, *Chaucerian and other pieces*, p. lix, in *Complete works*, vol. vii; E. Vollmer, *Das Mittelenglische Gedicht "The Boke of Cupide"*, *Berliner beitrage zur Germanischen und Romanischen Philologie 18, Germanische Abteilung*, 8 (1989), 59; A. Brusendorff, *The Chaucer tradition* (1924), 443; L. C. Ward, 'The authorship of the *Cuckoo and the Nightingale*', *MLN* 44 (1929), 217–26, p. 217. Ethel Seaton argues that Richard Roos was the author, *Sir Richard Roos—Lancastrian poet* (Oxford, 1961), 388.

[14] See Walsingham, *Historia Anglicana*, ii. 159; K. B. McFarlane, *Lancastrian kings and Lollard knights* (Oxford, 1972), 162–6; 171–6; 183–4.

their views.[15] While it has usually been Clanvowe's religious treatise *The Two Ways* that has provided the focus of examination for accusing, or exculpating, Clanvowe from the taint of Lollardy,[16] I hope to argue that the perceived disjunction between *Cupide* and *Two Ways*—one a poetic courtly entertainment, the other, a dourly insipid work of piety in prose—may be something of a chimera.[17] Examining the textuality of the poem sheds as much light on the religious attitudes of Clanvowe as working from author to prose text.

In the case of *Mum*, there would appear to be no alternative to working from the text back to its putative author. For a start, we have no name even to conjure with. All the same, the probable provenance of *Mum* is one that is rather intriguing. Many factors suggest that the author of *Mum* may have had some connection with the circle of Sir Thomas Berkeley of Gloucester.[18] The evidence is various. First is the authorial relationship between *Mum and the Sothsegger* and *Richard the Redeless*. Examination of their subliminal habits of composition suggest a strong likelihood that both poems were written by the same author, even if the range and scope of *Mum* is much greater than the earlier poem.[19] The opening lines of *Richard* locate the action to Bristol and show a detailed knowledge of the layout of the city,[20] and the dialect of

[15] The spectrum of religious sensibilities at Richard II's court is examined by J. A. Tuck, 'Carthusian monks and Lollard knights: religious attitudes at the court of Richard II', *SAC* 1 (1984), 149–61. Cf. Strohm, *Chaucer's fifteenth century audience*. Jill Havens argues that Clanvowe has suffered through years of 'guilt by association' with Lollard knights, but that while there is substantial evidence for the Lollardy of Sir Thomas Latimer, Sir William Neville, and Sir Lewis Clifford, there is nothing in the records to condemn Sir John Clanvowe, 'Instruction, devotion, meditation, sermon: a critical edition of selected English religous texts in Oxford University College MS 97, with an ideological examination of some related MSS', D.Phil. thesis (Oxford University, 1995), 179.

[16] e.g. *Lancastrian kings*, 199–206; cf. Hudson, *Premature reformation*, 422–3. Havens argues that the tract is not convincingly Lollard: 'when the text is compared with well-known heterodox and orthodox texts, the text's orthodoxy is convincing, its heterodoxy is not', 'Instruction, devotion, meditation', 219.

[17] See e.g. David Burnley, *Courtliness and literature in medieval England* (London, 1998), 136; Havens, 'Instruction, devotion, meditation', 190–1; Glending Olson, 'Chaucer' in *CHMEL* 566–88, p. 571.

[18] The comments that follow are deeply indebted to the discussion in Ralph Hanna III, 'Sir Thomas Berkeley and his patronage', *Speculum*, 64 (1989), 878–916.

[19] See Helen Barr, 'The relationship of *Richard the Redeless* and *Mum and the Sothsegger*, *YLS* 4 (1990), 105–33.

[20] All quotations from the poem are from *The Piers Plowman tradition*, ed. Barr. See ll. 1–4, which correctly locates Holy Trinity Church, popularly known as Christ's Church, to the crossroads at the centre of the town (see notes on pp. 247–8).

both poems points to a provenance of the south-west Midlands.[21]
Further, both poems show a knowledge of contemporary events that
would have been directly accessible to a member of Berkeley's circle.
Thomas Berkeley took a leading role in the deposition proceedings
against Richard II, and in 1400, also captured some of the leaders of the
Cirencester revolt against Henry IV.[22] *Richard* shows very detailed
knowledge of the articles of deposition against *Richard* (I. 88–106) and
also alludes to the Cirencester uprising (II. 17).[23] In 1392, Berkeley
betrothed his only child Elizabeth to Richard Beauchamp, son of the
Lord Appellant, Thomas, earl of Warwick. *Richard*'s narration of how
Henry reversed the former king's punishment of Beauchamp focuses on
the interests of his heirs:

> He blythid the beere and his bond braste,
> And lete him go at large to lepe where he wolde.
> But tho all the berlingis brast out at ones
> As fayne as the foule that flieth on the skyes
> That Bosse was vbounde and brouute to his owen.   (III. 94–8)

Only the Beauchamp family (whose heraldic sign was the bear) in the
poem's narration of the fates of the Lords Appellant is singled out as
having heirs (berlingis),[24] and they are particularly concerned to avenge
themselves on Henry Grene:

> They gaderid hem to-gedir on a grette roughte,
> To helpe the heeris that had many wrongis;
> They gaglide forth on the grene for they greued were.   (III. 99–101)[25]

Grene was one of the property grantees for parts of the seized
Beauchamp estates,[26] and such detailed knowledge of the treatment of
Richard Beauchamp might well be expected from someone who was
part of his father-in-law's circle.

---

[21] See *Mum and the Sothsegger*, ed. Day and Steele.

[22] Hanna, 'Sir Thomas Berkeley', 888 and 882.

[23] This allusion provides the latest *terminus ad quem* for the poem, see Barr, 'The dates of *Richard the Redeless* and *Mum and the Sothsegger*'.

[24] Line III. 26 refers to Arundel's sons Richard and Thomas ('coltis') who were placed in the custody of the duke of Exeter after their father's execution. But they are not described as heirs.

[25] *On King Richard's ministers* shows knowledge of Richard Beauchamp's marriage: 'The berewardes sone is tendur of age | He is put to mariage'. He is said to want to lead the 'beres' at 'his wille'. Grene, who is figured as green grass in the poem, is said to have 'sclayn a stede', referring to the treatment of Arundel, not Warwick; *Political poems and songs*, ed. Wright, I. 364.   [26] See Goodman, *The loyal conspiracy*, 71.

Berkeley also had the right to parliamentary summons, and was a member for two years of Henry's privy council, though his attendance was infrequent.[27] In both poems, there is detailed understanding both of the workings of parliament and knowledge of important matters of the business of government.[28] Both poems also show extensive knowledge of legal matters and deploy legal diction: Berkeley had the right to hold a local court, a privilege normally reserved to the king, and employed an extensive entourage which included lawyers.[29]

As Hanna notes, the Berkeley parish alone employed fifteen clerics. One of these, until his death in 1402, was John Trevisa.[30] The author of *Mum* quotes Trevisa in the analogy of the hive of bees towards the end of the poem, and, as I shall discuss in greater detail below, the account in *Mum* is influenced by Trevisa's translation of the *De Proprietatibus Rerum*. The analogy also discusses the formation of political community and legal responsibility in a fashion which is commensurate with the treatment of these matters in Trevisa's translation of Giles of Rome's *De Regimine Principum*.[31] Trevisa himself, as Anne Hudson has shown, presents a rather interesting case in assessing late fourteenth-century associations with Wycliffism. Trevisa's commitment to translation activity, the books with which he is associated, and circumstantial evidence of his acquaintance with Wyclif and Hereford are suggestive, but while Hudson argues that a verdict of 'not proven' must be returned, this is less interesting than 'the evidence that the case provides of the centrality of Wycliffite figures and Wycliffite thought to the concerns of the late fourteenth century'.[32]

Berkeley was personally caught up in this centrality. He served on numerous commissions to extirpate Lollardy from Redcliffe, a renowned Lollard centre from the earliest days of the sect.[33] If the author

---

[27] Hanna, 'Sir Thomas Berkeley', 891. It is tempting (to me, at any rate), to read *Mum*, 151, 'For with the king-is cunseil I come but silde', as a wry comment on Berkeley's intermittent appearances.

[28] See Helen Barr, 'A study of Mum and the Sothsegger in its political and literary contexts', D.Phil. thesis (Oxford University, 1989), ch. 1 (this covers *Richard* as well as *Mum*), and notes (passim) to my 1993 edition.

[29] Hanna, 'Sir Thomas Berkeley', 881. For the coverage of legal issues see Helen Barr, 'The treatment of natural law in *Richard the Redeless* and *Mum and the Sothsegger*', *LSE* 23 (1992), 49–80, and *Signes and sothe*, ch. 5.

[30] Hanna, 'Sir Thomas Berkeley', 892–3.

[31] See Barr, 'The treatment of natural law'.

[32] Hudson, *Premature reformation*, pp. 396–7, quotation from p. 397.

[33] Hanna, 'Sir Thomas Berkeley', 896. Cf. Hudson, *Premature reformation*, 122–3, on Bristol.

of *Mum* were a member of Berkeley's circle, he would have had easy access to Wycliffite ideas, both from his geographical location, and from contact with people. And while the connection with the Berkeley circle that I have sketched is obviously conjectural, it is from exactly that kind of provenance, if not the very one, that *Richard* and *Mum* were likely to have been produced.

Speculation concerning its author aside, the textuality of *Mum* suggests an even stronger connection with Wycliffism. I have argued elsewhere that while the scope of *Mum* is much larger than being an occasion for the penning of a Lollard tract, nevertheless, the narrator's criticisms of the friars, monks, and priests can be seen to be Wycliffite inflected.[34] I now think that the same is true of the model of civic society that is narrated towards the end of the poem with the exemplum of the hive of bees. It is intriguing that a Wycliffite view of society emerges from the part of the poem which is so heavily indebted to Trevisa. The details of this exemplum, and the figure of the beekeeper within it, reproduce key features of the typical Wycliffite model of society, political responsibility, and representation of the third estate. While there are some differences from the usual Lollard formulations, to a reader familiar with Wycliffite textuality, the bee exemplum can be seen to offer an unorthodox picturing of civic society.

Most strikingly, the exemplum of the bees portrays a society where there is no second estate; there is the king, and there are his bees, who work assiduously for common profit. The bees also show the utmost loyalty to their king, and this is consonant with the Wycliffite stress on civil obedience to the secular lord, and obeying the law:[35]

> The bee of alle bestz beste is y-gouuerned
> Yn lowlynes and labour and in lawe eeke.
> Thay haue a kyng by kinde that the coroune bereth,
> Whom they doo sue and serue as souurayn to thaym alle,
> And obeyen to his biddyng, or elles the boke lieth.   (997–1001)

The beekeeper quotes his source faithfully here. In the section on bees

---

[34] See Barr, *Signes and sothe*, ch. 4.

[35] The account of the behaviour of Ghengis Khan (ll. 1414–56) is consonant with a Wycliffite view that a king must be obeyed, even if he were a tyrant, as examined in the previous chapter, but the eagerness of the nobles to slay their sons and seise Khan with their lands is troubling. It reads like a rather over-enthusiastic attempt to defend Henry's tenure of the throne in the teeth of Ricardian disquiet. This is one of the occasions in the poem where Wycliffism and Lancastrianism are held together in an uneasy tension.

in *De Proprietatibus Rerum*, the commonality of the bees is stressed, together with their unstinting loyalty to the king:

Been makeþ amonge hem a kynge and ordeyneþ among hem comyn peple. Ande þouȝ þey ben iput and iset vndir a kyng, ȝit þey beþ free and louiþ hire kyng þat þey makeþ by kynde loue and defendiþ hym wiþ ful greet diffens and holdeþ feire and worschipe to perische and be ispilt for here kyng. And þey doþ hire kyng so greet worschipe þat noon of hem dar gone out of her hous noþir to gete mete but ȝif þe kyng passe out and take þe principalte of fliȝt.[36]

The poet omits the detail in Bartholomaeus that if a bee finds himself disloyal to the king, then he will kill himself with his own sting (perhaps not having a taste for such Roman stoicism (p. 610/29–31)), but he does reproduce the account of the bees physically bearing up the king when he wishes to fly out of the hive (1038–43). Added to Bartholomaeus is the comment that each section of the hive has 'a principal' who keeps peace within his jurisdiction, and musters his retinues to correct wrongdoing (1012–15). While the poet is perfectly happy to add detail to introduce the nobility into the commonality of the hive, the lack of alteration to introduce the second estate creates a rather telling absence.[37]

But perhaps it is not strictly accurate to talk about the *absence* of the second estate. Another of the changes made to the source is the considerable expansion of the treatment of the drones. Bartholomaeus does include the drones in his account: they are figured as the idle bees which get thrown out of the company of workers. They are situated outside the hive and the bees within it have to keep a watch and fight the drones to prevent them from stealing their honey:

And þe schorter been fiȝtiþ wiþ þe lengere wiþ strong fiȝt whanne
þey eteþ moch hony and trauayllen not noþer gaderen nouȝte hony.

(p. 612/19–21)

In an account which runs to 150 lines, only seven are devoted to the subject of the idle bees. In *Mum*, by contrast, almost as much space is devoted the drones as to the bees. As in *Bartholomaeus*, the drones are situated outside the hive, and as in *Bartholomaeus*, they are 'long and lene' (1069). Further:

---

[36] M. C. Seymour *et al.*, eds., *On the properties of things: John Trevisa's translation of* Bartholomaeus Anglicus, De Proprietatibus Rerum (Oxford, 1975), 2 vols., i. 610/17–24.

[37] The addition presumably reflects the contemporary political climate in which there were baronial uprisings against Henry's perceived usurpation, e.g. the battle of Shrewsbury in 1403, the York uprising in 1405, and general unrest which focused on reports that Richard was still alive and purposing to return to claim his rightful throne.

> They haunten the hyue for hony that is ynne,
> And lurken and licken the liquor that is swete,
> And trauelyn no twynte but taken of the beste
> *Qui non laborat non manducet. Bernardus.*   (983–5)

The accompanying quotation (which I believe to be authorial) is from 2 Thessalonians, 3: 10: 'If any man will not work, neither let him eat'. This quotation also appears as a gloss to *Piers Plowman* B. Prol 39 in MS Oriel College 79 and CUL MS Ll.4.14.[38] In *Piers*, the gloss describes deceitful minstrels. In *Mum*, I think it describes the friars.

The analogy is built around the contrast between the bees and the drones. The beekeeper has nothing but praise for the work of the bees, and their civic organization. Bees surpass all other beasts in working hard, and are the most skilful 'to profite of the peuple' (991). They are also the best governed of all beasts (997); a fact that the narrator emphasizes by adding their obedience to law (998). So intent are the bees about 'comune profit' and labouring whenever they can that the drones are sometimes able to enter the hive without being noticed. But, says the beekeeper, as soon as the bees realize that their 'swynke' has been stolen then they gather into a swarm and kill the drones to requite their injuries (1078–86).

While a Lollard with pacifist leanings might blench at the readiness of the bees to imbrue their steely stings with blood, they might also recognize a very familiar textual dynamic in operation in this exemplum.[39] The honest and necessary toil of the bees is appropriated by the idle drones who are not part of the hive, but an invasive threat from outside. Not only do the drones fail to contribute to the sustenance of society, but they devour 'that deue is to other' (1066). 'Deue' is a legal term[40] and casts the drones as thieves. Bees work according to the law; lazy drones break it. The allegory reproduces exactly the Wycliffite representation of how the toil of the essential labourer is appropriated by fraternal orders who contribute nothing to society. The positioning of the drones outside the hive matches the way that Lollard texts figure the friars as

[38] See *Piers Plowman: the B version*, ed. George Kane and E. Talbot Donaldson (London, 1975), 224 and 229; CUL MS Ll.4.14 is the sole surviving witness to *Richard the Redeless*.

[39] Pacifism appears to have been a belief held by Lollards on the extreme of the movement. Ecclesiastical participation in war is hotly condemned, especially in light of the 1382 Despenser Crusade, but neither Wyclif nor Wycliffite writers routinely condemn military intervention if peace and justice cannot be secured by other means. For the range of views, see Hudson, *Premature reformation*, 367–70.

[40] *MED* 'due' 2(a) 'prescribed by law or custom'.

superfluous, and alien; descendants of Cain and 'put in' by the devil, as *Pierce the Ploughman's Crede* so pithily terms it (506). An earlier section on the friars in *Mum* traces their origins back to Cain, and produces a satirical snapshot of the failings of all the four orders by riddling with the CAIM acrostic (498–505). Further, the cryptic lines at 516–20, once decoded with the help of the Latin quotations appended to the passage, claim that the friars will have no place in the Church Triumphant, and will fetch up in hell.[41]

The drones in the bee exemplum extend this coded Wycliffite representation of the friars. As mentioned in the preceding chapter, *Pierce the Ploughman's Crede* also likens the friars to drones; they gobble up the first fruits that should belong to the husbandman (726–9). In *Mum*, the drones' theft of the lawful labour of the commonality of bees is permeated with many of the typically Wycliffite features of the representation of the friars. The drones are 'wastours that wyrchen not but wombes forto fille' (1017). They are perceived as the sole threat to society:

> For in thaire wide wombes thay wol hide more
> Thenne twenty bees and trauaillen not to tyme of the day,
> But gaderyn al to the gutte and growen grete and fatte
> And fillen thaire bagges brede-ful of that the bees wyrchen.
> *Quorum deus venter est et gloria in confusione. Paulus.*   (1045–8)

The Latin quotation is from Philippians 3: 19: 'whose God is their belly and whose glory is in their shame'. This is quoted by Thought in *Piers* IX. 61*a* to describe those who abuse their minds through gluttony. Because they serve Satan, says Thought, he shall have their souls (IX. 62). In *Mum*, it is the friars who will end their days in Satan's company,[42] and the lines quoted expand Bartholomaeus's account considerably. The description recalls the passage on the false beggars in *Piers*, B. Prol. 40–1: 'Bidderes and beggeres faste aboute yede | Til her bely and hire bagge were bredful y-crammed'. I suggest that in *Mum*, the 'bagges' of the drones are an ironic reference to how the friars flout the ideal of apostolic poverty. Christ sent out his disciples as labourers into the harvest, and commanded them to carry: 'no purse, no bag, no sandals'.[43] For St Francis, possession of a bag was a sign of a false apostle like Judas, who was distinguished from the other apostles by his sole custody of the

---

[41] See Barr, *Signes and sothe*, 126–9 for more detailed discussion of both these passages.

[42] The Summoner figures the friars as bees, whose final lodging place is in Satan's arse, *The Summoner's Prologue*, III. 1690–8.

[43] Luke, 10: 2–4. The friars' violation of this precept recurs in anti-fraternal literature, see Szittya, *The antifraternal tradition*, 47–50.

bag. True apostles ought to sell all they had in order to follow Christ.[44] That the drones fill their 'bagges' from the true labour of the bees casts them as pseudo-apostolic friars. Contemporary readers might be expected to pick up on 'bagges' as a marked lexical item in the debate over how the friars acquired financial support for their existence.[45]

Although accusations of gluttony and idleness are not peculiar to friars, and it might be argued that the bee exemplum simply presents a model of society in which true labourers (the bees) are contrasted to wicked loafers (the drones), the fact that the drones are outside the hive and distinctively carry 'bagges' (not in Bartholomaeus), complicates such a reading. I think that *Mum* performs the same reregistration of the traditional features of anti-peasant discourse, in transferring their properties to the friars, as do other Wycliffite texts. The beekeeper states that the drones acquire access to the hive by 'deceipt' (1050) and 'subtilite' (1053). Although peasants were framed as cunning, able to outwit their superiors, 'subtilite' is a word with rather different resonances, and associated especially with ungrounded clerics in Wycliffite texts.[46]

There are further anti-fraternal resonances. Intrigued by the workings of these drones, the narrator asks the beekeeper to describe their characteristics to him so that he can recognize them:

> 'Yit wolde I wite' cothe I, if your wil be,
> Hough to knowe kindely, thorough crafte of your scole,
> The drane that deuoureth that deue is to other,
> By colour or by cursidnesse or crie that he maketh.
> Kenneth me the cunnyng, that I may knowe after'.
> 'Thay been long and lene', cothe he, 'and of a lither hue,
> And as bare as a bord, and bringen nought with thaym;
> But haue thay hauntid the hyve half yere to th'ende,
> Thay growen vnder gurdel gretter than other,
> And noon so sharpe to stinge ne so sterne nother.'
> *Nichil asperius paupero cum surget in altum. Gregorius*   (1064–73)

There is no counterpart to this in Bartholomaeus. The narrator's initial question may recall that asked by Will to Holy Church at the beginning of Passus II: 'Kenne me by som craft to knowe the false' (4). If this is a deliberate echo, then the drones are further identified through literary

---

[44] See ibid. 49–50.

[45] This criticism of the friars appears explicitly in *Crede*, 600–1.

[46] e.g. Matthew, 'sotil ypocrisie' (p. 9); 'soteltees and queyntese'(p. 20); 'false sotiltes' (p. 25); *Lanterne*, p. 13/4; 27; p. 26/20; *Lollard sermons*, ed. Cigman, p. 14/32; p. 42/436; p. 46/65; p. 89/323; 121/8.

allusion with the devil, and also with Mede. That the drones bring nothing with them to the hive may be seen as a coded allusion to their vow of poverty, a vow that is about as binding as the girdle fastened around their expanding girth; indeed, 'gurdle' (1063) suggests the rope tied round a friar's habit. In contrast to the king, who has no sting, the drones are seen to be ready to sting at the first opportunity, and fiercely. This may be an allusion to the sexual licentiousness of the friars; Gower makes a similar pun,[47] but it could also allude either to the friar's intolerance of criticism,[48] or to the fact that some of the fiercest critics of Wyclif and Wycliffism were friars.[49] The Latin quotation 'Nothing is harsh as a pauper when he is raised to prosperity' could readily be glossed to refer to the advancement of lowly born friars to elevated social positions. It is a criticism, as we have seen, made in *Crede* (744–61).[50]

There is one further detail which suggests that the bee analogy encodes a Wycliffite view of civic society. In a fashion which recalls Chaucer's use of Lollius in *Troilus and Criseyde*, the beekeeper, at one point, attributes to Bartholomaeus information which is not only absent from that account, but also unparalleled in any other bestiary:

> The bomelyng of the bees, as Bartholomew vs telleth,
> Thair noyse and thaire notz at eue and eeke at morowe,
> Lyve it wel, thair lydene the lest of thaym hit knoweth.   (1028–30)

Bartholomaeus tells us that the only noise made by bees is the sound of their wings in the air (p. 613/22–4). He stresses that the bees have many things in common: nature, habitation, travail, food, flight, virginity, and reproduction (p. 610/6–13), but *not* a common language. It is not hard to see why the *Mum*-poet takes refuge in a spurious authority here. A state united by a common tongue resonates powerfully with the Wycliffite demand for the Bible to be in English so that all could understand it. A guarded allusion to this sentiment is entirely explicable given the outlawing of scriptural translation in 1401 and the dangers of possessing books in the vernacular after Arundel's *Constitutions* of 1409. No heterodox statement is explicitly articulated in l. 1030, and an

---

[47] Gower, *Vox*, IV. 878–80.

[48] *Crede* states that no wasp in the world will sting more readily for stepping on the toe of a stinking friar (648–9). *On the leaven of the Pharisees*, Matthew, p. 18, states that a friar will offer to fight anyone who reproves him for his sinful life.

[49] For instance, of the seventeen doctors of theology present at the 1382 Blackfriars Council which condemned Wyclif's teaching, sixteen were friars, four from each order.

[50] See Chapter 6.

allusion to Lollard views on biblical translation becomes possible only
when read through the social knowledge constituted by Wycliffism:
'lydene' is a term available to be invested with cultural significance. This
(admittedly) circular mode of decoding is true of the bee exemplum in
its entirety. A reading informed by Lollard ideology allows the analogy
to yield a message that is consonant with the typically Wycliffite representations of civic society examined in the previous chapter. United
by a common language, with no second estate to claim a clerical
monopoly over Latin, sustained by hard-working labourers, staunchly
loyal to their king, and with the friars expelled, the community of bees
is a Lollard utopia.

There remains the figure of the beekeeper, however, a complex
figure, who can be seen to be both representative of, and also to depart
from, normative Wycliffite treatments of the third estate. He has no
counterpart in Bartholomaeus. There is a reference to a 'wardeyne'
who will feed the bees with figs if the honey runs out, but that is all
(p. 613/15–17). The beekeeper is not identical to the typical Wycliffite
idealization of the poor rural labourer, and its apotheosis in the ploughman figure. He is introduced first as a gardener of the land of a franklin's
freehold, but agricultural resonances are grafted on to his horticultural
activities:

> 'I am gardyner of this gate', cothe he, 'the grovnde is myn owen,
> Forto digge and to delue and to do suche deedes
> As longeth to this leyghttone the lawe wol I doo,
> And wrote vp the wedes that wyrwen my plantes;
> And wormes that worchen not but wasten my herbes,
> I daisshe thaym to deeth and delue out thaire dennes.
>
> (976–81)

'Gate' (976) is the manuscript reading which Day and Steele emended
to 'garth', meaning 'garden'. 'Garth' is the easier reading, although
'gate' is possible in the sense of 'plot of land', by extension from the
MED definition of 'furrow/track to be ploughed'.[51] The choice of reading has a material effect on constructing the figure of the beekeeper. To
have the beekeeper/gardener owning a 'gate' partially invests him with
the characteristics of the ploughmen who owned their bit of land, rather
like *Piers Plowman* and his half-acre.[52] Further, while to dig and to delve
(977), describes spadework which is a part of a gardener's job, it is a

---

[51] *MED* 'gate' (n), 2.1(c).
[52] See n. 12, Chapter 6 above.

collocation which normally describes agricultural labour.[53] Apart from 'plantes' (979) and 'herbes' (980), specialized horticultural vocabulary is conspicuously absent from the passage. One might have expected the gardener to 'sette and sowe', or to 'graffe'; 'sclatt' (prune), or to 'kutte', 'dyȝte', or 'bynde'.[54] Instead, he is figured more as a destroyer than a cultivator: 'wrote' (979); 'daisshe' and 'delue' (981).[55] The *Mum*-poet certainly knew the lexis of the more nurturing side of gardening activity because he uses it in a later passage; not to describe the beekeeper, however, but Lucifer:

> For Lucifer the lyer that lurketh aboute
> Forto gete hym a grounde that he may graffe on
> And to sowe of his seede suche as he vsith,
> That groweth al to grevance and gurdyng of heedes,
> He leyeth his lynes along that luste may be clepid
> Of oure foule flessh that foundrith ful ofte,
> And of gloire of this grounde his griefz been y-made,
> That who be hente in his hoke he shal be holde faste
> Til he be caste with couetise or sum croke elles.
> *Seminator zizanne et agricola diaboli*

(1157–65)

In an allegorical slippage typical of *Piers Plowman*, Lucifer metamorphoses from husbandman to fisherman and back again to ploughman in the Latin quotation: a sower of tares and a farmer of devils, Lucifer is cast here as a sower of civil dissension that is not exclusively Wycliffite; the beheadings (1160) probably allude to the punishment of nobles who revolted against Henry IV;[56] there is also a moral dimension to the allegory which need not be read with cultural specificity: 'luste' (1161), and 'couetise' (1165). The imagery, however, sets up an oppositional contrast between Lucifer as the cultivator of sin and dissent, and the beekeeper as the protector of the garden by exterminating pests. The tenor

---

[53] Cooper notes that the usual formulaic pairing is to dike and to delve, 'Langland's and Chaucer's Prologues', *YLS* 1(1987), 76, but see entries in *MED* for 'diggen' and 'delven' which customarily describe activities in fields.

[54] These are the verbs which recur in a fifteenth-century gardening treatise in verse. The chief occupations are listed by month throughout the year, see A. M. T. Amherst, 'On a fifteenth century treatise on gardening', *Archaeologia*, 54 (1894), 157–72.

[55] Cf. the sermon attributed to John Ball where he urges his followers to be like good husbandmen, tilling his field and uprooting the tares that threaten to destroy the grain but killing great lords, justices etc.; see Dobson, *The Peasants' Revolt*, 375.

[56] See Chapter 3 above.

of the imagery reproduces the figurative terrain fought over by the Lollards and their opponents. For defenders of the institutional Church, Lollards were heretics who sprinkled 'cockel' in 'clene corn',[57] while for Wycliffites, the false clergy were weeds that had to be cleared from the vineyard.[58] Rival sides in the religious debate competed for control of the discourse of corruption and pollution, each figuring the other as the pest that had infiltrated what was pure.[59]

While in *Mum* the discussion is more expansive than this debate, it is enmeshed in the rhetorical tropes that nourished it. In Wycliffite texts, Satan is the father of the false clergy, and the corrupt Church on earth is the 'fiend's church' in contrast to the Church which Christ founded and the Church triumphant in heaven.[60] The contrast between Lucifer and the beekeeper in *Mum* resonates with this opposition. Just as there are ploughman resonances in the portrait of the beekeeper, so too, are there details which point to a Christ-like figure. Christ was sometimes figured as a gardener: in his role as a second Adam, reversing the punishment of the Fall, and in his appearance to Mary Magdalen on the morning of his resurrection (John, 20:15). According to Gregory the Great, Christ planted the seeds of virtue in her breast. This image was well known in the Middle Ages.[61] In devotional texts, the heart or soul is sometimes figured as a garden which either belongs to Christ, or is tended by his father.[62] This tradition informs the Tree of Charity episode in *Piers Plowman* in which the soul is figured as a garden with Piers as its gardener:

---

[57] *The Epilogue to the Man of Lawe's Tale*, II. 1183.

[58] See *Lollard sermons*, ed. Cigman, p. 30/704–5.

[59] e.g., 'For I purposide noon oþerwise in þe bigynnyng of my sermoun but, aftir þe meenyng and vndirstonding of my teeme, to enpungne synne and bastard sectis or braunchis þat bi alien seed. and not bi þe pure seed of Iesu Crist þat is spouse of þe chirche, ben brouȝt into þe chirche', *SEWW* 96/122–6. See also discussion in Strohm, *England's empty throne*, 37–9.

[60] This opposition is frequent in Wycliffite writings. For a fully developed example, see e.g. *Epistola Sathanae ad cleros* in *Selections from English Wycliffite writings*, no. 17, pp. 89–93.

[61] See Freedman, *Images*, 224; e.g. Nicholas Love, *Mirror*, 'And thouȝ oure lorde was not bodily, as sche supposed, a gardyner, neuerþeles . . . he was so . . . goostly to hir, for he planted in the gardyn of hir herte þe plantes of vertues and of trewe loues', p. 268, cited from *MED*, 'gardiner' (b).

[62] e.g., Misyn, *Fire of Love*, 'þe saule truly þat boyth is swete be schynynge of consciens, & fayr be charite of endles lufe, cristis gardyn may be cald', p.65/10, and *Aȝenbite of Inwit*, ; 'Þe traw of uirtue þe god þe uader . . . zet ine þe gardyne and his wetereþ of þe welle of his grace', p.97/31, cited from *MED*, 'gardin' (b).

'It groweþ in a gardyn', quod he, 'þat God made hymselue;
Amyddes mannes body þe more is of þat stokke.
Herte highte þe herber þat it inne groweþ,
And *Liberium Arbitrium* haþ þe lond to ferme,
Vnder Piers þe Plowman to piken it and to weden it'.

(B. XVI. 13–17)

I do not think that the beekeeper in *Mum represents* Christ in the sense
that there is a hermetically sealed allegorical equation between the two
figures, but in ways reminiscent of the figure of Piers in *Piers Plowman*,
he is invested with some Christ-like characteristics which confirm him
as a source of truth and authority in opposition both to Mum and to
Satan.

The beekeeper recalls Piers in further ways. The agricultural overlay
recalls the figure of Piers ploughing his half-acre, and the beekeeper's
treatment of wasters recalls Piers's chastisement of the skiving labourers
in Passus VI. His explanation of the working of the hive seems indebted
to Piers's explanation of the Tree of Charity to Will. The scope is
drastically reduced in *Mum*, although the allegorical correspondences
are almost as organic and unwieldy. The tree in Passus XVI moves from
a diagrammatic allegory of the states of life on earth to a dynamic
account of the Incarnation and the course of providential history.[63] In
Mum, the account moves from dynamic action by the beekeeper to his
diagrammatic exposition of the bees, back to his interventionist role in
protecting the hive. This last chiefly takes the form of picking off the
drones before they have a chance to enter the hive by hitting them over
the head and crushing them with his thumb (968 and 1061). The beekeeper advises the narrator that it is very important not to let the drones
enter the hive, for once in, they will prevent the bees from working
in accordance with their natural disposition, through their deceitful
practices (1059–63).

If the drones are friars in code, then this casts the beekeeper as a
defender of the society against them. Presumably, his killing of the
drones is not meant to be taken literally, though the tenor rather
disturbs the Wycliffite inflection of the passage. It seems to me that
the beekeeper may be seen as a reformer, one who defends common
profit by purging society of superfluity and parasitic pests, rather as the

---

[63] For discussions of the allegorical shifts in the Tree of Charity scene see David Aers, *Piers Plowman and Christian allegory* (London, 1975), ch. 5; and Peter Dronke, 'Arbor caritatis', in P. L. Heyworth, ed., *Medieval studies for J. A. W. Bennett* (Oxford, 1981), 207–53. See also Simpson, *Piers Plowman*, 186–90.

Wycliffite sermon for Septuagesima Sunday figures the ungrounded clergy as evil plants and bastard branches which must be weeded and cut out of the Lord's vineyard.[64] The beekeeper is a true member of the third estate, and while he is not an idealized poor labourer, his contrast to the corruption of the second estate recreates a textual dynamic which is prevalent in demonstrably Lollard works.

Most crucially, perhaps, the beekeeper is the truthteller for whom the narrator has spent the poem searching. While in Wycliffite texts, the corrective voice is typically figured as coming from 'pore men',[65] here it comes from a worker who is not figured as needy, but fiercely wise. The Christ-like resonances invest the beekeeper with authority, but they do not turn him into a type of Christ. Rather, he can be seen to be a type of 'true man'.[66] At the start of his account to the narrator of how Mum is the source of all the trouble and misrule, the beekeeper authorizes his speech with reference to the Bible:

> 'Swete soon, thy seching', seide the freke thenne,
> 'And thy trauail for thy trouthe shal tourne the to profit,
> For I wol go as nygh the ground as gospel vs techeth
> For to wise the wisely to the waie-is ende.　　　　　　　(1111–14)

'Ground' is frequently used in Lollard texts to describe what is lawful and authorized by Christ in contrast to the ungrounded practices of men.[67] The beekeeper bases his speech on the gospel appeals to biblical truth in contrast to the fraudulent and self-serving speech of those that 'fikelly fablen and fals been withynne' (1203). It would be reductive to confine this opposition to a reading in which a representative Wycliffite 'true man' exposes the corruptions of the contemporary Church; the scope of the beekeeper's ensuing criticisms encompass all the estates of society. Nevertheless, the beekeeper as voice and source of truth in the poem can be seen to be consonant with Wycliffite representations of the corrective voice, even though there are differences both in detail and in range.

One of the chief differences is that the beekeeper is much closer to the figure of Piers in *Piers Plowman* than he is to *Pierce* in *Crede*, especially in recalling social tensions in the labouring estate through the

---

[64] See discussion of this sermon in Chapter 4.

[65] See discussion in Chapter 4.

[66] In Wycliffite texts, this is the term which the Lollards used to describe themselves, see Hudson, 'A Lollard sect vocabulary', in ead., *Lollards and their books*, 166–7.

[67] Ibid. 171–2.

resonances of Piers's treatment of the workers in Passus VI. While the opposition between the poor true ploughman and the friars in *Crede* is straightforwardly polemical, and constitutes the principal narrative strategy of the poem, in *Mum*, the discussion is more complex: the treatment of the contemporary Church is a part of larger vision (just as it is in *Piers*), but also, the Wycliffite resonances are available only by decoding the poem through a knowledge of typical features of Lollard textuality. To my mind, a Wycliffite reading of the community of bees, given the absence of the second estate, and the reregistration of anti-peasant discourse to describe the drones/friars, is available. It is more difficult to accommodate the beekeeper into the normative Lollard representations of members of the third estate, but the figure (apart from his brutal methods of dealing with pests) is not incompatible with them. The narrator, in a reprise of Will's frequent bafflement in *Piers*, claims that the bee exemplum is 'to mistike for me' (1089). He has a point! But drawing attention to the opaqueness of the narration (and we might recall the beekeeper himself passing over other 'pryvy poyntz' (1055)), foregrounds the evasiveness of the account. It reminds me of the refusal to explain the rat fable in the Prologue to *Piers Plowman*.[68] Responsibility for making sense of the exemplum is passed to the reader. Given the date of *Mum*,[69] it would be understandable for its author to let his audience decode Wycliffite sentiments in his coverage of the ills of early fifteenth-century society rather than to blazon his colours too brazenly. After all, that the bag of books which the narrator reads from at the end of the poem has been confiscated for many years by Mum and his confederates (Mum, a figure who menaces the narrator with his mitre earlier in the poem (579; cf. 1236)) points to one thing that is not a matter of speculation: the author of *Mum* was not ignorant of the contemporary cultural censorship of material which institutions found uncomfortable.

When *The Boke of Cupide* was written, the battle-lines had not been so starkly drawn, though tenets of Wyclif's teaching had been condemned both by Papal Bull in 1377, and by the Council at Blackfriars in 1382. While there was yet no provision for burning heretics, or the destruction of books, references to such measures shows that such consequences were part of the 'social imagination' of late fourteenth-

---

[68] '(What þis metels bymeneþ, ye men þat ben murye. | Deuyne ye, for I ne dar, by deere God in heuene)!' (B. Prol. 209–10).

[69] Between 1402–10, most probably after Arundel's *Constitutions* and the subsequent letter exempting the friars from their terms; see Barr, 'The dates'.

century society, and hence part of the social knowledge through which texts might be decoded.[70] I think that *Cupide* incorporates features of the social knowledge of emergent Lollardy in ways very similar to Chaucer in *The Wife of Bath's Tale*, *The Pardoner's Tale*, and most especially in the *Prologue to the Legend of Good Women*, as I have discussed above.[71]

The Prologue to the *Legend* is one of the sources of *Cupide*. Another possible source is *La Messe des Oiseaux*, composed by the mid-fourteenth-century French poet John de Condé.[72] There are only two surviving manuscripts of this work,[73] however, and I can find no references to its ownership and readership in the late fourteenth century.[74] That said, bequests of a 'Frensch boke' in wills are hardly informative, and given the well-documented French literary tastes of Clanvowe's circle of friends at the court of Richard II,[75] it is not impossible that he, and his friends, knew the work, and that it influenced both the writing and the reception of *The Boke of Cupide*.

La Messe is an allegorical love dream vision. It is also a piece of estates satire. The lechery of the nuns and canonesses, for instance, is obvious from their appeal to be in the service of Venus, who listens to their petitions in the poem.[76] More subtle is the religious satire in the Mass which is sung by the birds in the opening of the poem. The narrator has nothing but admiration for their performance: 'it was a fine thing to hear such a choir' (p. 106), though given that he is complicit in admir-

[70] See Strohm, *England's empty throne*, 36–40.

[71] See Chapter 4 above; and Alcuin Blamires, 'The Wife of Bath and Lollardy', *Medium Aevum*, 58 (1989), 224–42; Peggy Knapp, *Chaucer and the social contest* (London, 1990), ch. 5; Paul Strohm, 'Chaucer's Lollard joke: history and the textual unconscious', *SAC* 17 (1995), 23–42; and Hudson, *Premature reformation*, 390–4.

[72] See *Chaucer's dream poetry*, ed. Phillipps and Haveley, 226–7; and Minnis, *Medieval theory*, 15.

[73] Jean de Condé, *Messe des Oiseaux et le Dit des Jacobins et de Fremeneurs*, ed. Jacques Ribard (Geneva, 1970), p. xvi.

[74] There is no mention of the work in S. H. Cavanaugh, *A study of the books privately owned in England 1300–1450* (Ann Arbor, 1980).

[75] See V. J. Scattergood, 'Literary culture at the court of Richard II', in Scattergood and Sherborne, eds., *English court culture in the later middle ages* (London, 1983), 29–43; James Sherborne, 'Aspects of English court culture in the late fourteenth century', ibid. 1–27; Richard Firth Green, *Poets and princepleasers: literature and the English court in the late middle ages* (Toronto, 1980), 101–34; Minnis, *Medieval theory*, 9–19.

[76] References are to the translation of *La Messe* in B. A. Windeatt, ed., *Chaucer's dream poetry: sources and analogues* (Cambridge, 1982), 104–19. The ecclesiastical satire in the poem is discussed by Yvan G. Lepage, 'La dislocation de la vision allégorique dans la *Messe des Oiseaux* de Jean de Condé', *Romanische Forschungen*, 91 (1979), 43–9.

ing the services of Venus, and also, rather as the narrator of *Wynnere and Wastoure*, gets completely drunk halfway through the poem (p. 108), his powers of judgement are not exactly sober. The author moralizes his tale in his own voice at the end of the poem (pp. 116–19). He explicitly contrasts the devout services of the birds with the lecherous behaviour of the female religious (p. 118), but it seems hard to avoid the conclusion that there is some light-hearted ecclesiastical satire in the earlier description of the Mass sung by the birds but to which he does not overtly draw attention.

For a start, it is Venus who commands the nightingale to commence the Mass and to preside over it. Many other birds join in: the thrush chants the epistle, for example, for which he is esteemed by the lovers present (p. 105). The birds are very keen to put in a good performance: the goldfinch, linnet, finch, and wagtail sing an alleluia; 'and each was striving to surpass his fellows in singing beautifully and strongly' (p. 106). Everything in the service is sung or chanted, including the Epistle and Gospel. The narrator comments on the blackbird's rendition of the gospel 'that he had never heard a chant more melodious, more agreeable or graceful' (p. 106). There is nothing in the narrator's response to this avian Mass which draws attention to the devotional or doctrinal substance of what is being sung. There is plenty of art, but no matter. At the moment of the Elevation of the Host, the nightingale lifts up a red rose (p. 107). While John de Condé explains and defends the doctrine of transubstantiation at the end of the poem (p. 116), here the nightingale's actions seem like a wholly irreverent parody of this most crucial sacrament.[77] The narrator tells us that the nightingale knew well how to set down the flower gracefully, and muses on the beauty, fragrance, and grace of the flower that was so pleasing to look at (p. 107). Sensuous pleasures of sight and smell dominate the narrator's attention; the doctrinal significance of this moment in the Mass passes him by.

There is one bird, however, whom Venus expels from the Mass because of his criticisms of lovers: the cuckoo. He is forced to flee in terror, chased fiercely by the other birds. He returns to exact his revenge later in the poem, flying over the lovers who are kneeling to make their petitions to Venus, calling out 'Cuckoo! Cuckolds!' (p. 107). The lovers complain to Venus about the cuckoo, which precipitates the conventional symbolic account of the evils of the bird, his unnaturalness

---

[77] Especially as the poem post-dates *The Romance of the Rose*, the choice of this flower, and the nightingale's sensuous devotion to it, recalls the Lover's winning of the rose at the conclusion of the earlier poem.

and treacherous nesting habits and his dubious lineage.[78] Everyone lines up against the cuckoo (pp. 107–8). But given the foolishness with which the lovers are depicted in the poem, and how the Mass is performed with more gallantry and ostentatious display than deep-felt piety, whatever the narrator's sympathies, it is hard for the reader to accede to an interpretation which champions the nightingale at the expense of the cuckoo. The symbolic associations are not commensurate with the narrative action of the poem. In his epilogue, Condé allegorizes the Mass. He praises the birds for their holy devotions, and interprets the cuckoo as symbolic of those who sin in so many ways against Holy Church that they are condemned (p. 116). But rather as Henryson's 'moralities' reopen the plentitude of the narrative in his fables even as they purport to close it down,[79] so here, Condé's allegorical exposition does not replace, or cancel out, the equivocal treatment of the nightingale and the cuckoo earlier in the poem. While the allegorical discourse polarizes the birds, the nightingale as a devout priest, and the cuckoo as an enemy of the Church, the narrator's admiration for the preening and pirouetting singing of the nightingale, and for the parody of the Mass, undermines such stability of interpretation.

If Clanvowe did not know this poem, then the coincidences between it and his own are remarkable. *Cupide* is composed of the same ingredients: love dream vision; petitions to Venus; debate; a cuckoo and a nightingale; and, I think, discussion of religious song and the persecution of those perceived to be opponents of Holy Church. In Clanvowe's own cultural climate, inclusion of these kinds of issues situates the poem right at the heart of the debates concerning the emergence of Lollardy. I want to suggest that *Cupide* is written by a poet who was cognisant of these issues, and written for an audience who would be able to decode them. The resonances would be especially sharp if both the audience and Clanvowe did know *La Messe des Oiseaux*, but I think that they could have been teased out if they did not.

---

[78] The characteristics of the cuckoo are discussed by David Chamberlain, 'Clanvowe's cuckoo' in David Chamberlain, ed., *New readings of late medieval love poems* (Lanham, Md., 1993), 41–65, pp. 50–3. He draws attention to the identification of the cuckoo with Christ in pastoral debate literature and the cuckoo as the symbol of redemption in the lyric *Sumer is I-cumen In*. There is also a conventional derogatory tradition of representing the nightingale. In *The Knight's Tale*, the cuckoo sits on the hand of Jealousy, I. 1930–1; in *The Manciple's Tale*, the cuckoo is associated with cuckoldry in the crow's speech, IX. 243; and in *The Parlement of Foules* the cuckoo is 'euer unkynde' (356) and foul (505).

[79] On the complexity of the relationship between tales and morality in the *Fables*, see Douglas Gray, *Robert Henryson* (Leiden, 1979), 118–61.

The narrator in *Cupide*, as in *La Messe*, sides with the nightingale against the cuckoo. But, as Chamberlain and Patterson have demonstrated,[80] we should be very wary indeed of accepting his viewpoint. One of the Chaucerian features of the poem is the creation of an unreliable, love-lorn narrator, whose aged infatuation with the nightingale is a sign that, as in *La Messe*, interpretation of the poem should not be driven by the symbolic associations of these birds, associations which tend to privilege the attractiveness of the nightingale over the foul habits of the cuckoo.[81]

At the start of the poem, the narrator is prompted by the delights of May, and an unsatisfied love-sickness, to go in search of a nightingale so he might hear it sing. As he sits down amongst the flowers, he hears the other birds sing:

> Ther sat I dovne amonge the feire floures
> And sawe the briddes crepe out of her boures,
> Ther as they had rested hem al nyght.
> They were so ioyful of the dayes lyght,
> That they began of May to don her houres.
>
> They coude that seruise alle bye rote.
> Ther was mony a lovely note:
> Somme song loude, as they hadde playned.
> And somme in other maner voys yfeyned.
> And somme al out, with al the fulle throte.
>
> They pruned hem, and made hem ryght gay,
> And davnseden, and lepten on the spray.   (66–77)

The narrator thinks that the birds' harmony is the best melody ever heard. But some of the diction used here should make us cautious about accepting the narrator's evaluation. The birds sing the canonical 'houres' (70) of May. As in *La Messe*, there is a synthesis of spiritual and erotic singing. And there is a similar emphasis on the self-satisfied performance of the singers, 'pruned' (76). There is a singular absence of devotion, despite the comparison to the singing of divine office. There service is sung by 'rote' (71) and by some, in a 'feyned' voice. *Cupide* is

[80] See Chamberlain, 'Clanvowe's cuckoo', 41–65; and Lee Patterson, 'Court politics and the invention of literature: the case of Sir John Clanvowe', in David Aers, ed., *Culture and history 1350–1600: essays on English communities, identities and writing* (Hemel Hempstead, 1992), 7–41.

[81] Cf. the debate in *The Owl and the Nightingale* which starts with the nightingale's criticism of the foul habits and appearance of the owl, *The Owl and the Nightingale*, ed. E. G. Stanley (Manchester, 1972), 29–40. The owl responds in kind (46–54).

not the only English bird poem which likens birdsong to musical practices in church; it is a feature of the thirteenth century. *Owl and the
Nightingale*, for example, and just as the rivalry between the birds on this
subject may reflect the contemporary debate over the merits of plain-
song and Gregorian chant, so too, in *Cupide*, the discussion of singing
practices may inhere in late fourteenth-century discussions on musical
practices in church.[82]

   As Chamberlain has noted, the description of the singing in *Cupide* is
more prominent than that of the grass.[83] And when the nightingale and
the cuckoo begin their altercation, singing is again one of the topics
about which they spar. The narrator is delighted by the 'lusty' singing of
the nightingale and despises the 'foule voyse' of the cuckoo (94). The
nightingale, for her part, tells the cuckoo to clear off out of the forest
because everyone shuns his boring song (112–15). This is the cuckoo's
reply:

> 'What!' quoth he, "what may the eyle now?
> Hit thynkes me I syng as wel as thow;
> For my songe is bothe trewe and pleyn,
> Al thogh I can not breke hit so in veyne,
> As thou dost in thy throte, I wote ner how.
>
> And euery wight may vnderstonde me,
> But, nyghtyngale, so may they not the,
> For thou has mony a nyse, queynte crie.
> I haue herd the seye 'ocy! ocy!'
> Who myght wete what that sholde be?"   (116–25)

Conlee notes that the contrast in singing here is intended to suggest
the differences between the monophonic and polyphonic music of the
Middle Ages.[84] Others have drawn parallels (usually in a footnote) to
Wycliffite condemnations of elaborate singing in church, which I think
is nearer the mark.[85] The exchanges between the cuckoo and the
nightingale, if read with knowledge of the contemporary climate of

---

   [82] *The Owl and the Nightingale* (854–932). The conclusion of the thirteenth-century poem
The Thrush and the Nightingale also turns on a point of religious debate, though not about
singing; the nightingale wins the argument against the misogynist thrush by arguing that he
has slandered the Virgin Mary; see John W. Conlee, ed., *Middle English debate poetry: a critical
anthology* (East Lansing, Mich., 1991), 239–48, ll. 169–92.

   [83] See Chamberlain, 'Clanvowe's cuckoo', 47.

   [84] Conlee, *Debate Poetry*, 257.

   [85] e.g. Patterson, 'Court politics', 39 n. 89; and Chamberlain, 'Clanvowe's cuckoo', 63
n. 35.

religious debate, can be seen to encode issues that were hotly disputed between Wycliffites and their opponents. Elaborate singing in church is condemned in a number of Wycliffite texts. *Of Prelates* has this to say:

Also prelatis disceyen lordis & alle cristene men bi veyn preieris of mouþ, & veyn knackyng of newe song & costy . . . [lords are blinded into maintaining open traitors of God] . . . for here stynkynge & abhomynable blastis & lowd criynge; for bi þer grete criyng of song, as deschaunt, countre note & orgene, þei ben lettid fro studynge & prechynge of þe gospel; & here owene fyndynge vp, þat crist & his apostlis spoken not of, as is þis newe song, þei clepen it goddis seruyce, & magnyfien it at þe fulle, but good lif & techynge of þe gospel þei setten at nouȝt . . . for þei don not here sacrifices bi mekenesse of herte & mornynge & compunccion for here synnes & þe peplis, but wiþ knackynge of newe song, as orgen or deschant & motetis of holouris.[86]

Walter Brut, in his *Defence*, marvels at the fact that while Christ and his apostles command the preaching of the word of God, priests now are more bound to celebrate the Mass and say the canonical hours.[87] Given the cultural knowledge of Lollardy in Clanvowe's circle, it is not fanciful, I think, to argue that the nightingale's 'vayne crakil' (trilling) and also its volume, such that it makes the whole wood echo (100), could suggest Wycliffite condemnations of over-elaborate false singing. The self-satisfied performance of the canonical hours by the other birds suggests the empty chanting produced by the lips, but not issuing from the heart, which Lollards so abhorred. Towards the end of the poem, the nightingale promises the narrator that if he remains faithful to her, then she will sing him 'oon of thy songis newe, | For love of the as loude as I may crie' (247–8). The contrast with the true and plain singing of the cuckoo reproduces the Wycliffite preference for plain, true preaching over new song. *De Precationibus Sacris* includes a passage which could be read as a hostile rejoinder to the narrator for taking so much pleasure in the singing of the nightingale and the other birds:

Wonder it is whi men presisen so moche þis newe preiynge, bi gret criynge and hey song, and leven stille manere of preynge, as Crist and his apostils diden. It semeþ þat we seken oure owene likynge and pride in þis song more þan þe devocion and understondynge of þat þat we syngen, and þis is gret synne . . . þerfore seiþ Poul, I have levere fyve wordis in my witt þan ten þousand in tonge . . . O Pater Noster seynge wiþ devocion and goode

---

[86] Matthew, 77 and 91; cf. *The order of priesthood*, 169; *Three things that destroy this world*, 183; and *Of feigned contemplative life*, 191.

[87] See John Foxe, *The acts and monuments of John Foxe*, ed. S. R. Cattley and J. Pratt (London, 1853–70), 8 vols., iii. 181.

understondynge, is beter þan many þousand wiþouten devocion and undirstondynge.[88]

It is not just the empty elaboration that is at stake in the interchange between the cuckoo and the nightingale. The 'queynte'-ness (123) of the nightingale's 'crie' prevents everyone from understanding her. The cuckoo, by contrast, may be understood by all. The significant bar to comprehending the nightingale is that she sings in a foreign language. True, the language is French, not Latin, but just as the debate over biblical translation is displaced in *The Prologue to the Legend of Good Women* into an accusation of heresy against the narrator for having translated *The Romance of the Rose*,[89] so here, the cuckoo's criticism of the nightingale's foreign incomprehensibility, in the context of the opposition between plain truth and proud ornament, may be seen as a displacement into a courtly love debate of the Wycliffite concern for the Bible to be translated into English so that it was accessible to all.[90]

The choice of 'Oci' for the nightingale's cry is also significant. French poems use the same word.[91] On one level, this is because of its onomatopoeic qualities, but 'oci' is also the imperative of the Old French verb 'ocire'—to kill. The nightingale explains as much to the narrator, chastising him for his ignorance:

> 'O fole,' quoth she, "wost thou not what that is?
> When that I sey 'ocy! ocy!' iwisse,
> Then mene I that wolde wonder fayne
> That alle tho wer shamefully slayne,
> That menen oght ayen love amys.
>
> And also, I wold alle tho were dede,
> That thenke not her lyve in love to lede,
> For who that wol the god of love not serve,
> I dar wel say he is worthy for to sterve,
> And for that skille 'ocy! ocy!' I grede.   (126–35)

The cuckoo responds that: 'this is a queynt lawe, | That eyther shal I loue or elles be slawe' (136–7). Especially if this exchange were read, or heard, with knowledge of the characteristics of the cuckoo and the nightingale in *La Messe*, its resonance with defining who belongs, or does not belong, within Holy Church would be striking. In *La Messe*, it

---

[88] Arnold, iii. 228.

[89] See discussion in Chapter 4 above.

[90] See Chapter 4.

[91] It is used by Froissart and Deschamps, see *The works of John Clanvowe*, ed. Scattergood, 84.

is the cuckoo, against the narrative dynamic of the poem, whose disdain for the service of love Condé identifies as an action which slanders the Church. In *Cupide*, the cuckoo refuses to be bound to love's service, even if it means death, concluding: 'What nedith hit ayens trweth to strive?' (145). Patterson has read the cuckoo's plain speech to represent the plight of the truthteller in a secular court where it is impossible to speak the truth and to thrive.[92] Such a reading is certainly tenable, but, as Justice has briefly suggested, the plain speech of the cuckoo is also suggestive in cultural religious terms.[93] The narrator calls the cuckoo a 'cherl', intending as an insult an attribution that Wycliffite texts granted positive merit.[94] The cuckoo's 'lewde voys', in contrast to the sophisticated but unintelligible and murderous cry of the nightingale, can be seen to reproduce the opposition between the corrective voice of the Wycliffite 'trewe man' and the institutionalized language of the material Church.

That both the narrator and the nightingale wish to expel the cuckoo from the wood because of his 'pleyn' song resonates with the Church's beginning to define true doctrine against false.[95] Even though the argument between the birds centres around love, the diction used in the debate is drawn from religious discourse. The nightingale, defending love's servants, claims that her position is true:

> And that ys sothe, alle that I sey.
> In that *beleve* I wol bothe lyve and dye.
>
> (161–2; italics mine)

'Beleve' is a term used frequently in Lollard texts to assert that their views constitute God's law, a claim that is contested in the works of their opponents.[96]

Both the nightingale and the narrator line up against the cuckoo with increasing violence. As soon as the narrator hears the cuckoo's song, he curses him:

[92] Patterson 'Court politics', 19–25.

[93] 'The nightingale cherishes the same "ese and . . . lust" condemned in *The Two Ways*; and the cuckoo, a plain-speaking bird (he doesn't know French (124–5)), is despised as a "cherl" (147), much as the world, in the prose tract, despises the devout as "lolleris and loselis"', 'Lollardy', *CHMEL* 671.

[94] Cf. the Wycliffite approbation of the honest labourer discussed in the previous chapter.

[95] Expulsion from the wood is a common motif in bird debate poems. See in addition to the expulsion of the cuckoo in *La Messe des Oiseaux*, *The Thrush and the Nightingale*, 84, and *The Owl and the Nightingale*, 150–2.

[96] See Barr, *Signes and sothe*, 101.

> 'Now God,' quod I, that died vponn the croise,
> Yive sorrowe on the, and on thy foule voyse,
> For lytel ioy haue I now of thy crie."   (93–5)

This riposte would hardly commend the narrator's treatment of the cuckoo to a Wycliffite reader. That needless swearing would have been recognized by Clanvowe and his circle as a sign of Lollardy may be inferred from the interchange between the Parson and Harry Bailly in *The Canterbury Tales*, where Parson's rebuke for swearing prompts the Host to smell a Lollard in the wind, and to fear an outburst of preaching.[97] When the nightingale appears, the narrator continues his attack on the cuckoo, continuing to use diction that is socially suggestive:

> 'A lytell hast thou be to longe hen,
> For her hath be the lewede cukkow,
> And songen songes rather then hast tho.
> I prey to God that euel fire him brenne."   (102–5)

Heretics were burnt on the continent, and though no Lollard had yet been burned in England, the *idea* of doing so was current in England at this time.[98] The narrator's wish to see the 'lewed' cuckoo burnt for his tedious singing resonates with the emergent discourse of heretic-burning which would pave the way for the death of William Sawtry in 1401. The narrator's polarization of the nightingale and the cuckoo, and his desire to eliminate the latter, may be seen to reproduce the incipient moves by the Church to eradicate Wycliffism. The nightingale tells the narrator to '*leve* not the cukkow' (237), arguing that everything he has said is 'strong *lesing*' (238), and when she takes her leave of the narrator he prays that God will shield us from 'the cukkow and his *lore*; for ther is non so *fals* a brid as he' (259–60). The italicized vocabulary is all to be found bandied back and forth in the writings of Wycliffites and their opponents, and the opposition between truth and falsehood reproduces exactly the non-negotiable exchange of views that characterized the debate between orthodoxy and heresy. There was no 'middle weie'.[99]

The nightingale's 'medecyne' for the narrator's having had to endure the cuckoo is for him to go every day to gaze upon 'the fresshe flour daysye' (243). Presumably this is an intertextual reference to *The*

---

[97] *The Epilogue of the Man of Lawe's Tale*, II. 1170–7. On Wycliffite attitudes to oaths and swearing, see Hudson, *Premature reformation*, 371–4.

[98] See Strohm, *England's empty throne*, 38–40.

[99] See further discussion in Barr, *Signes and sothe*, 100–4.

Prologue to the Legend of Good Women. There, the daisy is described as a
'relyke' and the narrator's worship of it described, as in *Cupide*, as an act
of ritual devotion.[100] In *Cupide* this daily worship of a flower is set up in
opposition to hearing the 'lore' of the cuckoo. The nightingale tells
the narrator, that even if he be 'for wo in poynt to dye, | That shal ful
gretly lyssen the of thy pyne' (244–5). She commits the narrator to
an act of blind devotion to an image ('loke vpon' (243)), which will
greatly lessen his torment if he feels on the point of death. There is a
fusion of courtly love and spiritual discourses here that is reminiscent of
that in *La Messe* (especially the erotic treatment of the rose/Eucharistic
host), which situate the poem in the midst of the contemporary debate
over image worship and acts of devotional piety. Wycliffites deplored
devotion to images and empty ritual, and examinations of Lollards
frequently tested suspects for their views on this subject.[101]

The cuckoo has been banished from the poem at this point, though
it is not hard to imagine his reaction to such behaviour. The narrator
and the nightingale are left holding the stage, though scarcely as victors.
In reply to the cuckoo's refusal to serve Cupid, and his lament that truth
is absent from his court, the nightingale bursts into tears 'for tene' and is
speechless (201–10). Archbishop Arundel's exasperated cupboard-
thumping in his exchange with the wily Thorpe might be considered
an action in a similar vein.[102] In *Cupide*, the nightingale has lost the
argument; it was a rule of medieval school's debate that arguing one's
adversary into silence conferred victory.[103] The nightingale's charitable
spirit can be inferred from her immediate concern to be avenged on the
cuckoo (215), a desire which the narrator promptly satisfies by throwing
a stone at the bird, forcing him to flee.

Neither the nightingale or the narrator come out well in this
incident. Proverbially, it was bad luck to throw a stone at a cuckoo, and

---

[100] *The Legend of Good Women*, F. 40–63; 308–21; the word 'relyke' is used at l. 321. It does
not appear in G.

[101] See Hudson, *Premature reformation*, 92–4; ead. *Lollards and their books*, 126, and on
p. 134, from the register of Thomas Polton: '26: Item an veneraciones crucis et ymaginum
sint faciende. 27. Item an oblaciones facte ad ymagines in ecclesijs in honore sanctorum illo-
rum quos ipse ymagines representant sint meritorie'; Aston, *Lollards and reformers*, 177–87. *The
Testimony of William Thorpe* (in *Two Wycliffite texts*, ed. Hudson) puts the case succunctly: 'þei
þat comen to þe chirche for to preie deuoutli to þe lord God moun in her inward wittis be
þe more feruent, þat alle her outward wittis ben schit fro alle vyward seeing and heeringe,
and fro alle disturbaunce and lettygis', p. 59/1146–49.

[102] *The Testimony of William Thorpe*, p. 88/70–01.

[103] *Works of John Clanvowe*, ed. Scattergood, 85.

further, to resort to violence, having lost the argument, shows the narrator, like the nightingale, to be guilty of the sin of anger. As in the narrator's desire to see the cuckoo burnt, here, the narrative enacts a physical expulsion of a speaker characterized as 'true', 'plain', and 'lewed'. Clanvowe's textuality here is only a stone's throw away from the burning barrel at Smithfield in 1401.

In contrast to Condé's moralization at the end of *La Messe*, Clanvowe offers no interpretation of the preceding debate. Instead, on the advice of 'oon brid' (271), the debate is referred, in the absence of the cuckoo, to the lord and peers of parliament (271–5) for judgement. Clanvowe is writing before the *Twelve Conclusions of the Lollards* were posted on the doors of Westminster Hall in 1395, and although a Wycliffite petition to Richard II and his lords does survive, its date is uncertain and its format differs from the conventional mode of presenting a formal petition to parliament.[104] No record survives of any such Lollard petition being presented but a bill for the disendowment of the clergy had been put to parliament in 1385, however, and Walsingham has left us an account of it. It was rejected.[105] The conclusion to *The Boke of Cupide* may have no connection whatsoever with requests to parliament to reform the Church; the means of adjudication may simply be a literary debt to *The Parliament of Fowles*. All the same, to mobilize the concept of a parliament meeting to adjudge an argument which resonates so powerfully with contemporary religious debate suggests that such a connection cannot be dismissed totally out of hand.[106] That Queen Anne is chosen to arbitrate may also be a purely literary debt; to the intercessory figure of Alceste in the *Prologue to the Legend of Good Women*. After all, her reputed ownership of a Bible in English has been shown to be a Lollard fabrication.[107] Facts, however, as Chaucer's *House of Fame* demonstrates so graphically, are not always extricable from fictions, especially in a community which might be supposed to share assumptions conditioned by social knowledge. The narrative denouement of *Cupide*, like the rest

---

[104] One version of the petition is in Arnold, iii. 507–23; a section from the end of the petition is included at the end of *Of feigned contemplative life*, see Matthew, 187–96. The Latin version is in I. H. Stein, ed., 'The Latin text of Wyclif's complaint', *Speculum*, 7 (1932), 87–94. For discussion of these tracts, see Somerset, *Clerical discourses*, 3–9, and Hanna, 'Two Lollard codices', in *Pursuing history*, 48–59.

[105] See *Historia Anglicana*, ii. 139–40.

[106] Justice briefly suggests that the end of *Cupide* may refer to the 1388 Merciless Parliament, *Lollardy*, CHMEL 673.

[107] Hudson, *Premature reformation*, 248.

of the poem, inheres very suggestively in issues that were germane to the emergence of Lollardy.

It might be objected that all of the above proceeds from an over-active olefactory sense rather than prudent literary judgement. But, as Anne Hudson has argued, 'authors other than Chaucer make it clearer that [Wycliffite] concerns also extended into the areas of social, theological and ecclesiastical questions'.[108] Clanvowe's *Boke of Cupide* is no clearer than Chaucer, but if I am right in sniffing out Lollard resonances in this poem, then we have an example of how awareness of Wycliffite issues permeates a courtly love poem. *Cupide* has been described as a 'jeu d'esprit', with no serious moral message intended.[109] It is, I think, an extremely playful poem, especially if the range of literary allusiveness in the text includes *La Messe des Oiseaux*. While *The Two Ways* has been suspected of Lollardy chiefly because of its silence about the importance of sacraments, *Cupide* may be seen to give voice to demonstrably Wycliffite concerns. One can no more claim Clanvowe as a Lollard on the basis of this poem, however, than one can claim Chaucer. None-theless, as Hudson argues, this bypasses the more interesting questions. To my mind, *Cupide* resembles the kind of love literature that Gary Waller examines with reference to the court of Henry VIII. The songs and sonnets of Wyatt, for example, use the diction of 'fin amour' but may be read as part of a coded courtly game where all the participants are aware that the subject of the verse is as much about the dangers and favours of court as the dark disdain and anguish of being rejected by one's beloved mistress.[110] Clanvowe's friends and fellow literary enthusiasts would have been well placed to read his poem both as a debate about love, and a half-serious staging of issues of religious debate in the late fourteenth century. Less than twenty years separate Clanvowe's birds from *Mum*'s bees, but the measures passed to extirpate Lollardy during that time make a significant difference to how we might interpret the use of coded religious views in literary works. While in *The Boke of Cupide*, shared sets of assumptions about the social knowledge of Wycliffism mobilize a discourse of solidarity for a pleasurable literary game, in *Mum*, sentiments commensurate with pro-Lollard ecclesiastical reform are articulated more guardedly—and in earnest.

[108] Ibid. 391–3.
[109] Charles Rutherford, '*The Boke of Cupide* reopened', *Neuphilogische Mitteillungen*, 78 (1977), 350–58, p. 357.
[110] Gary Waller, *English poetry of the sixteenth century* (London, 1993), 103–34.

Afterword: 'Adieu Sir Churl': Lydgate's *The Churl and the Bird*[1]

LYDGATE'S SHORT DEBATE between a churl and a bird[2] employs many of the formal features of literary language which I have discussed in the previous chapters of this book. His poem aptly illustrates the social mobility and inherent positionality of literary discourses. The poem is a translation. Lydgate tells us that he takes the tale 'out of Frenssh' (34).[3] While Lydgate apologizes for the quality of his translation, calling it a 'rude makyng' (382), invoking the well-worn topoi of authorial modesty, and the inferiority of English,[4] at no point is there any suggestion that the activity of translation is subversive or dangerous. In contrast to the associations made between translation and heresy that I examined in *The Prologue to the Legend of Good Women*, here a French tale is translated in order to deliver a lesson in social quietism and to sanction a conservative ordering of society as natural and God-given.

As much is said at the outset. The narrator begins by defending telling a tale which utilizes 'liknessis & ffigures' (1). He licenses his use of figurative diction and allegory with 'auctoritees groundid on scriptures' (3).

---

[1] The quotation is from l. 362 of *The Churl and the Bird*, cited from *The minor poems of John Lydate*, Part Two, ed. Henry N. MacCracken (EETS OS 192 1934).

[2] Walter F. Schirmer, in *John Lydgate: a study in the culture of the XVth century*, trans. Ann E. Keep (London, 1961), argues that the poem is one of Lydgate's early works, written during the reign of Henry IV. Derek Pearsall, *John Lydgate* (London, 1970), 200, says that it is not possible to date the poem, but it is usually regarded as early. The poem is amongst Lydgate's most popular works; it survives in at least twelve MSS dating from the fifteenth to sixteenth centuries, and five early printed editions; see Derek Pearsall, *John Lydgate: a biography* (Victoria, BC, 1977), 80–4.

[3] On the sources of the poem see Leonora D. Wolfgang, ' "Out of the Frenssh": Lydgate's source of *The Churl and the Bird*', *ELN* 32 (1995), 10–19; and Neil Cartlidge, 'The source of John Lydgate's *The Churl and the Bird*', *Notes and Queries*, 44 (1997), 22–4. Wolfgang argues that Lydgate's ultimate source is the thirteenth-century Anglo-Norman poem *Les Tres Savoirs*. Cartlidge argues that Lydgate was working directly from the version of the fable contained in *Tres Savoirs* and the thirteenth-century Anglo-Norman poem *Donnei des Amants* but not from either of the surviving copies of these texts.

[4] See discussion of these issues in the Introduction.

Grounding one's practice in Scripture deploys diction familiar from Wycliffite tracts[5] but the narrator's 'purpose' (33) is very far removed from the Lollard reregistering of the language of social description seen in the Wycliffite tracts I examined in Chapter 6, or the account of the social community offered up by the beekeeper in *Mum and the Sothsegger*. Having called upon biblical authority to license the use of allegory (1–14), the narrator of *Churl* defends the use of 'dirk parables' in beast fables (16), explicitly to endorse social hierarchy. He observes that in the natural world 'som . . . haue lordship, and som . . . obey' (21): eagles have lordship because they fly highest, the cedar is the tallest of trees, and the laurel 'of natur' is evergreen (22–5).[6] 'Of natur' stresses that sovereignty and power are naturally ordained, a phrase which articulates a normatively rigid vision of social relationships from a completely different narrative position from the use of the natural world and natural properties in *The Nun's Priest's Tale*, *The Book of Cupid*, and *Mum*.

The social quietism of the prologue is reinforced by the teaching of the bird in the debate which follows. Because, she argues, each thing in the natural world belongs in its rightful place—the fish in the sea, the birds in the air, animals on land—so too, is it right for a 'plowman for to tyle his londe | And a cherl, a mookfork in his honde' (260–6). In language which recalls the strain of anti-peasant discourse which associates them with muck and dirt,[7] the bird claims that the place of peasants and churls is ordained by nature. The bird herself, however, is described as having feathers 'brihter than gold wer' (59),[8] singing from a laurel tree in a garden which is described using many features of the 'locus amoenus' topos; references to 'sote herbis', (52); 'siluer stremys', (54); 'fressh laurer' (57); and the 'heuenly melodie' of birdsong (71).[9] The bird is located within a courtly discourse of writing,[10] and consequently, when she is caught by the churl in a trap, his action is explicitly seen to be one which violates natural and social order (85–126).

[5] See discussion in the Introduction.

[6] Cf. ll. 106–10 where the bird stresses the natural sovereignty of the lion and the eagle.

[7] See discussion in Chapter 6.

[8] In the *Donnei des Amants* the bird has yellow feathers, see Cartlidge, 'The source', 23. If the extant copies of the poem represent what Lydgate was working from, then he has intensified the courtliness of the bird by using diction which compares the sun-like feathers to gold wire. The courtliness of the description bears resemblances to the portrayal of Cupid and Alceste in *Prologue to the Legend of Good Women*, see Chapter 4 above.

[9] See Chapter 2 above.

[10] The courtliness of the garden setting causes some complications to the overt social moralizing of the poem, and I discuss these later.

In the debate which follows, the bird strenuously maintains an opposition between her own social position and that of the churl. While in the beast fable told by Chaucer's Nun's Priest, the quarrel between the fox and the cockerel is between animals whose rhetorical social standings are scrambled, and in *Wynnere and Wastoure*, a debate happens between participants whose social roles are discontinuous and contradictory, in *The Churl and the Bird*, the social disparity between the actants is consistently spelled out. The bird's speeches frame the churl with many of the characteristics of the anti-peasant strain of labouring discourse. He is associated with bodily appetite (145–7), illicit gain (267–8), accused of wanting to erase social distinctions (140), and to better his position (288–94), and delighting in 'ribaudrye' (356). Above all, the churl is accused of being stupid.

The bird taunts the churl with his 'lewdnesse' in allowing her to escape, but more significant, in terms of the use of literary materials in this poem, she baits the churl for his inability to comprehend orders of discourse which are associated with superior social positions. She tricks the churl into believing that she carries a jacinth inside her body which he has lost by giving her her liberty and rubs salt into his wounds by enumerating the qualities of precious stones, only to lament, at several points, that she is wasting her time trying to educate a churl with knowledge of gemstones:

> I am a fool to telle þe al attonys,
> Or teche a cherl the prys of precious stonys   (251–2)

> I lese my tyme any moor to tarye,
> To telle a bovir of the lapidarye   (265–6)

As the word 'lapidarye' in l. 266 makes clear, what the churl is unable to understand is a learned discourse, a systemized body of knowledge which inheres beyond his cultural ken.[11] While in *Pearl*, the Maiden's speeches to the Dreamer which try to re-educate his understanding of aristocratic materials and practices nevertheless encode social mobility and uncertainty,[12] in *The Churl and the Bird*, the use of jewel discourse asserts social division.[13] Rather as Hoccleve buttresses his social normativeness in *Oldcastle* by appeal to several dominant discourses, so too

---

[11] For examples, see *English Medieval Lapidaries*, ed. J. Evans and M. J. Serjeantson (EETS OS 190 1933).

[12] See Chapter 2 above.

[13] Cf. the bejewelled courtly artefacts discussed above in Chapters 3 and 4.

does the bird in Lydgate's poem. First, she reinforces her point by conjoining biblical citation with lapidary discourse:

> Men shuld nat put a precious margarite
> As rubies, saphires or othir stonys ynde,
> Emeroudes, nor othir perlis whihte
> To fore rude swyn, that love draff of kynde;
> For a sowe delitith, as I fynde,
> Moore in fowle draff his pyggis for to glade,
> Than all the perre, that cometh of Garnade   (253–9)

The injunction from Matthew not to cast pearls before swine[14] is cross-fertilized with a lapidarian enumeration of jewels, which are seen to be clearly distinct from animal muck. Significantly, the biblical image is feminized, which implicitly locates the biblical and lapidarian discourses within a masculine preserve in a discursive move which performs similar ideological work to Hoccleve's criticism of Oldcastle's feminized reading practices.[15] And just as Hoccleve invokes the discourses of reason and madness to impugn Bible reading by members of the third estate, the bird states that anyone who attempts 'to teche a cherl termys of gentilnesse' is 'mad' (342–3).[16]

The churl is also excluded from knowledge of liturgical discourse. Anyone who sings 'a fool a masse' is also 'mad' (341). In *The Book of Cupid* the singing of Mass is freighted with Wycliffite resonances,[17] but in Lydgate's poem sung liturgy is invoked to spell out the dull-wittedness of the churl, likened to an 'asse' (340). The bird also mocks the churl for his ignorance of clerical discourses. 'As clerkes specifie' (349), she says, everything in the natural world has its proper time and place, and its distinctive properties (349–57). This is adduced as the reason why the hunters delight in speaking of 'venerye' and the churl of 'ribaudrye' (356–67).[18] But more than this, she accuses the churl of not

---

[14] Matthew 7: 6. In criticizing Wyclif for having translated the gospel into English, Knighton accuses him of having made 'common and open to the laity, and to women who were able to read, which used to be for literate and perceptive clerks, and spread the Evangelist's pearls to be trampled by swine', *Chronicle*, 251.

[15] See Chapter 1 above.

[16] Cf. her taunt to the churl that he raves (330) and that he has forgotten her moral lesson to him because of his 'madnesse' (335).

[17] See Chapter 7 above.

[18] Some MSS readings make the social distinctions here more clear-cut: 'The gentylman tretyth of genterye | The cherl delyteth to speke of Rybawdrye' (*Minor poems*, ed. Mac-Cracken, p. 483).

being able to distinguish, as clerics can, between different species in the natural world:

> All oon to the a ffaucon & a kyte,
> As good an oule as a popyngay,
> A donghyl doke, as deynte as a snyte   (358–60)[19]

The churl's ignorance of natural lore results in social levelling. The bird's recourse to a tissue of normative discourses endorses a conservative socioliterary hierarchy.[20]

One further important discourse which is invoked in this poem is that of moral exempla. While in *The Nun's Priest's Tale*, clear moralities are confounded, the bird offers her lesson of 'thre wisdamys' (320) as examples of unambiguous teaching which the churl is simply too stupid to comprehend (319). The tone of her teaching, like that of the narrator in *Oldcastle*, is insistently propositional and axiomatic. There is a similar absence of modality which presents her moral teaching as given and not subject to interrogation or question. Axiomatic statements on the rightful ordering of the social world coexist with assertive truisms, for example:

> It sitt a mayster to have his liberte   (166).

> He is a foole, that skapid is daunger
> Hath brooke his ffeteris, & fled is from prisoun,
> For to resort; for brent child dredith fyer   (174–6)

> Whoo dredith no perel, in perel he shal falle;
> Smothe watres beth oft-sithis deepe   (183–4)

> All is nat gold that shewith goldissh hewe,
> Nor stoonys all bi natur, as I fynde,
> Be nat saphires that shewe colour ynde.   (306–8)

---

[19] There may be an echo here of the tercelet's words to the goose in *The Parlement of Foules*: '"Now fy, cherl!" . . . Out of the donghil cam that word ful right!' (596–7). He answers the goose, but the duck has also spoken in the preceding stanza.

[20] The social emphasis of the section of the poem from which the preceding lines are quoted, ll. 337–64, is all the more telling given that there is no counterpart in the *Donnei*. In *Savoirs*, there is a ten-line passage which corresponds to this section in which the bird states that there is no point in teaching a cuckoo to play an instrument well; he will still end up only being able to say 'cuckoo'. The cuckoo, along with the ass, are the churl's natural companions; see Wolfgang, '"Out of the Frenssh"', 17–18. Unless there was a version of the fable available to Lydgate which accentuated the social significance of this preaching far more than in the *Savoirs*, then Lydgate has taken the opportunity to introduce explicit social moralizing by adapting his sources. In any case, it is clear, as I discuss below, that his framing of the tale reads it very clearly as a socially conservative exemplum.

The syntactical construction of these statements, and of the three morals which the bird proclaims to the churl (196–217), present a world-view in which the use of the present tense brooks no contradiction. Speakers in other poems that I have discussed use identical linguistic formulations, for instance, the Pearl-maiden, Winner and Waster, and the Cuckoo and the Nightingale in *Cupide*, but a crucial difference between the propositional formulations of these speakers and of the bird in *The Churl and the Bird* is that there is no explicit narrative endorsement of their statements. In contrast, the narrator's comments in the envoi to *The Churl and the Bird*, which cannot be foisted off onto the responsibility of a translated 'auctor' (44), reinforces the axiomatic conservatism of one of the actants in the debate at the expense of the other. While the resolution in these other disputant poems is left indeterminate, the envoi to Lydgate's poem clearly sides with the bird's derision of the churl and reproduces her characteristically propositional mode of speech:

> Ye folk that shal this fable seen & rede
> New forgid tales councelith yow to flee,
> For losse of good takith no gret heede,
> Beeth nat to sorwefful for noon aduersite,
> Coveitith no-thyng that may nat bee,
> And remembrith, wheer that euer ye gon,
> A cherlis cherl is alwey woo-begon.   (365–71)

The syntax is imperative and moral instruction is fused with social truism. Explicitly, the narrator endorses the lesson of social quietism which the bird so emphatically delivers. The audience which is projected is one whose social alignments, in contrast to the projected audience of *Wynnere and Wastoure*,[21] are clear-cut.

The final stanza replicates this model of social hierarchy by reconfiguring the bird's social mandates into the domain of literary patronage and the production of text:

> Go, litel quaier, & recomaunde me
> Vn-to my maister with humble affeccioun;
> Beseche hym lowly, of mercy & pite,
> Of thi rude makyng to have compassioun;
> And as touchyng thi translacioun
> Out of the Frenssh, how-euyr the English be,
> All thyng is seide vndir correccioun
> With supportacioun of your benygnyte.   (379–86)

[21] See discussion in Chapter 1.

The diction of this passage figures the relationship between patron and writer as ruler and ruled. The patron is flatteringly co-opted into the normative pattern of social relationships which the poem endorses. The modesty topos also figures a relationship between text and 'maister' which confirms the power of the patron at the expense of the text. The aureate diction of ll. 385–6, 'correccioun; supportacioun and benygnyte', contrasts in register to the vernacular provenance of 'rude makyng' (382); and this contrast of register is reinforced by the fact that the patron is addressed with the polite second person pronoun 'your' (386), whereas the author addresses his translation with the intimate or inferior 'thi' (382).

The opening and closing frame of the fable can be seen as an attempt to create a declarative text, one which 'works diligently towards the suppression of any contradiction between its overt thematic project and the challenges posed to that project by the work's constitutive discourses'.[22] While in *Wynnere and Wastoure*, *Cupide*, *The Nun's Priest's Tale*, or even *Pearl*, there is no formal attempt to arrest the social play of signification generated by the medley of discourses and registers in the poem, Lydgate's framework can be seen to attempt to police the reading of the fable he translates. Perhaps he recognized that constitutive discourses in the fable might be seen to challenge the overt project of recommending social normativeness? For the fable certainly does encode challenges to the neat and tidy social frame which Lydgate supplies to his translation.

For all the bird's attempts to lay claim to privileged social discourses and assert their inaccessibility to the churl, the opening of the tale figures the churl, not as a dirty serf, pitchfork in hand amongst filthy swine, but as a gardener, and a gardener of a very beautiful courtly garden (50–63). While a gardener is still a member of the third estate, and, as we have seen, this is important in *Mum*,[23] the depiction of the gardeners in *Mum* and *The Churl and the Bird* is very different. The gardener in *Mum* is a labourer, and the garden is in part of a franklin's land.[24] In *Churl*, the courtliness of the garden bears many resemblances to aristocratic 'erber' in the *The Floure and the Leaf*,[25] and the elaborate

---

[22] See R. Barton Palmer, 'The narrator in *The Owl and the Nightingale*: a reader in the text', in Trigg, ed., *Medieval English poetry* (London, 1993), 156–71, p. 158.

[23] See Chapter 7 above.

[24] See Chapter 7 above.

[25] *The Flour and the Leaf*, ed. Derek Pearsall (Kalamazoo, Mich., 1990), ll. 49–112.

water features remind us of those at which the jeweller gawps in *Pearl*.[26] It is extremely unusual for the description of a fine garden to include mention of the labour, or labourer who created it. Accounts of splendid gardens, castles, and feasts delete reference to the sources of production.[27] Even more discordant, however, is that the garden *belongs* to the churl; he is not working it for someone else; he is a 'cherl which hadde lust & gret corage | Withyne hymsilf, bi diligent travaile | Tarray *his* gardeyn with notable apparaile' (45–7, my emphasis). Lydgate explicitly acknowledges his 'auctor' in the preceding line (44), and I wonder whether this is a caveat because he recognized that the description of the churl's garden is constituted from conflicting constituent discourses. One could, I suppose, read the lines as social satire at the expense of the churl who has tricked out his garden in a style inappropriate to his social position, but even with this reading, it is clear that the literary materials which Lydgate has chosen to translate encode a social mobility which is more unruly than the social quietism proclaimed by the bird and by the frame.

The pronominal economy of the fable is also much more unstable than that of the envoi. While Lydgate is very strict in observing the rules of pronominal decorum in his supplication to his 'maister', the use of second-person pronouns in the story fails to acknowledge crucial social distinctions. The bird consistently addresses the churl with the 'thou' pronoun (e.g. 113; 156; 165; 225), which is what we might expect from a bird framed as courtly to a speaker who is a peasant. But, the churl also consistently addresses the bird as 'thou' (e.g. 143; 145; 154; 170). There is no acknowledgement from him of the bird's superior social status. Again, one might read this at the expense of the churl, and see his use of pronouns as an instance of his attempt to erase social distinctions. But rather as the crow in *The Manciple's Tale* insults Phoebus, the god of poetry, as much through its insistent use of 'thy' as the use of the word 'swyve',[28] thus scrambling social distinctions maintained in language, so in *The Churl and the Bird*, the churl's insistent use of 'thou' creates a pronominal discourse within the poem in which social distinctions are upset. It is also worth noting that the gendering of the speakers in the

---

[26] See Chapter 2 above.

[27] As noted by Freedman of romances, *Images*, 31. He notes that where rustics appear in these works, it is usually as deformed peasants in forests. He notes a change, however, as the period progresses, for instance in the *Trés Riches Heures* of the Duke de Berry in which peasants are depicted going about their business while the nobility go about theirs.

[28] See *The Manciple's Tale*, IX. 256.

poem, rather as in *Pearl*, creates potential social confusion. While the unlearned are classified as sows in order to maintain learned discourses as a masculine preserve, the debate presents a female bird instructing a male human being. Beast fables are designed to instruct humans, as the prologue to the poem makes clear. It upsets traditional notions of hierarchy to have a human, however low in the social scale, taught by an animal.[29]

Further, there are two very significant points of emptiness in the poem. Despite the confidence of the bird and the narrator in the value of moral instruction, the churl learns nothing from the bird's lesson (299–308). Of course, one way to read this is to see it as a confirmation of the innate stupidity of churls. But the failure of moral instruction comes about because the bird has in fact tricked the churl. As in *The Nun's Priest's Tale*, there is a fusion of moral plenitude with trickery and guile. The bird's claim to carry a jacinth inside her body (232–45) is performative; it sounds convincing enough, but it invents a reality which the bird subsequently denies. If the bird can perform a narrative about her possession of a gemstone, then why should we take the rest of her speech as authoritative?[30] The recitation of moral instruction at the expense of churlish ignorance rings hollow, and with it, the efficacy of the discourse of moral instruction per se. Moral instruction is revealed as a constructed discipline.

Obviously, that is a very 'suspicious' reading of the poem, but it is one which is supported, I think, by another crucial emptiness, or silence, in the poem. The bird mocks the churl for his ignorance of distinctions in the natural world (358–60) but at no point in the poem are we ever told what *kind* of bird we are listening to. She sings both day and night (58), is far too small to carry a jacinth inside her (312–13), and is located within a courtly setting. But then, so too does the churl inhabit a setting which is courtly. While the bird sits on the conventionally courtly laurel tree, it is a tree which is owned by the churl. Her singing is heavenly, and she has feathers which are like gold wire, but as the bird solemnly acknowledges, all that glisters is not gold (306). In a poem which expressly asserts normative social hierarchy through appeal to classifications in the natural world, that the bird remains unlocated

---

[29] See discussion of this in Chapter 5 above.

[30] Especially in light of the fact that the bird explicitly tells the churl earlier in the poem not to give too hasty credence to any tale, for 'Mong many talis is many grett lesyng' (200).

creates a telling lacuna.[31] The bird assumes a courtly and learned status through linguistic description, which, as we have seen from Chaucer's *Manciple*, creates social reality at the same time as it encodes it.[32] And, for all the policing of discourse in the poem, that the bird can address the churl with the honorific title 'sir' in bidding adieu to him (362) shows how language constructs social reality. 'Sir churl' is, perhaps, a rather appropriate coinage to describe the apparent contradiction of a peasant owning a courtly garden?

The bird's claim to status is also constituted through her knowledge of socially elevated discourses: lapidarian, biblical, and moral. The bird claims power, not from her position within avian classification, but through her possession of dominant discourses. Discourses remain dominant, however, only if passed off as given and natural, and guarded jealously by their makers, but as Chaucer's *General Prologue* tells us, 'a jay | Kan clepen "Watte" as wel as kan the pope' (642–3).[33] Subversive mimicry has the power to destabilize the status quo.[34]

Even as the frame to *The Churl and the Bird* attempts to edit out confrontation between the constituent discourses of the fable, the faultlines are still visible. The declared aim of the poem is to peg literary materials to conservative social order, but perhaps its author was more alert to the social spillage than he lets on? To offer moral instruction and social normativeness to the audience of a poem with linguistic performativeness at its centre might be interpreted as an elaborate literary joke. Lydgate shows us elsewhere that he is not averse to larking around with normative discourses, for instance, the insertion of Latin in his mock-poem for the instruction of laundresses.[35] And so it may be too that in this French translation, for all its resemblances to Hoccleve's assertive social moralizing, the position of the translator is one, not of 'earnest', but of 'game'. Whatever reading is adopted, however, what the *Churl*

[31] Rather as the absence of the white hart sign in Gower's *Tripartite Chronicle* exposes and dismantles Ricardian sign-construction, so in *The Churl and the Bird*, there is a crucial absence in the natural world seen as a sign system endorsing conservative hierarchy.

[32] See discussion in Chapter 1 above.

[33] David Aers ('"Vox populi"', 442) notes of these lines that the governing classes kept jays as decorative cagebirds able to pick up and regurgitate fragments of human speech. In *Vox*, as Aers observes, Gower depicts Wat Tyler as a jackdaw (I. 9), 'the people's orator, the rival to the "vox populi" of Gower's poem'.

[34] Judith Butler discusses drag as a form of subversive mimicry in her analysis of how gender is 'a stylized repetition of acts', *Gender trouble*, (London, 1990), 140.

[35] *A Tretise for Laundres*, in *The minor poems*, ed. MacCracken, ii. 723. (I am grateful to Rosemary Appleton for drawing my attention to this playful poem.)

and the Bird demonstrates so well is not just that literature is social discourse, but that literary materials are socially positioned discourse. Socioliterary practice is simultaneously material and endlessly open to negotiation. Given all that I have said about the positionality of propositional statements, however, to end with one is probably an act of social imprudence.

Works Cited

UNPUBLISHED PRIMARY SOURCES

Bodleian Library, Oxford, MS Bodley 938.

PRINTED PRIMARY SOURCES

The alliterative Morte Arthure, in *King Arthur's Death*, ed. Larry D. Benson (Exeter, 1986).

The Anonimalle Chronicle, ed. V. H. Galbraith (Manchester, 1970).

ARNOLD, THOMAS, ed., *Select English works of John Wyclif* (Oxford, 1869–71), 3 vols.

BRINTON, THOMAS, *The sermons of Thomas Brinton, Bishop of Rochester*, ed. M. A. Devlin (Camden Society, London 4, ser. 3).

CHAUCER, GEOFFREY, *The complete works of Geoffrey Chaucer*, ed. W. W. Skeat (Oxford, 1900). 7 vols.

—— *The Riverside Chaucer*, ed. L. D. Benson *et al.* (Oxford, 1988).

—— *Chaucer's dream poetry*, ed. Helen Phillipps and Nick Haveley (London, 1997).

—— *The Legend of Good Women*, ed. J. Cowan and G. Kane (London, 1995).

The Chester Mystery Cycle, ed. R. M. Lumiansky and David Mills (EETS SS 3 1974).

CLANVOWE, JOHN, *The Works of Sir John Clanvowe*, ed. V. J. Scattergood (Cambridge, 1975).

CONDÉ, JEAN DE, *Messe des Oiseaux et le Dit des Jacobins et de Fremeneurs*, ed. Jacques Ribard (Geneva, 1970).

CONLEE, JOHN W., ed., *Middle English debate poetry: a critical anthology* (East Lansing, Mich., 1991).

Death and Liffe, ed. J. P. Donatelli (Cambridge, Mass., 1989).

The Dieulacres Chronicle, ed. M. V. Clark and V. H. Galbraith, *Bulletin of the John Rylands Library*, 14 (1930), 164–81.

DYMOCK, ROGER, *Liber contra XII errores et hereses Lollardorum*, ed. H. S. Cronin (London, 1922).

English Medieval Lapidaries, ed. J. Evans and M. J. Serjeantson (EETS OS 190 1933).

English Wycliffite sermons, vols. i and iii, ed. Anne Hudson; vol. i (Oxford, 1983; repr. Oxford, 1990), vol. ii, ed. Pamela Gradon (Oxford, 1988); vol iv, ed. Pamela Gradon and Anne Hudson (Oxford 1996).

Eulogium historiarium sive temporis, ed. F. S. Haydon, Rolls Series 9 (London, 1858–63), 3 vols.

The Flour and the Leaf, ed. Derek Pearsall (Kalamazoo, Mich., 1990).

FORDE, SIMON N., ed., 'Nicholas Hereford's Ascension Day sermon 1382', *Medieval Studies*, 51 (1989), 205–41.

Four English political tracts of the later Middle ages, ed. J.-P. Genet (Camden Society, 4th series 18, London, 1977).

FOXE, JOHN, *The acts and monuments of John Foxe*, ed. S. R. Cattley and J. Pratt (London, 1853–70), 8 vols.

Sir Gawain and the Green Knight, ed. J. R. R. Tolkien and E. V. Gordon (Oxford, 1967), 2nd edn. rev. Norman Davis.

GIVEN-WILSON, CHRIS, ed., *Chronicles of the revolution* (Manchester, 1993).

A good short debate between Winner and Waster: an alliterative poem on social and economic problems in England in the Year 1352 with modern English rendering, ed. Israel Gollancz (Select Early English Poems, 3, 1920).

GOWER, JOHN, *The complete works of John Gower: the French works*, ed. G. C. Macaulay (Oxford, 1899).

—— *The complete works of John Gower: the Latin works*, ed. G. C. Macaulay (Oxford, 1902).

—— *The English works of John Gower*, ed. G. C. Macaulay (EETS ES 81 1900).

—— *The major Latin works of John Gower*, ed. and trans. E. W. Stockton (Seattle, 1961).

—— *Mirour de L'Omme,* trans. William Burton Wilson (East Lansing, Mich., 1992).

GRAY, DOUGLAS, ed., *A selection of religious lyrics* (Oxford, 1975).

The Harley Lyrics, ed. G. L. Brook (Manchester, 1956).

HARRISON, TONY, *Continuous* (London, 1981).

Historia Vitae Ricardi Secundi, ed. G. Stow (Philadelphia, 1977).

Historical poems of the XIVth and XVth centuries, ed. R. H. Robbins (New York, 1959).

HOCCLEVE, THOMAS, *The Regement of Princes*, ed. F. J. Furnivall (EETS ES 72 1987).

—— *The minor poems*, ed. F. J. Furnivall and I. Gollancz rev. Jerome Mitchell and A. I. Doyle (EETS ES 67, 73 1970).

Jack Upland, Friar Daw's Reply and Upland's Rejoinder, ed. P. L. Heyworth (Oxford, 1968).

JOHANNIS DE TROKELOWE et HENRICI DE BLANEFORDE, *Chronica et Annales*, ed. H. T. Riley (London, 1886).

JOHN OF SALISBURY, *Policraticus*, ed. Markland Murray (New York, 1979).

KAIL, J., ed., *Twenty six political and other poems* (EETS OS 124 1904).

The Book of Margery Kempe, ed. S. B. Meech and H. E. Allen (EETS OS 212 1940).

KNIGHTON, HENRY, *Chronicon*, ed. J. R. Lumby (Rolls Series, 2 vols. 1889–95).

The Lanterne of Li3t, ed. Lilian M. Swinburn (EETS OS 151 1917).

Lollard sermons, ed. Gloria Cigman (EETS OS 294 1989).

LYDGATE, JOHN, *The Minor poems of John Lydgate*, Part Two, ed. Henry N. MacCracken (EETS OS 192 1934).

MAIDSTONE, RICHARD, *Concordia inter regem Ricardum Secundum et civitatem London*, in *Political poems and songs*, ed. Thomas Wright (Rolls Series, London, 1859–61), ii. 282–300.

Middle English romances, ed. A. V. C. Schmidt and Nicolas Jacobs (London, 1980).

Mum and the Sothsegger, ed. M. Day and R. Steele (EETS OS 199 1936).

Octovian, ed. F. M. McSparran (EETS OS 289 1986).

The Owl and the Nightingale, ed. E. G. Stanley (Manchester, 1972).

The Parlement of the Thre Ages, ed. M. Y. Offord (EETS OS 246 1959).

Pearl, ed. E. V. Gordon (Oxford, 1953).

Piers Plowman: the B version, ed. George Kane and E. Talbot Donaldson (London, 1975).

Piers Plowman: A parallel text edition of the A, B, C and Z versions, ed. A. V. C. Schmidt (London, 1995).

The Piers Plowman tradition, ed. Helen Barr (London 1993).

The poems of the Pearl manuscript, ed. Malcolm Andrew and Ronald Waldron, rev. edn. (Exeter, 1987).

Political poems and songs, ed. Thomas Wright (Rolls Series, London, 1859–61), 2 vols.

Registrum Johannis Trefnant, ed. W. W. Capes (Canterbury and York Society 1916).

RICHARD OF CIRENCESTER, *Ricardi de Cirencestria Speculum Historiale*, ed. J. E. B. Mayor (London, Rolls Series, 1863–9).

Rotuli Parliamentorum (London, 1832), 7 vols.

Secreta Secretorum: nine English versions, ed. M. A. Manzalaoui (EETS OS 276 1977).

M. C. SEYMOUR *et al.*, ed., *On the Properties of things: John Trevisa's translation of Bartholomaeus Anglicus, De Proprietatibus Rerum* (Oxford, 1975), 2 vols.

Selections from English Wycliffite writings, ed. Anne Hudson (Cambridge, 1978).

Six Ecclesiastical satires, ed. James Dean (Kalamazoo, Mich., 1991).

Speculum Historiale, ed. J. E. B. Mayor (Rolls Series 30, London, 1863).

Statutes of the realm (10 vols., London, 1810–28).

Stein, I. H., ed., 'The Latin text of Wyclif's complaint', *Speculum*, 7 (1932), 87–94.

TURVILLE-PETRE, THORLAC, ed., *Alliterative poetry of the later Middle ages* (London, 1989).

Two Wycliffite texts, ed. Anne Hudson (EETS OS 301 1993).

USK, ADAM, *Chronicon de Adae de Usk*, ed. and trans. E. Maunde Thompson (London, 1904), 2nd edn.

Von Nolcken, Christina, ed., *The Middle English translation of the Rosarium Theologie* (Heidelberg, 1979).

The Wakefield pageants in the Townley Cycle, ed. A. C. Cawley (Manchester, 1958).

Walsingham, Thomas, *Chronicon Angliae*, ed. E. M. Thompson (London, Rolls Series, 1874).

—— *Historia Anglicana*, ed. H. T. Riley (Rolls Series, 2 vols., 1863–4).

The Westminster Chronicle 1381–1394, ed. and trans. B. Harvey and L. C. Hector (Oxford, 1982).

Wilkins, D., ed., *Concilia Magnae Britanniae et Hibernae* (4 vols., London, 1737).

Wimbledon's Sermon: Redde rationem villicationis tue: a Middle English sermon of the Fourteenth Century, ed. I. K. Knight (Pittsburgh, 1967).

Wyclif, John, *The English works of John Wyclif hitherto unprinted*, ed. F. D. Matthew (EETS OS 74 1880, 2nd rev. edn., 1902).

—— *Trialogus*, ed. G. Lecher (Oxford, 1869).

Wynnere and Wastoure, ed. Stephanie Trigg (EETS OS 297 1990).

SECONDARY SOURCES

Abraham, David H., '"Cosyn and cosynage": pun and structure in the *Shipman's Tale*, *Chaucer Review*, 11 (1977), 319–217.

Ackerman, Robert W., 'The *Pearl*-maiden and the penny', in John Conley, ed., *The Middle English Pearl* (Notre Dame, Ind., 1970), 149–62.

Aers, David, *Piers Plowman and Christian allegory* (London, 1975).

—— *Chaucer, Langland and the creative imagination* (London, 1980).

—— 'The self mourning: reflections on *Pearl*', *Speculum*, 68 (1993), 54–73.

—— '"Vox populi" and the literature of 1381', in *CHLME* 440–51.

Alexander, Jonathan J. G., 'The portrait of Richard II in Westminster Abbey', in D. Gordon, L. Monnas, and C. Elam, eds., *The regal image* (London, 1997), 197–206.

Alford, J. A., ed., *A companion to* Piers Plowman (Berkeley, 1988).

Althusser, Louis, 'Ideology and ideological state apparatuses', in *Lenin and Philosophy*, trans. Ben Brewster (London, 1971), 121–73.

Ames, Ruth, 'The feminist connections of Chaucer's *Legend of Good Women*', in Julian N. Wasserman and Robert J. Blanch, eds., *Chaucer in the Eighties* (Syracuse, NY, 1986), 57–74.

Amherst, A. M. T., 'A fifteenth century treatise on gardening', *Archaeologia*, 54 (1894), 157–72.

Anderson, M. D., *The medieval carver* (Cambridge, 1935).

Aston, Margaret, *Lollards and reformers: images and literacy in late medieval religion* (London, 1984).

—— 'Lollardy and sedition', in *Lollards and reformers* (Hambledon, 1984), 1–47.

—— 'Wyclif and the vernacular', *Studies in Church History*, Subsidia 5 (1987), 281–330.

—— 'Caim's castles: poverty, politics and disendowment', in *Faith and fire: popular and unpopular religion* (London, 1993), 95–131.

—— 'Corpus Christi and corpus regni: heresy and the Peasants' Revolt', *Past and Present*, 143 (1994), 3–47.

BALIBAR, ETIENNE, and MACHEREY, PIERRE, 'On literature as an ideological form', in Robert Young, ed., *Untying the Text* (London, 1981), 79–99.

BARNEY, STEPHEN A., 'The plowshare of the tongue: the progress of a symbol from the Bible to *Piers Plowman*', *Medieval Studies*, 35 (1973), 261–93.

BARR, HELEN, 'A study of Mum and the Sothsegger in its political and literary contexts', D.Phil. thesis (Oxford University, 1989).

—— 'The dates of *Richard the Redeless* and *Mum and the Sothsegger*', *Notes and Queries*, 235 (1990).

—— 'The relationship of *Richard the Redeless* and *Mum and the Sothsegger*', *YLS* 4 (1990), 105–33.

—— 'The treatment of natural law in *Richard the Redeless* and *Mum and the Sothsegger*', *LSE* 23 (1992), 49–80.

—— *Signes and sothe: language in the Piers Plowman tradition* (Cambridge, 1994).

BARRON, CAROLINE, 'The tyranny of Richard II', *BIHR* 41 (1968), 1–18.

—— 'Introduction', in D. Gordon, L. Monnas, and C. Elam, eds., *The regal image* (London, 1997), 9–17.

—— 'Richard II and London', in Anthony Goodman and J. L. Gillespie, eds., *Richard II: the art of kingship* (Oxford, 1999).

BARTHES, ROLAND, 'Rhetoric of the image', in *Image, music, text*, trans. Stephen Heath (Glasgow, 1977), 32–51.

BELL, D. M., *L'idéal éthique de la royauté en France au moyen âge* (Paris, 1962).

BENNETT, MICHAEL J., *Community, class and careerism: Cheshire and Lancashire society in the age of* Sir Gawain and the Green Knight (Cambridge, 1983).

—— 'The court of Richard II and the promotion of literature', in Barbara Hanawalt, ed., *Chaucer's England: literature in historical context* (Minneapolis, 1992), 3–20.

—— 'The historical background', in D. Brewer and J. Gibson, eds., *A companion to the* Gawain-*poet* (Cambridge, 1997), 71–90.

—— 'Richard II and the wider realm', in A. Goodman and J. L. Gillespie, eds., *Richard II: the art of kingship* (Oxford, 1999), 187–204.

BESTUL, T. H., *Satire and allegory in* Wynnere and Wastoure (Lincoln, Nebr., 1974).

BILDERBECK, J. B., *Chaucer's* Legend of Good Women (London, 1902), 85–7.

BINSKI, PAUL, *Westminster Abbey and the Plantagenets* (New Haven and London, 1995).

BISHOP, IAN, Pearl *in its setting* (Oxford, 1968).

BISHOP, IAN, '*The Nun's Priest's Tale* and the Liberal Arts', *RES* 30 (1979).

BISSON, LILLIAN M., *Chaucer and the late medieval world* (London, 1998).

BLAMIRES, ALCUIN, 'The Wife of Bath and Lollardy', *Medium Aevum*, 58 (1989), 224–42.

BLANCH, ROBERT J., 'The current state of *Pearl* criticism', *Chaucer Yearbook*, 3 (1996), 21–33.

—— YOUNGERMAN, MIRIAM, and WASSERMAN, JULIAN N., eds., *Text and matter: new critical perspectives on the* Pearl-*Poet* (New York, 1991).

—— and JULIAN N. WASSERMAN, *From* Pearl *to* Gawain*: 'forme to fynisment'* (Gainesville, Fl., 1995).

BLENKNER, LOUIS, 'The theological structure of *Pearl*', in John Conley, ed., *The Middle English Pearl*, (Notre Dame, Ind., 1970), 220–71.

BOFFEY, JULIA, and COWEN, JANET, eds., *Chaucer and fifteenth century poetry* (London, 1991).

BOGDANOS, THEODORE, Pearl: *image of the ineffable* (University Park, Pa., and London, 1983).

BOITANI, PIERO, '"My tale is of a cock"—or the problem of literal interpretation', in Richard G. Newhauser and J. A. Alford, eds., *Literature and religion in the later Middle ages: philological studies in honor of Siegfried Wenzel* (New York, 1995), 25–42.

BOLTON, J. L., *The medieval English economy 1150–1500* (Totowa, NJ, 1980).

BORN, L. K., 'The perfect prince: a study in thirteenth and fourteenth century ideals', *Speculum*, 3 (1928), 470–504.

BOURDIEU, PIERRE, *Language and symbolic power*, ed. John B. Thompson (Cambridge, 1991).

BOWERS, JOHN M., 'The politics of *Pearl*', *Exemplaria*, 7 (1995), 419–441.

—— '*Pearl* in its royal setting: Ricardian poetry revisited', *SAC* 17 (1995), 111–55.

—— '*Piers Plowman* and the police: notes toward a history of the Wycliffite Langland', *YLS* 6 (1992), 1–50.

BRADY, SR. M. TERESA, '*The Pore Caitif*: an introductory study', *Traditio*, 10 (1954), 529–48.

—— 'Lollard interpolations and omissions in manuscripts of *The Pore Caitif*', in Michael G. Sargent, ed., *Cella in seculum: religious and secular life and devotion in late medieval England* (Cambridge, 1989), 183–203.

BREEZE, ANDREW, 'A Welsh addition to the *Piers Plowman* group?', *Notes and Queries*, 238, NS 40 (1993), 142–51.

BREWER, DEREK, 'The ideal of feminine beauty in medieval literature, especially *The Harley Lyrics*, Chaucer, and some Elizabethans', *MLR* 50 (1955), 257–69.

—— and JONATHAN GIBSON, eds., *A companion to the* Gawain-*poet* (Cambridge, 1997).

BROWN, A. L., 'Parliament c.1377–1422', in R. G. Davies and J. H. Denton, eds., *The English parliament in the middle ages* (Manchester, 1981), 109–40.

BROWN R., and GILMAN, A., 'The pronouns of power and solidarity', in Piero Paolo Giglioli, ed., *Language and social context* (Harmondsworth, 1982), 252–82.

BURLIN, ROBERT, *Chaucerian fiction* (Princeton, 1977).

BURNLEY, DAVID, *Courtliness and literature in medieval England* (London, 1988).

BURROW, J. A., *Ricardian poetry* (London, 1971).

—— 'Hoccleve's *Series*: experience and books', in R. F. Yeager, ed., *Fifteenth century studies: recent readings* (Hamden, Conn., 1984).

BUTLER, JUDITH, *Gender trouble* (London, 1990).

CAMERON, DEBORAH, 'Demythologising sociolinguistics: why language does not reflect society', in John E. Joseph and Talbot J. Taylor, eds., *Ideologies of language* (London, 1990), 79–93.

CAMILLE, MICHAEL, 'Labouring for the lord: the ploughman and the social order in the Luttrell Psalter', *Art History*, 10 (1987), 423–54.

—— *Mirror in parchment: the Luttrell Psalter and the making of medieval England* (London, 1998).

CAMPBELL, MARIAN, 'Gold, silver and precious stones', in John Blair and Nigel Ramsay, eds., *English medieval industries: craftsmen, techniques, products* (London, 1991), 107–66.

—— 'White harts and coronets: the jewellery and plate of Richard II' in D. Gordon, L. Monnas, and C. Elam, eds., *The regal image* (London, 1997), 95–114.

CANNON, CHRISTOPHER, *The making of Chaucer's English* (Cambridge, 1998).

CARTLIDGE, NEIL, 'The source of John Lydgate's *The Churl and the Bird*', *Notes and Queries*, 44 (1997), 22–24.

CAVANAUGH, S. H., *A study of the books privately owned in England 1300–1450* (Ann Arbor, 1980).

CHAMBERLAIN, DAVID, 'Clanvowe's cuckoo', in David Chamberlain, ed., *New readings of late medieval love poems* (Lanham, Md., 1993), 41–65.

CHANCE, JANE, 'Allegory and structure in *Pearl*: the four senses of the "Ars Praedicandi" and fourteenth century homiletic poetry', in R. J. Blanch, M. Youngerman, and J. N. Wasserman, eds., *Text and matter* (New York, 1991), 31–59.

CHROUST, A. H., 'The corporate idea and the body politic in the middle ages', *Review of Politics*, 9 (1947), 423–52.

CIGMAN, GLORIA, ' "Luceat lux vestra": the Lollard preacher as truth and light', *RES* ns 40 (1989), 479–96.

COLEMAN, JANET, *English literature in history 1350–1400* (London, 1981).

COLEMAN, JOYCE, *Public reading and the reading public in late medieval England and France* (Cambridge, 1996).

CONLEY, JOHN, ed., *The Middle English Pearl* (Notre Dame, Ind., 1970).

COOKE, W. G., and BOULTON, D'A. J. D., '*Sir Gawain and the Green Knight*: a poem for Henry of Grosmont?', *Medium Aevum*, 68 (1999), 42–51.

COOPER, HELEN, *The structure of 'The Canterbury Tales'* (London, 1983).

—— 'Langland's and Chaucer's Prologues', *YLS* 1 (1987), 71–81.

—— *Oxford guides to Chaucer: The Canterbury Tales* (Oxford, 1996), 2nd edn.

COPELAND, RITA, 'The fortunes of "non verbum pro verbo": or why Jerome is not a Ciceronian', in Roger Ellis, ed., *The medieval translator: the theory and practice of translation in the middle ages* (Cambridge, 1989), 15–35.

—— *Rhetoric, hermeneutics and translation in the later middle ages: academic traditions and vernacular texts* (Cambridge, 1991).

COULTON, C. G., *The medieval village* (Cambridge, 1925).

COX, CATHERINE S., '*Pearl*'s "precios pere": gender, language and difference', *Chaucer Review*, 32 (1998), 377–90.

COX, JEFFREY N., and REYNOLDS, LARRY J., eds., *New historical literary study: essays on reproducing texts, representing history* (Princeton, 1993), 3–38.

CRANE, SUSAN, 'The writing lesson of 1381', in Hanawalt, ed., *Chaucer's England* (Minneapolis, 1992), 201–21.

CUNNINGHAM, J. V., 'The literary form of the Prologue to the *Canterbury Tales*', *Modern Philology*, 49 (1952), 172–81.

DAHLBERG, C., 'Chaucer's cock and fox', *JEGP* 53 (1954), 277–90.

DAVENPORT, W. A., *The art of the* Gawain-*poet* (London, 1978).

DAVIDSON, CLIFFORD, *Drama and art* (Kalamazoo, Mich., 1977).

DAVIES, MORGAN THOMAS, 'Plowmen, patrons and poets: Iolo Goch's *Cwydd y Llafurwr* and some matters of Wales in the fourteenth century', *Medievalia et Humanistica*, 24 (1997), 51–74.

DAVIES, RICHARD G., 'Richard II and the church', in A. Goodman and J. L. Gillespie, eds., *Richard II: the art of kingship* (Oxford, 1999), 83–106.

DE MAN, PAUL, *The resistance to theory* (Manchester, 1987).

DELANY, SHEILA, *Medieval literary politics: shapes of ideology* (Manchester, 1990).

—— *The naked text: Chaucer's* Legend of Good Women (Berkeley, 1994).

DOBSON, R. B., ed., *The Peasants' Revolt of 1381* (London, 1983).

DOUGLAS, MARY, *Purity and danger: an analysis of the concepts of pollution and taboo* (London, 1966).

DRONKE, PETER, 'Arbor caritatis', in P. L. Heyworth, ed., *Medieval studies for J. A. W. Bennett* (Oxford, 1981), 207–53.

DU BOULAY, R. H., and BARRON, C., eds., *The reign of Richard II* (London, 1971).

DUGGAN, HOYT, 'Langland's meter', *YLS* 1 (1987), 41–71.

DULS, LOUISA D., *Richard II in the early chronicles* (The Hague, 1975).

DYER, CHRISTOPHER C., '*Piers Plowman* and plowmen: a historical perspective', *YLS* 8 (1995), 155–76.

DYER, GILLIAN, *Advertising as communication* (London and New York, 1982).

EASTHOPE, ANTHONY, *Poetry as discourse* (London, 1983).

EBERLE, PATRICIA J., 'The politics of courtly style at the court of Richard II', in Glyn S. Burgess and Robert A. Taylor, eds., *The spirit of the court* (Cambridge, 1985).

——'Richard II and the literary arts' in A. Goodman and J. L. Gillespie, eds., *Richard II: the art of kingship* (Oxford, 1999), 231–53.

ECHARD, SIÂN, 'With Carmen's help: Latin authorities in the *Confessio Amantis*', *Studies in Philology*, 95 (1998), 1–40.

ECO, UMBERTO, *The role of the reader: explorations in the semiotics of texts* (London, 1981).

EDWARDS, ROBERT, ed., *Art and context in late medieval narrative* (Cambridge, 1994).

ELDREDGE, LAWRENCE, 'The state of *Pearl* studies since 1933', *Viator*, 6 (1975), 171–94.

ELLIOTT, R. W. V., 'The topography of *Wynnere and Wastoure*', *English Studies*, 48 (1967), 1–7.

ELLIOTT, THOMAS J., 'Middle English complaints against the times: to contemn the world or to reform it?', *Annuale Medievale*, 14 (1973), 22–35.

ELLIS, ROGER, 'Chaucer, Christine de Pizan and Hoccleve: *The Letter of Cupid*', in Catherine Batt, ed., *Essays on Thomas Hoccleve* (Brepols, 1996), 29–54.

EVANS, JOAN, *English art 1307–1461* (Oxford, 1949).

——*A history of jewellery 1100–1870* (Boston, 1953).

EVERETT, DOROTHY, *Essays on Middle English literature* (Oxford, 1955).

FAIRCLOUGH, NORMAN, *Language and power* (London, 1989).

FARAL, E., ed., *Les arts poétiques du xiie et du xiiie siècle* (Paris, 1924).

FEHRENBACHER, RICHARD W., ' "A yeerd enclosed al aboute": literature and history in *The Nun's Priest's Tale*', *Chaucer Review*, 29 (1994), 134–48.

FEIN, SUSANNA GREER, 'Twelve line stanza forms in Middle English and the date of *Pearl*', *Speculum*, 72 (1997), 367–98.

FINNEGAN, RUTH, *Oral poetry: its nature, significance and social context* (Cambridge, 1977).

FISHER, CELIA, 'A study of the plants and flowers in the Wilton Diptych', in D. Gordon, L. Monnas, and C. Elam, eds., *The regal image* (London, 1997), 155–63.

FISHER, JOHN H., *John Gower: moral philosopher and friend of Chaucer* (New York, 1964).

——'A language policy for Lancastrian England', *PMLA* 107 (1992), 1168–80.

FLEMING, JOHN V., 'The moral reputation of the *Roman de la Rose* before 1400', *Romance Philology*, 18 (1965), 430–5.

FLETCHER, ALAN J., *Preaching and politics in late medieval England* (Dublin, 1998).

FOUCAULT, MICHEL, *Madness and reason: a history of insanity in the age of reason*, trans. Richard Howard (New York, 1965).

——'The order of discourse', in Robert Young, ed., *Untying the text* (London, 1981), 48–78,

FOUCAULT, MICHEL, 'What is an author?', in David Lodge, ed., *Modern literary criticism and theory* (London, 1988), 196–210.

FOWLER, ROGER, *Literature as social discourse* (London, 1981).

FRANK, R. W., *Chaucer and the* Legend of Good Women (Cambridge, Mass., 1972).

FREEDMAN, PAUL, *Images of the medieval peasant* (Stanford, Calif., 1999).

FRIEDMAN, ALBERT B., ' "Whan Adam delved" . . . contexts of an historic proverb', in Larry D. Benson, ed., *The learned and the lewed: studies in Chaucer and medieval literature* (Cambridge, Mass., 1974), 213–30.

FYLER, JOHN, *Chaucer and Ovid* (New Haven, 1979).

GALLOWAY, ANDREW, 'Gower in his most learned role and the Peasants' Revolt of 1381', *Medievalia*, 16 (1993), 329–47.

GANIM, JOHN M., 'Chaucer and the noise of the people', *Exemplaria*, 2 (1990), 71–88.

GILBERT, A. H., 'Notes on the influence of the *Secreta Secretorum*', *Speculum*, 3 (1928), 84–93.

GIVEN-WILSON, CHRIS, *The royal household and the king's affinity: service, politics and finance in England, 1350–1413* (London, 1986).

—— *The English nobility in the late middle ages: the fourteenth century political community* (London, 1987).

GODDEN, MALCOLM, 'Plowmen and hermits in Langland's *Piers Plowman*', *RES* NS 35 (1984), 129–63.

GOLDSTEIN, R. JAMES, 'Chaucer, Freud, and the political economy of wit: tendentious jokes in *The Nun's Priest's Tale*', in Jean Jost, ed., *Chaucer's Humour* (New York, 1994), 145–62.

GOODMAN, ANTHONY, *The loyal conspiracy* (London, 1971).

—— 'Richard II's Councils', in A. Goodman and J. L. Gillespie, eds., *Richard II: the art of kingship* (Oxford, 1999), 59–82.

—— and GILLESPIE, JAMES L., eds., *Richard II: the art of kingship* (Oxford, 1999).

GORDON, DILLIAN, *Making and Meaning: the Wilton Diptych* (London, 1993).

—— MONNAS, LISA, and ELAM, CAROLINE, eds., *The regal image of Richard II and the Wilton Diptych* (London, 1997).

GRADON, PAMELA, *Form and style in early English literature* (London, 1971).

—— '*Piers Plowman* and the ideology of dissent', *PBA* 66 (1980), 179–205.

GRAY, DOUGLAS, *Robert Henryson* (Leiden, 1979).

GREEN, RICHARD FIRTH, *Poets and princepleasers: literature and the English court in the late middle ages* (Toronto, 1980).

—— 'John Ball's letters: literary history and historical literature', in B. Hanawalt, ed., *Chaucer's England* (Minneapolis, 1992), 176–200.

GREETHAM, D. C., 'Self-referential artefacts: Hoccleve's persona as a literary device', *Modern Philology*, 86 (1989), 242–51.

GROSS, CHARLOTTE, 'Courtly language in *Pearl*', in Robert J. Blanch, Miriam Youngerman, and Julian N. Wasserman, eds., *Text and matter: new critical perspectives on the* Pearl-*poet* (New York, 1991), 79–91.

GROVER, JAN ZITA, 'AIDS: Keywords' in Christopher Ricks and Leonard Michaels, eds., *The state of the language: 1990s edition* (London, 1990), 142–62.

GWYNN, AUBREY, *The English Austin friars in the time of Wyclif* (Oxford, 1940).

HANAWALT, BARBARA, ed., *Chaucer's England: literature in historical context* (Minneapolis, 1992).

—— and WALLACE, DAVID, eds., *Bodies and disciplines: intersections of literature and history in fifteenth century England* (Minneapolis, 1996).

HANDELMAN, SUSAN, *The slayer of Moses: the emergence of rabbinic interpretation in modern literary theory* (New York, 1982).

HANNA, RALPH III, 'Sir Thomas Berkeley and his patronage', *Speculum*, 64 (1989), 878–916.

—— 'Miscellaneity and vernacularity: conditions of literary production in late medieval England', in Stephen G. Nichols and Siegfried Wenzel, eds., *The whole book: cultural perspectives on the medieval miscellany* (Ann Arbor, 1996), 37–52.

—— 'Pilate's voice/Shirley's case', in *Pursuing history: Middle English manuscripts and their texts* (Stanford, Calif., 1996), 267–79.

HANRAHAN, MICHAEL, 'Seduction and betrayal: treason in the *Prologue* to *The Legend of Good Women*', *Chaucer Review*, 30 (1996), 229–40.

HARRINGTON, DAVID V., 'Indeterminacy in *Winner and Waster* and *The Parlement of the Thre Ages*', *Chaucer Review*, 3 (1986), 246–57.

HARVEY, JOHN H., 'Richard II and York', in R. Du Boulay and C. Barron, eds., *The reign of Richard II* (London, 1971).

HARWOOD, BRITTON J., 'Language and the real: Chaucer's Manciple', *Chaucer Review*, 6 (1972), 268–79.

HAVENS, JILL, 'Instruction, devotion, meditation, sermon: a critical edition of selected English religious texts in Oxford University College MS 97, with an ideological examination of some related MSS', D.Phil. thesis (Oxford University, 1995).

HICKS, ERIC, *Le débat sur le Roman de la Rose* (Paris, 1977).

HIEATT, CONSTANCE B., '*Winner and Waster* and *The Parliament of the Three Ages*', *American Notes and Queries*, 4 (1966), 100–4.

HILTON, R. H., *Bondmen made free: medieval peasants and the English rising of 1381* (London, 1973).

—— *The decline of serfdom in medieval England* (London, 1983).

—— *Class conflict and the crisis of feudalism: essays in medieval social history* (London, 1985).

—— and T. H. ASTON, eds., *The English rising of 1381* (Cambridge, 1984).

HODGE, ROBERT, and KRESS, GUNTHER, *Language as ideology* (London, 1979).

—— *Social semiotics* (Cambridge, 1988).

HOWARD, DONALD R., *The idea of The Canterbury Tales* (Berkeley, 1976).

HUDSON, ANNE, *Lollards and their books* (Hambledon, 1985).

HUDSON, ANNE, *The premature reformation* (Oxford, 1988).

—— 'The legacy of *Piers Plowman*', in *A Companion to* Piers Plowman, ed. John A. Alford (Berkeley, 1988), 251–66.

—— '*Piers Plowman* and the Peasants' Revolt: a problem revisited', *YLS* 8 (1994), 85–106.

—— ' "Poor preachers, poor men; views of poverty in Wyclif and his followers', in *Häresie und vorzeitige reformation im spätmittelalter: herausgegeben von František Šmahel undet Elisabeth Müller-Luckner* (Munich, 1998), 41–53.

HUGHES, GEOFFREY, *Words in time* (Oxford, 1988).

HUNT, TONY, 'The trilingual glossary in MS London BL Sloane 146 ff.69v–72r', *English Studies*, 70 (1989), 289–310.

HUPPÉ, B. F., *A reading of the Canterbury Tales* (New York, 1967).

ISER, WOLFGANG, *The act of reading: a theory of aesthetic response* (Baltimore, 1978).

JACOBS, NICOLAS, 'The typology of debate and the interpretation of *Wynnere and Wastoure*', *RES* 36 (1985), 481–500.

JAMES, JERRY D., 'The undercutting of conventions in *Wynnere and Wastoure*', *MLQ* 25 (1964), 243–58.

JAUSS, H. R., 'Literary history as a challenge to literary theory', *New Literary History*, 2 (1970), 11–19.

JOHNSON, LYNN STALEY, 'The *Pearl* dreamer and the eleventh hour', in R. J. Blanch, M. Youngerman, and J. N. Wasserman, eds., *Text and Matter* (New York, 1991), 3–15.

JOHNSON, VENDELL STACY, 'The imagery and diction of *The Pearl*: toward an interpretation', *ELH* 20 (1953), 161–80.

JONES, R. H., *The royal policy of Richard II* (Oxford, 1968).

JORDAN, R. M., *Chaucer's poetics and the modern reader* (Berkeley, 1987).

JUSTICE, STEVEN, *Writing and rebellion: England in 1381* (Berkeley, 1994).

—— 'Lollardy', in *CHMEL* 662–89.

KANE, GEORGE, 'The text of the *Legend of Good Women* in CUL MS Gg.4.27', in D. Gray and E. G. Stanley, eds., *Middle English studies presented to Norman Davis in honour of his seventieth birthday* (Oxford, 1983), 39–58.

KANTOROWICZ, E. H., *The king's two bodies: a study in medieval political theology* (Princeton, 1957).

KEAN, P. M., The Pearl: *an interpretation* (London, 1967).

KEEN, MAURICE, 'The Wilton Diptych: the case for a crusading context', in D. Gordon, L. Monnas, and C. Elam, eds., *The regal image* (London, 1997), 189–96.

KENNY, ANTHONY, *Wyclif* (Oxford, 1985).

KERBY-FULTON, KATHRYN, '*Piers Plowman*', in *CHMEL* 513–38.

KIPLING, GORDON, 'Richard II's "sumptuous pageants" and the idea of civic triumph', in D. M. Bergeron, ed., *Pageantry in the Shakespearean theater* (Athens, Ga., 1985), 83–103.

KIRK, ELIZABETH D., 'Langland's plowman and the recreation of fourteenth-century religious metaphor', *YLS* 2 (1988), 1–21.

KISER, LISA J., *Telling classical tales: Chaucer and the* Legend of Good Women (New York, 1983).

KNAPP, PEGGY, *Chaucer and the social contest* (London, 1990).

KNIGHT, STEPHEN, *Ryming craftily: meaning in Chaucer's poetry* (Sydney and London, 1973).

——'Chaucer and the sociology of literature', *SAC* 2 (1980), 15–51.

KRATZMANN, GREGORY, and SIMPSON, JAMES, eds., *Medieval English religious and ethical literature: essays in honour of G. H. Russell* (Cambridge, 1986).

KRESS, GUNTHER, *Linguistic processes in sociocultural practice* (Oxford, 1989), 2nd edn.

KROCHALIS, JEANNE E., 'The books and reading of Henry V and his circle', *Chaucer Review*, 23 (1988), 59–60.

LACLAU, ERNESTO, and MOUFFE, CHANTAL, *Hegemony and socialist strategy: towards a radical democratic politics*, trans. Winston Moore and Paul Cammack (London, 1985).

LAMPE, DAVID, 'The satiric strategy of *Peres the Ploughman's Crede*', in B. S. Levy and P. S. Szarmach, eds., *The alliterative tradition in the fourteenth century* (Kent, Oh., 1981), 69–80.

LAWTON, DAVID, 'The date of two Middle English alliterative poems', *Parergon*, 18 (1977), 17–25.

——'Lollardy and the *Piers Plowman* tradition', *MLR* 76 (1981), 780–93.

——ed., *Middle English alliterative poetry and its literary background* (Cambridge, 1982).

——'Alliterative style', in J. A. Alford, ed., *A Companion to* Piers Plowman (Berkeley, 1988), 223–49.

LEE, DAVID, *Competing discourses* (London, 1992).

LE GOFF, JACQUES, 'Merchant's time and church's time in the middle ages', in *Time, work, and culture in the Middle ages* (Chicago, 1980).

LEICESTER, H. MARSHALL, 'The art of impersonation: a General Prologue to the *Canterbury Tales*', *PMLA* 95 (1980), 213–24.

LEPAGE, YVAN G., 'La dislocation de la vision allégorique dans la *Messe des Oiseaux* de Jean de Condé', *Romanische Forschungen*, 91 (1979), 43–9.

LEVY, B. S., and ADAMS, G. R., 'Chauntecleer's paradise lost and regained', *Medieval Studies*, 29 (1967), 178–92.

LINDLEY, PHILLIP, 'Absolutism and regal image in Ricardian sculpture', in D. Gordon, L. Monnas, and C. Elam, eds., *The regal image* (London, 1997), 61–83.

LOWES, J. L., 'The Prologue to the *Legend of Good Women* as related to the French *Marguerite* poems and the *Filostrato*', *PMLA* 19 (1904), 593–683.

——'The Prologue to the *Legend of Good Women* considered in its chronological relations', *PMLA* 20 (1905), 749–864.

McAlpine, Monica E., 'The triumph of fiction in "The Nun's Priest's Tale"', in Robert R. Edwards, ed., *Art and context in late medieval narrative* (Cambridge, 1994), 79–92.

Macdonell, Diane, *A theory of discourse* (Oxford, 1986).

McFarlane, K. B., *Lancastrian kings and Lollard knights* (Oxford, 1972).

—— *The nobility of later medieval England* (Oxford, 1973).

Machan, T. W., 'Textual authority and the works of Hoccleve, Lydgate and Henryson', *Viator*, 23 (1992), 281–99.

—— 'Language contact in *Piers Plowman*', *Speculum*, 69 (1994), 359–85.

Mainzer, H. C., 'A study of the sources of the *Confessio Amantis* of John Gower', D.Phil. thesis (Oxford University, 1967).

Mann, Jill, *Chaucer and medieval estates satire* (Cambridge, 1973).

—— 'The *Speculum Stultorum* and the *Nun's Priest's Tale*', *Chaucer Review*, 9 (1975), 262–82.

—— 'Price and value in *Sir Gawain and the Green Knight*', *Essays in Criticism*, 36 (1986), 294–318.

Martin, Priscilla, *Chaucer's women* (London, 1996) 2nd edn.

Mathew, G., *The court of Richard II* (London, 1968).

Metcalf, Allan J., '*Gawain* and you', *Chaucer Review*, 5 (1971), 165–78.

Middleton, Anne, 'William Langland's "kynde name": authorial signature and social identity in late fourteenth-century England', in Lee Patterson, ed., *Literary practice and social change in Britain, 1380–1530* (Berkeley, 1990), 15–82.

—— 'Acts of vagrancy: the C version "autobiography" and the Statute of 1388', in Steven Justice and Kathryn Kerby-Fulton, eds., *Written work: Langland, labor and authorship* (Philadelphia, 1997), 208–317.

Miller, Jacques-Alain, 'Suture elements of the logic of the signifier', *Screen*, 18 (1977/78), 23–34.

Milroy, James, '*Pearl*: the verbal texture and the linguistic theme', *Neophilologus*, 55 (1971), 195–208.

—— James and Lesley, *Authority in language* (London, 1985).

Minnis, Alastair, *Medieval theory of authorship: scholastic literary attitudes in the later middle ages* (Aldershot, 1988), 2nd edn.

Mitchell, Jerome, *Thomas Hoccleve: a study in early fifteenth century English poetic* (Urbana, Ill., 1968).

Mitchell, Shelagh, 'Richard II: kingship and the cult of the saints', in D. Gordon, L. Monnas, and C. Elam, eds., *The regal image* (London, 1997), 115–24.

Mohl, Ruth, *The three estates in medieval and renaissance literature* (New York, 1933).

Monnas, Lisa, 'Fit for a king: figured silks shown in the Wilton Diptych', in D. Gordon, L. Monnas, and C. Elam, eds., *The regal image* (London, 1997), 165–77.

MOORMAN, CHARLES, 'The role of the narrator in *Pearl*', *Modern Philology*, 53 (1955), 73–81.

MORGAN, NIGEL, 'The signification of the banner in the Wilton Diptych' in D. Gordon, L. Monnas, and C. Elam, eds., *The regal image* (London, 1997), 179–188.

NARKISS, DORON, '"The fox, the cock and the priest": Chaucer's escape from fable', *Chaucer Review*, 32 (1997), 46–63.

NEUSE, R., *Chaucer's Dante: allegory and epic theater in the Canterbury Tales* (Berkeley, 1991).

NOLAN, BARBARA, 'A poet ther was: Chaucer's voices in the General Prologue to *The Canterbury Tales*', *PMLA* 101 (1986), 154–69.

NORBROOK DAVID, '"A liberal tongue": language and rebellion in *Richard II*', in J. M. Mucciolo, ed., *Shakespeare's universe: renaissance ideas and conventions; essays in honour of W. R. Elton* (London, 1996), 37–51.

OLSON, GLENDING, 'Chaucer', in *CHMEL* 566–88.

ORME, NICHOLAS, *Education and society in medieval and renaissance England* (Hambledon, 1989).

PALMER, F. R., *Semantics* (Cambridge, 1981).

PALMER, R. BARTON, 'The narrator in *The Owl and the Nightingale*: a reader in the text', in S. Trigg, ed., *Medieval English Poetry* (London, 1993), 156–71.

PARKES, M. B., 'The literacy of the laity', in David Daiches and Anthony Thorlby, eds., *Literature and western civilisation* (London, 1973), ii. 555–78.

PATTERSON, LEE, *Negotiating the past* (Madison, 1987).

—— ed., *Literary practice and social change in Britain, 1380–1530* (Berkeley and Los Angeles, 1990).

—— *Chaucer and the subject of history* (London, 1991).

—— 'Court politics and the invention of literature: the case of Sir John Clanvowe', in David Aers, ed., *Culture and history 1350–1600: essays on English communities, identities and writing* (Hemel Hempstead, 1992), 7–41.

PEARSALL, DEREK, *John Lydgate* (London, 1970).

—— *Old and Middle English Poetry* (London, 1977).

—— 'Gower's Latin and the *Confessio Amantis*', in A. J. Minnis, ed., *Latin and vernacular: studies in late medieval texts* (Cambridge, 1989), 13–25.

—— 'Interpretative models for the Peasants' Revolt', in Patrick J. Gallacher and Helen Damico, eds., *Hermeneutics and medieval culture* (New York, 1989), 63–71.

—— '"Lunatyk lollares" in *Piers Plowman*', in Piero Boitani and Anna Torti, eds., *Religion in the poetry and drama of the late Middle ages in England* (Cambridge, 1990), 163–78.

—— 'Hoccleve's *Regement of Princes*: the poetics of royal self-representation', *Speculum*, 69 (1994), 386–410.

—— *John Lydgate: a bio-biography* (Victoria, BC, 1977).

PECK, R. A., *Kingship and common profit in Gower's* Confessio Amantis (Carbondale, Ill., 1978).

PERCIVAL, FLORENCE, *Chaucer's legendary good women* (Cambridge, 1998).

PETTIT, T., ' "Here comes I, Jack Straw": English folk drama and social revolt', *Folklore*, 95 (1984), 3–20.

PINTI, DANIEL, ed., *Writing after Chaucer: essential readings in Chaucer and the fifteenth century* (New York and London, 1998).

POCOCK, J. G. A., 'Texts as events', in K. Sharpe and S. N. Zwicker, eds., *Politics of discourse: literature and history in seventeeth century England* (Berkeley, 1987), 21–34.

PORTER, ELIZABETH, 'Gower's ethical microcosm and political macrocosm', in A. J. Minnis, ed., *Gower's* Confessio Amantis*: responses and re-assessments* (Cambridge, 1983), 135–62.

POSTAN, M. M., 'Medieval agrarian society in its prime: England', in *The Cambridge economic history of medieval England*, vol. i: *The agrarian life of the middle ages* (Cambridge, 1966).

PRESCOTT, A. J., 'Writing about rebellion: using the records of the Peasants' Revolt of 1381', *History Workshop Journal*, 45 (1998), 1–27.

PRIOR, SANDRA PIERSON, *The* Pearl-*poet revisited* (New York, 1994).

—— *The fayre formez of the* Pearl-*poet* (East Lansing, Mich., 1996).

PUJMANOVÀ, OLGA, 'Portraits of kings depicted as magi in Bohemian painting', in D. Gordon, L. Monnas, and C. Elam, eds., *The regal image* (London, 1997), 247–66.

PUTTER, AD, *An introduction to the* Gawain-*poet* (London, 1996).

REID, IVAN, *Social class differences in Britain* (Glasgow, 1989) 3rd edn.

REISS, EDMUND, 'The symbolic plow and plowman and the Wakefield *Mactacio Abel*', *Studies in Iconography*, 5 (1979), 3–30.

—— 'Ambiguous signs and authorial deceptions in fourteenth century fictions', in Julian Wasserman and Lois Roney, eds., *Sign, sentence and discourse* (New York, 1989), 113–37.

RICHARDSON, H. G., 'Heresy and the lay power under Richard II', *EHR* 51 (1936), 1–26.

RIDDY, FELICITY, 'Jewels in *Pearl*', in D. Brewer and J. Gibson, eds., *A companion to the* Gawain-*poet* (Cambridge, 1997), 143–55.

RIGBY, S. H., *Chaucer in context: society, allegory and gender* (Manchester, 1996).

RONEY, LOIS, '*Winner and Waster's* "wyse wordes": teaching economics and nationalism in fourteenth century England', *Speculum*, 69 (1994), 1070–100.

RÖSENER, WERNER, *Peasants in the Middle ages*, trans. Alexander Stützer (Cambridge, 1992).

ROTHWELL, WILLIAM, 'The trilingual England of Geoffrey Chaucer', *SAC* 16 (1994), 45–67.

ROWE, DONALD, *Through nature to eternity: Chaucer's* Legend of Good Women (Lincoln, Nebr., and London, 1988).

Roy, Ashok, 'The techniques of the Wilton Diptych', in D. Gordon, L. Monnas, and C. Elam, eds., *The regal image* (London, 1997), 125–35.

Russell, J. Stephen, 'Is London burning? A Chaucerian allusion to the Rising of 1381', *Chaucer Review*, 30 (1995), 107–9.

Rutherford, Charles, '*The Boke of Cupide* reopened', *Neuphilogische Mitteillungen*, 78 (1977), 350–58.

Salter, Elizabeth, *Piers Plowman: an introduction* (Oxford, 1962).

—— '*Piers Plowman* and *The Simonie*', *Archiv*, 203 (1967), 241–54.

—— 'The timeliness of *Wynnere and Wastoure*', *Medium Aevum*, 47 (1978), 40–65.

—— 'Langland and the contexts of *Piers Plowman*', *Essays and Studies*, 32 (1979), 19–25.

Sandler, Lucy Freeman, 'The Wilton Diptych and images of devotion in illuminated manuscripts', in D. Gordon, L. Monnas, and C. Elam, eds., *The regal image* (London, 1997), 137–54.

Saul, Nigel, 'The kingship of Richard II', in A. Goodman and J. L. Gillespie, eds., *Richard II: the art of kingship* (Oxford, 1999), 38–57.

—— *Richard II* (New Haven and London, 1997).

—— 'Richard II's ideas of kingship' in Gordon *et al.*, eds., *The regal image* (London, 1997).

Scanlon, Larry, 'The authority of fable: allegory and irony in *The Nun's Priest's Tale*' , *Exemplaria*, 1 (1989), 43–68.

Scattergood, V. J., *Politics and poetry in the fifteenth century* (London, 1971).

—— and J. W. Sherborne, eds., *English court culture in the later middle ages* (New York and London, 1983).

—— 'Literary culture at the court of Richard II', in V. J. Scattergood and J. W. Sherborne, eds., *English court culture in the later middle ages* (New York and London, 1983), 29–43.

Scheps, Walter, 'Chaucer's anti-fable: "reduction ad absurdum" in *The Nun's Priest's Tale*', *LSE* 4 (1970), 1–10.

Scheifele, Eleanor, 'Richard II and the visual arts', in A. Goodman and J. L. Gillespie, eds., *Richard II: the art of kingship* (Oxford, 1999), 255–71.

Schirmer, Walter F., *John Lydgate: a study in the culture of the XVth century*, trans. Ann E. Keep (London, 1961).

Seaton, Ethel, *Sir Richard Roos—Lancastrian Poet* (Oxford, 1961).

Shepherd, Geoffrey, 'The nature of alliterative poetry in late medieval England', *PBA* 56 (1970), 57–76.

Sherborne, James, 'Aspects of English court culture in the late fourteenth century', in V. J. Scattergood and J. W. Sherborne, eds., *English court culture in the later middle ages* (New York and London, 1983), 1–27.

Shoaf, R. A., 'The play of puns in late Middle English poetry: concerning juxtology', in Jonathan Culler, ed., *On Puns* (Oxford, 1988), 44–61.

—— '*Purgatorio* and *Pearl*: transgression and transcendence', *Texas Studies in*

Language and Literature, 82 (1990), 152–68.

SIMPSON, JAMES, *Piers Plowman: an introduction to the B text* (London, 1990).

—— 'Madness and texts: Hoccleve's *Series*', in Julia Boffey and Janet Cown, eds., *Chaucer and fifteenth century poetry* (London, 1991), 15–26.

—— 'Ethics and interpretation: reading wills in Chaucer's *Legend of Good Women*, *SAC* 20 (1998), 73–100.

SOMERSET, FIONA, *Clerical discourse and lay audience in late medieval England* (Cambridge, 1998), 140–53.

SPEARING, A. C., *The Gawain-poet: a critical study* (Cambridge, 1970).

—— 'Symbolic and dramatic development in *Pearl*', in J. Conlee, ed., *Middle English Pearl*, 122–48.

—— *Medieval dream poetry* (Cambridge, 1976).

—— 'Father Chaucer', in D. Pinti, ed., *Writing after Chaucer* (New York and London, 1998), 145–66.

SPEIRS, JOHN, *Chaucer the maker* (London, 1951).

—— *Medieval English poetry: the non-Chaucerian tradition* (London, 1957).

STANBURY, SARAH, *Seeing the Gawain-poet: description and the act of perception* (Philadelphia, 1991).

—— 'Feminist masterplots: the gaze on the body of *Pearl*'s dead girl', in Linda Lomperis and Sarah Stanbury, eds., *Feminist approaches to the body in medieval literature* (Philadelphia, 1993), 96–115.

STANILAND, KAY, 'Extravagance or regal necessity: the clothing of Richard II' in D. Gordon, L. Monnas, and C. Elam, eds., *The regal image* (London, 1997), 85–94.

STEEL, A., *Richard II* (Cambridge, 1941).

STILLER, NIKKI, 'The transformation of the physical in the Middle English *Pearl*', *English Studies*, 63 (1982), 402–9.

STOREY, R. L., 'Liveries and commissions of the peace 1388–90', in R. H. Du Boulay and C. Barron, eds., *The reign of Richard II* (London, 1971).

STROHM, PAUL, *Social Chaucer* (Cambridge, Mass., 1989).

—— 'Form and social statement in *Confessio Amantis* and *The Canterbury Tales*', *SAC* 1 (1979), 17–40.

—— 'Chaucer's fifteenth century audience and the narrowing of the Chaucer tradition', *SAC* 4 (1982), 3–32.

—— 'Chaucer's audience(s): fictional, implied, intended, actual', *Chaucer Review*, 18 (1983), 137–64.

—— *Hochon's arrow: the social imagination of fourteenth-century texts* (Princeton, 1992).

—— '"Lad with revel to Newegate": Chaucerian narrative and historical meta-narrative', in Robert R. Edwards, ed., *Art and context in late medieval narrative* (Cambridge, 1994), 163–76.

—— 'Chaucer's Lollard joke: history and the textual unconscious', *SAC* 17 (1995), 23–42.

—— 'What happens at intersections?' in B. Hanawalt and D. Wallace, eds., *Bodies and disciplines* (Minneapolis, 1996), 223–32.

—— 'The trouble with Richard: The reburial of Richard II and Lancastrian symbolic strategy', *Speculum*, 71 (1996), 87–111.

—— *England's empty throne: usurpation and the language of legitimation* (New Haven, 1998).

—— 'Hoccleve, Lydgate and the Lancastrian court', in *CHMEL*, ed. David Wallace (Cambridge, 1999), 640–61.

SZITTYA, PENN R., *The antifraternal tradition in medieval England* (Princeton, 1986).

TANNER, LAWRENCE E., *The history and treasures of Westminster Abbey* (London, 1953).

TAYLOR, JOHN, 'Richard II's views on kingship', *Proceedings of the Leeds Philosophical and Literary Society*, 14 (1971), 189–205.

—— 'Richard II in the chronicles', in A. Goodman and J. L. Gillespie, eds., *Richard II: the art of kingship* (Oxford, 1999), 15–35.

THRUPP, SYLVIA, *The merchant class of medieval London* (Ann Arbor, 1962; repr. of 1948).

TRAVIS, PETER W., 'Chaucer's trivial fox chase and the Peasants' Revolt of 1381', *Journal of Medieval and Renaissance Studies*, 18 (1988), 195–220.

TRIGG, STEPHANIE, 'Israel Gollancz's *Wynnere and Wastoure*: political satire or editorial politics?' in Gregory Kratzmann and James Simpson, eds., *Medieval English Religious and ethical literature: essays in honour of G. H. Russell* (Cambridge, 1986), 115–27.

—— 'The rhetoric of excess in *Winner and Waster*', *YLS* 3 (1989), 91–108.

—— *Medieval English poetry* (London, 1993), 186–99.

TRUDGILL, PETER, *Sociolinguistics* (Harmondsworth, 1983).

TUCK, J. A., *Richard II and the English nobility* (London, 1973).

—— 'Richard II's system of patronage', in F. R. H. DuBoulay and Caroline Barron, eds., *The reign of Richard II: essays in honour of May McKisack* (London, 1971), 1–20.

—— 'Carthusian monks and Lollard knights: religious attitudes at the court of Richard II', *SAC* 1 (1984), 149–61.

TUDOR-CRAIG, PAMELA, 'The Wilton Diptych in the context of contemporary English panel and wall painting', in D. Gordon, L. Monnas, and C. Elam, eds., *The regal image* (London, 1997), 207–22.

TURVILLE-PETRE, THORLAC, *The alliterative revival* (Cambridge, 1977).

—— 'The Prologue to *Wynnere and Wastoure*', *LSE* 18 (1987).

—— *England the nation: language, literature and national identity, 1290–1340* (Oxford, 1996).

VON NOLCKEN, CHRISTINA, '*Piers Plowman*, the Wycliffites and *Pierce the Ploughman's Crede*', *YLS* 2 (1988), 71–102.

—— '"A certain sameness" and our response to it in English Wycliffite Texts', in Richard Newhauser and J. A. Alford, eds., *Literature and religion in the later Middle ages: philological studies in honour of Siegfried Wenzel* (Binghamton, NY, 1995), 191–208.

WALKER, SIMON, 'Richard II's views on kingship', in Rowena E. Archer and Simon Walker, eds., *Rulers and ruled in late medieval England: essays presented to Gerald Harriss* (Hambledon, 1995), 48–63.

WALLACE, DAVID, *Chaucerian polity: absolutist lineages and associational forms in England and Italy* (Stanford, Calif., 1997).

—— ed., *Cambridge history of medieval English literature* (Cambridge, 1999).

WALLER, GARY, *English poetry of the sixteenth century* (London, 1993).

WALTHER, HANS, *Lateinische sprichworter und sentenzen des mittelalters unter der frühen neuzeit* (Göttingen, 1986).

WARD, L. C., 'The authorship of the *Cuckoo and the Nightingale*', *MLN* 44 (1929), 217–26.

WASSERMAN, JULIAN, and RONEY, LOIS, eds., *Sign, sentence and discourse* (New York, 1989).

WATKINS, JOHN, '"Sengeley in synglere": *Pearl* and late medieval individualism', *Chaucer Yearbook*, 2 (1995), 117–36.

WATSON, NICHOLAS, 'The *Gawain*-poet as a vernacular theologian', in D. Brewer and J. Gibson, eds., *A companion to the* Gawain-*poet* (Cambridge, 1997), 293–314.

—— 'The politics of Middle English writing', in Wogan-Browne *et al.*, eds., *The idea of the vernacular* (Exeter, 1999), 331–52.

WATTS, JOHN, *Henry VI and the politics of kingship* (Cambridge, 1996).

—— 'Review of Nigel Saul, *Richard II*', *Notes and Queries*, 224 (1999), 91–3.

WAWN, ANDREW, 'The genesis of *The Plowman's Tale*', *YES* 2 (1972), 21–40.

—— 'Chaucer, *The Plowman's Tale* and reformation propaganda: the testimonies of Thomas Godfray and *I Playne Piers*', *Bulletin of the John Rylands Library*, 56 (1973), 174–92.

WETHERBEE, WINTHROP, 'Latin structure and vernacular space: Gower, Chaucer and the Boethian tradition', in Robert Yeager, ed., *Chaucer and Gower: difference, mutuality, exchange* (Victoria, BC, 1991), 7–35.

WHEATLEY, EDWARD, 'A selfless ploughman and the Christ/Piers conjunction in Langland's *Piers Plowman*', *Notes and Queries*, 40 (238) (1993), 135–42.

WHITROW, G. J., *Time in history* (Oxford, 1988).

WILSON, CHRISTOPHER, 'Rulers, artificers and shoppers: Richard II's remodelling of Westminster Hall, 1393–99', in D. Gordon, L. Monnas, and C. Elam, *The regal image* (London, 1997), 33–59.

WINDEATT, B. A., ed., *Chaucer's dream poetry: sources and analogues* (Cambridge, 1982).

WITTIG, MONIQUE, 'The mark of gender', in *The straight mind* (Hemel Hempstead, 1992), 76–89.

WOGAN-BROWNE, JOCELYN, WATSON, NICHOLAS, TAYLOR, ANDREW, and

EVANS, RUTH, eds., *The idea of the vernacular* (Exeter, 1999).

WOLFGANG, LEONORA D.,' "Out of the Frenssh": Lydgate's source of *The Churl and the Bird*', *ELN* 32 (1995), 10–19.

WRIGHT, LAURA, 'Macaronic writing in a London archive, 1380–1480', in Matti Rissanen *et al.*, eds., *History of Englishes: new methods and interpretations in historical linguistics* (Berlin, 1992), 582–91.

YEAGER, R. F., *Fifteenth century studies: recent readings* (Hamden, Conn., 1984).

——'English, Latin and the Text as "other": the page as sign in the work of John Gower', *Text*, 3 (1987), 251–67.

——*John Gower's poetic: the search for a new Arion* (Woodbridge, 1990).

——ed., *Chaucer and Gower: difference, mutuality, exchange* (Victoria, BC, 1991).

——'Learning to speak in tongues: writing poetry for a trilingual culture', in R. F. Yeager, ed., *Chaucer and Gower*, 115–29.

YOUNG, ROBERT, ed., *Untying the text* (London, 1981).

Index